Sampling and Remixing Blackness in Hip-Hop Theater and Performance

Sampling and Remixing Blackness in Hip-Hop Theater and Performance

Nicole Hodges Persley

University of Michigan Press
Ann Arbor

Published in the United States of America by
the University of Michigan Press
Manufactured in the United States of America
Printed on acid-free paper

First published October 2021

A CIP catalog record for this book is available from the British Library.

ISBN 978-0-472-07511-9 (hardcover : alk. paper)
ISBN 978-0-472-05511-1 (paper : alk. paper)
ISBN 978-0-472-12961-4 (ebook)

CONTENTS

Digital materials related to this title can be found on the Fulcrum platform via the following citable URL: https://doi.org/10.3998/mpub.7380849

ACKNOWLEDGMENTS

The idea seeds for this book began quite some time ago when I was in graduate school at the University of Southern California, in what was then the Program in American Studies and Ethnicity, and is now one of the most exciting American studies departments in the world. It was at USC that Dorinne Kondo helped these ideas take root along with other phenomenal mentors, Bruce Burningham, Meiling Cheng, Ruth Wilson Gilmore, Jane Iwamura, David Román, George Sanchez, Leiland Saito and Fred Moten, who all pushed me out of my comfort zones to explore to new aspects of performance. My USC PASE cohort, Jennifer Stover, Daniel Hosang, Reina Prado, Ulli Ryder, Luis Rodriguez, Lata Murti, and Phuong Nguyen, provided generous feedback in the early development of these ideas about sampling, hip-hop, and identity. Fellow USC Trojans Deborah Al-Najjar, Jungmiwha S. Bullock, Michan Connor, Imani K. Johnson, and Anthony Sparks; your encouragement, your creativity, and your scholarship have inspired me in countless ways. I am forever grateful for the knowledge, love, and support I received while at USC.

I am indebted to many artists who opened up to me about their work using hip-hop in the theater. Thank you to Danny Hoch, Sarah Jones, Nikki S. Lee, Jonzi D, and Matt Sax who shared their perspectives about performance influenced by hip-hop in personal correspondence with me. Toni Blackman and Rickerby Hinds, thank you for your groundbreaking perspectives about hip-hop, theater arts, and diplomacy. Daniel Banks, your scholarship and friendship have been a constant source of light and encouragement on this journey.

I am thankful for my Hip-Hop Archive family at the Hutchins Center for African & African American Studies at Harvard University. Thank you to Marcyliena Morgan, Larry Bobo, Henry Louis "Skip" Gates, Jr., Dionne Bennett, Alvin Carter, and Lisa B. Thompson(Univesity of Texas-Austin) for your continued support. Working at the intersection of American studies, performance studies, and theater means I have several scholars whose work keeps me sane as I work in these overlapping disciplinary circles. Deborah Elizabeth Whaley, your scholarship, art, sisterhood, and friendship have been a constant source of energy and inspiration. Monica White Ndounou, you are a constant collaborator and forever sister-friend. To Jonathan Shandell, Eunice Ferreira, Veronda Carey, Kaja Dunn, Baron Kelly, much love and appreciation for your support. Christie Dobson, Michelle Heffner Hayes, Leslie Bennett, Anne Dotter, Terri Murray, and Leticia Garcia, you are all a constant source of love and support. Nina Morgan, your mentorship continues to inspire me to pay it forward. E. Patrick Johnson, Harvey Young, Soyica Colbert, and Harry Elam, Jr. you have continued to mentor me from afar and to look out for me in ways that I can never repay. Thanks to Justin Williams and Joe Schloss for supporting my work as a theater artist and scholar in hip-hop studies.

To all of the hip-hop theater artists who I did not mention in this book, thank you for paving the way for all of us to tell more hip-hop theater stories. Special thanks to my editor, LeAnn Fields, who never gave up on the possibility of this book as I weathered tenure and administrative and professional arts opportunities. I would be remiss to not thank the incredible readers for this book who gave me invaluable feedback to help me realize this project.

I feel incredibly fortunate to have been embraced by several departments at my home institution, the University of Kansas. A New Faculty Research Grant and a Book Proposal Writing Fellowship at the Hall Center for Humanities supported my shaping of the book. Special thanks to my colleagues in my former department at KU Theatre & Dance: Henry Bial, Jane Barnette, Leslie Bennett, Dennis Christilles, Rana Esfandiary, John Gronbeck-Tedesco, Michelle Heffner Hayes, Karen Hummel, Mechele Leon, Paul Meier, Kathy Pryor, Mark Reaney, Omofolabo Ajayi Soyinka, and Rebecca Rovit, who provided unwavering support. Sincere thanks to my colleagues in my new joint appointment departments at KU, American studies and African and African American studies. In

American studies, I am grateful to call Ben Chappell, Elizabeth Esch, Nishani Frazier, Randal Jelks, Margaret Kelly, Joo Ok Kim, Ray Pence, Christopher Perreira, David Roediger, Sherrie Tucker, and Robert Warrior colleagues and friends. In African and African American studies, Shawn Alexander, Tony Bolden, Abel Chikanda, Amal El Haimeur, Jessica Gershultz, Dorothy Hines, Randal Jelks, Elizabeth McGonagle, Peter Ojiambo, Dorthy Pennigton, Kathryn Rhine, Brenda Waywire, and Peter Ukpokodu are colleagues who always embrace my big ideas with zeal.

I would be remiss to not mention a terrific cohort of African and African American studies scholars and friends who attend (or cheer from afar) every stage play or film I direct, forward every news feature, and promote my creative work and scholarship tirelessly: Cécile Accilien (now at Kennesaw State University); Jennifer Hamer and Clarence Lang (now at Penn State University); and my KU crew, Shawn Alexander, Giselle Anatol, Tony Bolden, Ayesha Hardison, Darren Canady, Maryemma Graham, Randal Jelks, Clarence Lang, Peter Ukpokodu, Sherrie Tucker, and Kim Warren are all wonderful colleagues, audience members, and friends who have made my academic and creative journey at KU fantastic. Tanya Golash-Boza, you helped me to realize more writing dreams than I thought possible. Shantanu Duttahammed, your care helped birth this book. Saralyn Reece Hardy and Hume Feldman, thank you for your wisdom and guidance. Birgit Bauridl and Udo Hebel, thank you for making another intellectual home for me in Germany at the Universität Regensburg.

Wholehearted thanks to my family at KC Melting Pot Theater where I serve as artistic director. Harvey Williams, Linda Williams Lewis Morrow, Melonnie Walker, Doug Schroeder, and the KCMPT collective keep me sane by helping me make theater that matters to Black communities. Lewis Morrow our on-going creative collaboration inspires me to think about activism and black performance daily.

Many people in my immediate and extended families affirmed the ideas in this book and have been tireless supporters. To Ingrid Gessner, Nassim Ballestrini, and Raphaël Nkolwoudou thank you for being friends who are always there for me abroad making a home away from home for me. Ricarda Perez, Robyn Iverson, Colette Freedman, and

Anne Laure Guyard, you are my spiritual sisters. To my Kansas City lifelines, the Browns, the Garcias, the Murrays, and the Shanklands, I am so happy to have you in my life.

To my aunts Shirley, Evelyn, Roberta, Zelika, and Christina, and my uncles Zell, Ivan and Donald, the time and resources you have given to support me over the years have helped me more than you know. To my brother Mack Hodges and my sister Heather Bourne, thank you for being the best siblings I could ask for in life. To all of my family: the Hodges, Moores, Westmaas's, Bradys, Persleys, Bournes, Dyes, and Inces for being faithful supporters and prayer partners along my journey. To my nieces Heaven and Savannah, and my nephew Chris, Jr., I pray you will reach for your dreams and never stop striving. To my brother-in-law, Christopher A. Bourne, thank you for your powerful prayers over our huge family.

Lastly, thank you to my husband Jay and my daughter Ellington. Your love sustains and inspires me each day. To my in-laws, Ernestine Persley, Vincent Persley, and Valedenia Winn, thank you for your support for the past twenty years. I gain continued strength from my late grandparents Alma and Ben Moore. This book is dedicated to my amazing mother, Barbara Westmaas, and in memory of my father, the late Willie Mack Hodges, Jr.; without your love for one another, I would not be.

INTRODUCTION / Sampling and Remixing Hip-Hop's Blackness in Contemporary Hip-Hop Theater and Performance

> For much of the last century the burden of being Black in America was the burden of a systemic denial of human and constitutional rights and equal economic opportunity. It was also a century in which much of what America sold to the world as uniquely American in character in terms of music dance, fashion, humor, spirituality, grassroots politics, slang, literature and sports, was uniquely African-American in origin, conception and inspiration.
>
> —Greg Tate, *Everything But the Burden*

Work songs, Negro spirituals, blues, jazz, soul, rhythm and blues—at one point during the first part of the twentieth century, this was all called "race music," and it was uniquely associated with Black people in America. Early in my education at predominantly Black schools in Detroit, Michigan, our teachers taught us all about these genres and to be proud of the rich heritage that created such an incredible musical tradition. I was mesmerized by the stories of Billie Holiday, Duke Ellington, Josephine Baker, Ella Fitzgerald, Dorothy Dandridge, and Paul Robeson, artists who would later inspire my life's trajectory. At school we sang the Black National Anthem, "Lift Every Voice and Sing," and learned from W. E. B. Du Bois, by way of my drama teacher Mrs. Leona Fisher, that we were part of a legacy of music and theater created about, by, for, and near Black people in the United States.[1] Black music was full of theater, and I loved it. I loved performing throughout elementary and middle school, where I was lovingly affirmed by my teachers as a young Black girl who was charged to contribute to the world. I wanted to make art. I was told that the amazing artists that I'd learned about and loved had to make "a way out of no way" because institutional racism and systemic inequality allowed mainstream America to love Black theater, music, and dance, but segregate and diminish the people that made them. We young Black artists were told that we had to fight for our rights, our history, and our joy.

It wasn't until my mom, divorced with three children, moved my siblings and me to a predominantly White middle school in the suburbs of Detroit that I realized the positive feelings I had about theater and music created by Black people were not shared by all. As it turned out, music and theater were racialized in very specific ways that positioned all things "Black" and "other" in the margins as something abnormal. Yet everything I saw or heard, even in White theater spaces, contained elements of blackness. In the late 1970s and early 1980s, when hip-hop began to move from the inner cities to the suburbs and samples of blackness emerged in all aspects of popular culture, I hoped that my talent could overcome the socially imposed racial barriers and allow those positive feelings of pride I had about Black music and performance (specifically African American music and theater) to resurface. However, such hopes were challenged by my White teachers, who believed that a Black girl like me could never play Sandy in *Grease*. Hip-hop music, an important part of the soundtrack of my life, was often negatively categorized as "Black" and/or "ghetto" by the White peers who made up the majority of my theater and art friends. Curiously, these White friends were employing elements of hip-hop—language, dance, sartorial expression, and culture on a daily basis to shape their identities, while my blackness was read as less than, abnormal, something apart from the pleasure they gained from hip-hop. Despite the rich inheritance I brought to the American theater, my entrée to White theater spaces was relegated to backstage. I had to get in where I fit in and make my own way if I wanted to become a professional theater artist. Those early inklings and painful experiences followed me most of my life, but I held on to the teachings of my African American mentors. I was determined to work in theater by any means necessary. I believed that hip-hop would change the world.

Cut to the present. The two things I love the most, African American theater and hip-hop, have converged to create this hybrid thing called hip-hop theater. The international success of Latinx American actor, playwright, and composer Lin-Manuel Miranda's musical *Hamilton* in 2016 brought the genre, which had been underground since the mid-1990s, to the mainstream theater world by telling the story of an American founding father. Alexander Hamilton's biography is ventriloquized through the bodies and voices of African American, Asian American, and Latinx American actors. Miranda remixes hip-hop with other music derived from the African diaspora, such as jazz, soul, and reggae, along with show tunes from musical theater—the same historically White musical theater that had foreclosed most opportunities to the very bodies and people who now perform them in the Tony Award–winning musical. How do we reconcile the mashup of two genres that personify the Black–White binary and are diametrically opposed to one another in American history? Hip-hop, once regarded as the Blackest and most dangerous of all Black American music, and theater, still arguably one of the Whitest and most Eurocentric performance genres in the United States, come together in a musical that reminds us, as cultural critic Greg Tate observes, that "much of what America sold to the world as uniquely American in character in terms of music, dance, fashion, humor, spirituality, grassroots politics, slang, literature and sports, was uniquely African-American in origin, conception and inspiration."[2]

The artistic practices and identity negotiations I explore in *Sampling and Remixing Blackness in Hip-Hop Theater and Performance* are inspired by my own history of reconciling theatrical practice as an African American actor and director with the normative whiteness of American theater practices. It is my coming to terms with the tragic irony of African American expressions of hip-hop culture's Black history, specifically the African American and African diasporic specificity of that history, being distorted in American music and theater history at a moment when hip-hop is the soundtrack of the international protests against anti-Black violence in the wake of the deaths of George Floyd, Ahmaud Arbery, Breonna Taylor, Elijah McClain and so many others that came before and after these Black Americans. People love our music and our cultural contributions, but they just don't seem to like Black people. A tough pill to swallow, as so-called allies and accomplices say #BlackLivesMatter while consuming our cultural products, yet are often silent when our bodies are slain and our liberties are violated and ignored. The book attempts to make sense of similar questions I began to ask in the early

2000s about non-African American artists borrowing aspects of blackness in their expressions of hip-hop. I started to witness non-Black, non-African American, and non-Latinx people demonstrate cultural fluency of hip-hop culture that was akin to the history of White appropriation of Black culture through acts of racial mimicry, violence, and theft, but decidedly different. The incidents of appropriation and incorporation of African American culture that I witnessed were performed not only by Whites, but also by Asian and Asian American, Latinx, and Black artists of other nationalities and ethnicities. All of the borrowing—or sampling—of blackness was filtered through hip-hop and selectively isolated with vernacular language, styles of self-adornment, and gestures that are definitely recognizable as part of "Black" American culture. Yet, the people inhabiting the expressions of that culture were not African American Blacks. Nor were they trying to "be" Black. I noticed that non-Black artists had the capacity to disconnect hip-hop from blackness and to manipulate that relationship to express their relative experiences of marginalization. White artists who were claiming hip-hop as legitimate consumers and cultural producers became increasingly careful to disavow racism and to denounce cultural appropriation for fear of losing street credibility in the genre and culture. In his 2016 song "White Privilege," Macklemore reflects on his position as a White rapper in a predominantly African American cultural matrix:

> Where's my place in a music that's been taken by my race
> Culturally appropriated by the white face?
> And we don't want to admit that this is existing
> So scared to acknowledge the benefits of our White privilege
> [. . .]
> So where does this leave me?
> I feel like I pay dues, but I'll always be
> a white MC
> I give everything I have when I write a rhyme
> But that doesn't change the fact that this culture's not mine[3]

This book begins to explain how the same Black music that changed American culture has become at once Black and not Black. Adored and despised. American and African American. I explore performance practices by non-Black artists and non-African American Black artists (those of African descent from other locations in the diaspora) that both affirm and disavow the positive influence that African American cultural practices have on the construction of the American cultural experience through hip-hop. My argument moves through the spaces of contradiction that are enabled when we think of blackness as something that is scripted simultaneously on and beyond Black bodies. No matter how I define "blackness" as linguistic, embodied, stylistic, cultural, and emotional expression that allows Black people to articulate their experiences living as an oppressed people; no matter what my personal experiences as a straight African American woman living in the United States; no matter if blackness is measured by White theater producers and audiences in relationship to the stereotypical depictions of African American life in the United States; mainstream definitions of blackness by non-Black people are measured against, and inherited from, the master-slave dialectic of the plantation. We are produced by this dialectic, Black people fight daily to challenge it, but are constantly reminded that we are at the bottom of the hierarchy in the American racial imaginary.

Paul Gilroy's analysis of hip-hop as it relates to biopolitics and the Black public sphere in the early 2000s in *Against Race: Imagining Political Culture Beyond the Color Line* is important to revisit as I reference hip-hop's identarian roots and the influence of African American expressions of blackness in hip-hop on Black artists of non-African American ethnicity and non-Black racial and ethnic identities. Gilroy argues the "transgressive qualities in Hip-hop have led to its being identified not as one black culture among many but currently as the very blackest culture—the one that provides the measure on which all others can be evaluated."[4] Gilroy warned that the conflation of hip-hop with revolutionary praxis and marginality would mask the ways in which the music and culture are both culture-consuming and consumed by mass, capitalist enterprise. Such international visibility and audibility render hip-hop a complex site through which a specifically American-identified blackness is presented through hip-hop. Almost eighteen years after Gilroy asked us to rethink our relationship to the color line, hip-hop's blackness and its transgressive qualities are still part of what attracts non-African American artists and consumers. However, its stereotypes and popular vernaculars in language, style, and gesture, are always tethered to a violent, unrecognized history of slavery in the United States. Equally important is Gilroy's observation that hip-hop's "transracial popularity might be significant in political struggles against white supremacism."[5] No matter how people around the world consume, perform, and/or love hip-hop, its connection to blackness and its intrinsic political struggles for equality are always present, as hip-hop is the social theater of the hip-hop generation. The struggle to acknowledge the cultural contribution and creative impact of African American artistic production—the sonic, linguistic, and aesthetic codes of blackness that reside in hip-hop and its musical predecessors like jazz—is embedded in the African American fight for freedom throughout history. In the case of cross-racial performance within the Black–White binary that forms the racial imagination in the United States, Eric Lott argues that it is through imitation of stereotypically Black behavior that Whites define their identity in opposition to their conceptions of blackness. His concept of "symbolic crossings of racial boundaries" helps to explain appropriation of African American culture across racial and ethnic lines.[6] Through negative appropriation of Black cultural signifiers in various historical moments (e.g., performative indexes), Whites attempted to construct their own identity as distinct from these conceptions. Ironically, because they were so conscious of stereotypes of blackness, they incorporated blackness into their own identities, even as they worked to distance themselves from it. Lott engages with acts of mimicry by Whites in the United States; he argues that in the process of trying to act "Black," Whites ultimately engage in some process of learning about the power of blackness, which enables a temporary reversal of power between Black and White subjects.[7]

Sampling and Remixing Blackness works to disentangle hip-hop from ontological notions of Black identity while acknowledging that African Americans' cultural contributions to hip-hop and hip-hop's effect on non-African American identity formation is worthy of theorization. To this end, this book investigates three guiding questions: First, how are vernacular expressions of African American culture, expressed through hip-hop theater and performance, sampled and remixed to create alternative representations of racial identities on stage? Second, what do transracial performances of African American expressions of blackness across racial, ethnic, and national lines enable us to understand about the unifying power and labor of Black cultural production? Third, how do performances of blackness by non-African American artists impact how we understand the flexibility of blackness in the twenty-first century? I argue that hip-hop-inspired theater and dramatic pieces offer blueprints that use performance to map new identity formations that challenge the normative whiteness associated with mainstream theatrical practice, as performers rely upon blackness as expressed through African American culture in hip-hop to create their works. By identifying the linguistic, physical, and embodied hip-hop sampling by non-African American artists, I open a dialogue about the cultural production of artists who employ hip-hop aesthetics to locate themselves within the social justice ideologies of hip-hop's blackness through theatrical performance.

Hey Mr. D.J.[8]—Sampling and Remixing Blackness

My methodological approach operates as a mixtape, sampling from the theoretical observations that grant intersectional and shifting meanings of race, ethnicity, class, gender, disability, and sexuality in various national and international contexts. Working at the intersection of performance studies and American studies scholarship, I count embodied research as a platform from which to make theoretical connections within and between cultural practices that are able to speak with—not for or about—the experiences of other groups.[9]

Sampling is adapted in this book as a mode of theatricality that can be understood as the act of borrowing characteristics of racial identity to reproduce sonic, oral, visual, literary, or embodied expressions of mainstream understandings of how race is lived. Remixing is the act of recombining what has been borrowed and connecting it to existing aspects of identity and thus transforming both parts into a new configuration. Such acts of sampling and remixing have the potential to both reinscribe and subvert the saliency of categories of difference through performance. Performers sample sounds, gestures, and styles as select parts of their identities and then remix them to create a conversation between their lived experiences and the ones they borrow in performance. The process of transformation that occurs during the remix—the acts of improvisation that create connection between disparate and similar parts—changes the actual doing of blackness. Joseph Schloss's discussion of sampling sheds light on the performative connections forged when non-Black and non-African American artists perform hip-hop:

> Hip-hop developed in New York City in neighborhoods that were dominated by people of African descent from the continental United States, Puerto Rico and the West Indies. As a result, African derived aesthetics, social norms, standards and sensibilities are deeply embedded in the form, even when it is being performed by individuals who are not themselves of African descent.[10]

Schloss highlights the hybridity of hip-hop as he references the African diasporic contributions made by innovators in New York in the early 1980s whose cultural experiences informed the aesthetic impulses of the music and culture. When non-African American performers sample blackness in quests to become more hip-hop, they reveal the fictitious lines between racial identities, but they still run the risk of replaying the stereotypes associated with those speculative understandings of race. Black studies scholar Mark Anthony Neal discusses such acts of remaking the now as an act of "social improvisation" for African Americans.[11] Improvisatory practices of sampling in Black music styles, particularly jazz and hip-hop, can be read as social acts of self-fashioning performed in response to what Neal identifies as "impoverishment, racism, class hierarchies and a host of other everyday threats."[12]

An example that synthesizes sampling and remixing as modes of theatricality used to identify and embody gestures of blackness through hip-hop can be found in the work of non-African American, Black actor Idris Elba, who is of Ghanaian and Sierra Leonean ethnicity and was born and raised in Hackney, England. Elba received critical praise for his convincing performance of Stringer Bell, a fictional character on the David Simon-created drama *The Wire*, which ran on HBO from 2002 until 2008. Simon and the writers of *The Wire* worked to complicate stereotypes of African American men selling drugs in inner cities. In the show, Russell "Stringer" Bell is a drug dealer in Baltimore who moonlights as a community college student studying economics.

Stringer Bell is an African American male in the 1990s from a low-to-moderate income community who is deeply engaged in the aesthetics of hip-hop culture. To perform African American blackness, Elba and the show's writers had to locate particular linguistic and embodied samples of African American Black masculinity associated with hip-hop and Stringer's socioeconomic and political positions as a drug dealer. The vexed spaces between the actor's Englishness and blackness in a British context had to be negotiated by and through samples of African American expressions of blackness, masculinity, and class. Elba, like the other artists mentioned in this book, has been exposed to all types of hip-hop music from the United States and around the world. The actor could have easily drawn upon Black British samples of hip-hop within the context of his life in England to inform his characterization. However, the script called for specifically African American expressions of Black masculinity. Elba had to remix his performance by isolating his experiences as a Black British male and removing all traces of his accent, style of dress, and language in order to play back a combination of samples that could convince mainstream American television audiences that he was African American. Elba's blackness is mapped onto his body, but ethnicity, nation, class, and social-historical context determine its specificity. Many American fans of the show believed Elba was African American, not a Black actor from England. Even today, years after his performance as Stringer Bell, Elba is still read in multiple contexts based on his national location. He is read as Black, both African American and Black British, despite the fact that the former context is based solely on his portrayal of a character. In this book I look to performance in hip-hop-influenced theater to interrogate hip-hop's relationship to blackness as the sampling of vernacular codes that can be remixed to reveal hip-hop as a circuitous site of Black cultural production that opens opportunities for multiracial and ethnic coalitions building to fight anti-Black racism.

Greg Tate has written extensively about the range of ways that White Americans have stolen and incorporated African American culture into their everyday lives without the physical, social, and political burdens of blackness. Non-African American artists in hip-hop theater and performance use their bodies to locate sights and sounds of blackness associated with African American singularity. Alexander Weheliye argues that we must resist reducing blackness to its particularity in a given context that forecloses opportunities to think about multiple Black singularities that make up a larger whole. He contends that "to argue that black popular musics and their multifarious technological instantiations are only relevant to black people and not to American culture at large, or numerous other global cultural architectonics, simply misses the point, all of the points."[13]

Weheliye challenges discussing Black culture in terms of identarian perspectives that conflate African American particularity with a monolithic Black culture. Sampling and remixing, as theatrical technologies of identity construction in performance, have the potential to connect points of belonging that artists selectively identify in profound and superficial imaginings of hip-hop. This book's main subjects—Danny Hoch, Nikki S. Lee, Jonzi D, Matt Sax, Sarah Jones, and Lin-Manuel Miranda—improvise fluid social understandings of race that attempt to flip how we understand racial and ethnic identification. These fluid social understandings are directly connected to a longer history of improvisational practices of call-and-response in African American culture that are archived in hip-hop music.

In the twenty-first century, the Hip-Hop Arts Movement replays the activist past of the Harlem Renaissance and the Black Arts Movement in the present as it positions hip-hop music and culture as simultaneously Black and other. Blackness, in any national context, is tethered to a fraught racial past of violence, imperialism, and colonialism that cannot be edited out of any Black cultural production or experience. Black Studies scholar Imani Perry asserts that attempts to disassociate hip-hop from blackness constitute a strategic act to devalue Black American cultural productions. "The accuracy of the assertion that Hip-hop has multiracial and multicultural origins does not suggest that it is not black. Only a world-view that subjugates blackness marks the phrase 'it's just black' as offensive. Why can't something be black and be influenced by a number of cultures and styles at the same time?"[14] Perry alerts us that, despite its multiracial history, hip-hop is inextricably tied to Black racial and cultural identity. The struggle to keep conversations about African American musical and theatrical forms connected to the history of Blacks in the United States is often admonished by critics as "identarian" politics. However, disassociating hip-hop from African American cultural production in an attempt to remove its relationship to blackness works to undermine the importance of African American cultural production in shaping U.S. popular culture. The sonic, linguistic, and aesthetic codes of U.S. blackness that reside in hip-hop music and its musical predecessors, such as jazz, have been exported worldwide as American popular music and culture. In 1963, at the height of the Cold War, a similar type of sampling and remixing of Black music took place in the midst of shifting political tides and civil unrest in the United States. Jazz musician and composer Duke Ellington toured Sri Lanka, Egypt, India, Iraq, Jordan, Lebanon, Pakistan, Iran, and Turkey. His epic recording, *Far East Suite*, is a mix-tape of this journey and reflects the influences of his transnational tour on his identity as an artist. The album links the exchanges witnessed by Ellington of African American culture, jazz music, freedom, and democracy. For Ellington, culture was an ongoing process that found synergy with what Vijay Prashad calls polyculturalism, or the process of acknowledging the syncretism of cultural identities and their intersecting and overlapping connections.[15]

According to Greg Tate, Ellington's epic tour was "sold to the world as uniquely American in character."[16] Ellington's autobiographical reflections on the 1963 tour are documented in his "Notes on the State Department Tour." He recalls a reception at the U.S. Embassy in Damascus: "We [were] not required to restrain ourselves in the expression of our personal, political, social or religious views. As citizens of a great country, there were no restrictions on our tongues."[17] Referencing racial segregation in the United States, Ellington used the opportunity to assert the rights he was denied on U.S. soil. When asked about race in America, Ellington responded carefully, realizing the commodity of his blackness within particular international contexts and the socioeconomic privilege that he experienced. His response alerted the world that the "United States has a minority problem. Negroes are one of several minority groups, but the basis of the whole problem is economic rather than a matter of color."[18] Ellington's economic analysis of U.S. race struggles suggested that the racial and economic tension between blackness and Americanness was indeed a global problem. The problem that Ellington highlights emphasized the ways in which White Americans centralized the normative whiteness of America. He shifted the conversation on race to call for a more complex discourse that would consider the ways in which class and race are lived and produced by social relations. Ellington's analysis of how race and class connect in the identity politics he experienced is echoed by the late cultural studies scholar

Stuart Hall: "race is the modality in which class is 'lived,' the medium through which class relations are experienced, the form in which it is appropriated and 'fought through.'"[19]

When non-African American artists sample from African American blackness, they create performative conversations between the histories of their bodies and African American struggles for freedom. Thus, artists who are racially not Black and Black artists who are not African American are able to engage the individualities of African Americanness in various iterations and translations in performances that exceed current racial discourse. The theatrical process of the remix allows for spoken, written, and embodied recombination of lived histories that occur through selective sampling. Paul Gilroy's now classic argument on hybridity and blackness is relevant here:

> Regardless of their affiliation to the right, left, or centre, groups have fallen back on the idea of cultural nationalism, on the over integrated conceptions of culture which present immutable, ethnic differences as an absolute break in the histories and experiences of "black" and "white" people. Against this choice stands another, more difficult option: the theorization of créolisation, métissage, mestizaje, and hybridity. From the viewpoint of ethnic absolutism, this would be a litany of pollution and impurity. These terms are rather unsatisfactory ways of naming the process of cultural mutation and restless (dis)continuity that exceed racial discourse and avoid capture by its agents.[20]

Sampling and remixing both attempt to theorize notions of hybridity through performance. Another important contribution to performance studies scholarship that speaks to the performance of blackness and cultural discontinuities is E. Patrick Johnson's work on redemptive and transgressive Black appropriation. Johnson engages the dialectic between divergent and convergent racial scripts of authenticity. His asserts that no one person or group owns blackness, but rather, "individuals or groups appropriate this complex and nuanced racial signifier in order to circumscribe its boundaries or to exclude other individuals or groups."[21] This is a warning that we must not ignore that sampling can be appropriation, and that it can occur by diverse Black and non-Black subjects, within and outside U.S. national contexts, and over different social, historical, and political landscapes of production. Many of the hip-hop theater and performance artists in this book align themselves with struggles against anti-Black racism and social inequality embedded in hip-hop music. Cultural anthropologists Marcyliena Morgan and Dionne Bennett's suggestion that hip-hop has the capacity to inspire activism, social identification, and creative innovation supports the theory that sampling and remixing are tools that aid performers in contesting conventional identity constructions. The authors state, "Global Hip-hop has emerged as a culture that encourages and integrates innovative practices of artistic expression, knowledge production, social identification, and political mobilization. In these respects, it transcends and contests conventional constructions of identity, race, nation, community aesthetics, and knowledge."[22] Viewing hip-hop as a culture that encourages and integrates innovative practices of artistic expression allows for social realities to be navigated through hip-hop in exchanges that forge an alternative set of practices that challenge generic notions of a normatively White "universal" theater and performance. Sujatha Fernandes reflects on hip-hop as this kind of alternative space of identity negotiation and borrowing:

> The Hip-hop Nation as a transnational space of mutual learning and exchange may not have been a concrete reality. But the transient alliances that Hip-hoppers imagined across boundaries of class, race, and nation gave them the resources and the platform they needed to tell their stories and provided the grounds for their locally based political actions.[23]

Fernandes identifies hip-hop as a space for self-identified connections, yet warns that assuming all transient connections to hip-hop are for sociopolitical mobilization is naïve at best. Meiling Cheng's theory of multicentricity also asks us to think about the way that certain artistic exchanges connect and overlap, yet not arbitrarily so. Cheng argues that shifting the power hierarchies assumed between "majority" and "minority" cultures takes for granted "the boundary between 'majority' and 'minority,' between 'dominant' cultures and 'marginal' others."[24] This is not to suggest that any racial, ethnic, or national group selectively performs its racial identities in one particular way, but there are identifiable sights, sounds, and gestures associated with particular identity formations. The actors, performance artists, and dancers inspired by hip-hop in this book remix ideas about race, ethnicity, gender, and nation to cross socially constructed borders and offer social commentary about connections and disconnections between cultural experiences and practices. Performance studies scholar Richard Schechner's description of the ritual practices of rehearsal for performers to play with elements of everyday lived experiences suggests that in the act of performance notions of authenticity are obsolete and that artists have the freedom to assemble identities as they need them to be in a given performance. Schechner argues:

> Authenticity is a display of harmony/mastery of whatever style is being played. It is the work of rehearsal to prepare the strips of behavior so that when expressed by performers, they appear spontaneous, authentic, unrehearsed. [. . .] During rehearsals a past is assembled out of bits of actual experience, fantasies, historical research, past performances. Or a known score is recalled or replayed.[25]

The score that Schechner describes can be read as the linguistic, embodied, and visual codes used by artists in hip-hop theater and performance to assemble their unique version of hip-hop identity.

By the early 1990s hip-hop's influence on theater practices began to manifest in spaces across the United States and England. As a developing theater artist who played parts across racial, ethnic, and national identities, I struggled with my transgressive border-crossing. I began to train in the Stanislavsky method of acting between 1985 and 1992, the same period that Adam Bradley and Andrew Dubois label "The Golden Age of Hip-Hop."[26] I listened to all kinds of music growing up, from Motown and Barbra Streisand to Run-D. M. C. and U2. I will admit that I was a reluctant hip-hopper during my early years of performance training. My embrace of hip-hop as a soundtrack of my personal journey was produced by my discovery of the music in the 1980s when music was forced into the multicultural cipher of MTV, yet distinctly separated into neatly racialized categorizes. R&B was Black. Hip-hop was Black. Heavy metal was White. Country was White. New age was multicultural. One associated race with music in very specific ways while simultaneously "mixing it" up on MTV video shows. No one could have told me that hip-hop's blackness would be up for interpretation in the late

1980s. The specificity of my racial, ethnic, and gender identity shaped how I understood acting, performance, and music, but I was encouraged by my acting teachers to ignore race. Hip-hop eventually became a performance frame that allowed me the freedom to use its aesthetic practices to shape my worldview and my approach to theater practice. In 1993, I began to study sketch comedy in schools like the Groundlings in Los Angeles, seeking to escape the rigid structures of formal acting training that only seemed to legitimize European-derived performance aesthetics. In improv classes, I began to find an intersection between my process as an actor and that of hip-hop DJs. Just as DJs isolated musical samples from existing albums to create new songs in the remix, I used my body, borrowing samples of language, accents, gestures, and styles of other racial and ethnic groups to create characters. Particularly in hip-hop theater, codes used by hip-hop performers to articulate racial and ethnic difference were similar to sonic samples employed by DJs. An acting coach I worked with in Los Angeles compared my approach to that of a White actor from New York, Danny Hoch, whose solo show she had seen on HBO. Watching Hoch's show, I saw that the characters and experiences he expressed were mediated via a specific African American experience of blackness articulated in hip-hop through which many non-Black artists found shared community. Could non-African American artists engaged with hip-hop locate blackness as a site to rethink their own relationships to White oppression, and thus perform blackness in a way that was intended to build social and cultural connections? I began to locate other hip-hop-inspired plays and performances in which actors and performers played across boundaries of difference in order to connect themselves to the social and cultural experiences narrated in hip-hop.

The post–civil rights generation that created hip-hop in the early 1970s and ushered it into the mainstream in the 1980s was predominantly African American artists, of varying African diasporic backgrounds. These young, gifted African American (and many Afro-Latinx) artists who fashioned hip-hop into a malleable artistic movement were responding to deindustrialization, Reaganomics, and the rapid growth of the prison-industrial complex. As hip-hop moved into the mainstream and the White suburbs in the late 1980s and early 1990s, it became one of the most influential art forms in the world. As many Generation Xers, the children of baby boomers born between the mid-1960s and the early 1980s, came of age, they developed a critical consciousness—across racial lines—and understood hip-hop not simply as a music and culture, but as a way of knowing and making sense of the world around them. Through the late 1980s and early 1990s hip-hop's economic success and significant aesthetic impact prompted American media influencers to market hip-hop less as "Black" music and more as universal music, thus whitewashing or "multicultural-washing" hip-hop in ways that disconnected African American people from the genius of its creativity. In the early and mid-twentieth century the United States Department of State sponsored jazz tours showcasing African American artists (such as Duke Ellington, mentioned previously) who were charged to promote unity and peace in the wake of racial unrest that resulted from the systemic inequality of Black people in the United States. In the early 2000s, the State Department's hip-hop "diversity tours" mimicked similar efforts by the state to mask anti-Black racism and systemic inequality. Hip-hop artists were recruited to travel throughout the globe, in the early, and now mid-2000s. The influence of hip-hop on American and European popular culture produced an influx of non-Black and non-African American Black-identified, hip-hop-inspired artists and characters portrayed throughout popular culture, in music, theater, film, and television programs. Hip-hop theater was getting ready for its close-up.

Just as jazz music's relationship to African American expressions of blackness changed in popular culture when the music shifted from being read as "race" (or Black) music to be read as "American" music without racial signifier, so were the performative vernaculars associated with African American identity absorbed into representations of a hip-hop aesthetic. Both jazz and hip-hop music have been, and continue to be, read in- and outside the Black continuum. How might our view of blackness, specifically its historical location within U.S.-based hip-hop, change when we acknowledge its performance in newly embodied contexts? Writing in American Theatre in 2016 about *Hamilton*, African American cultural critic John McWhorter states:

> For 125 years, American musical theatre language has been driven by serial infusions of black pop energy, creating the sound of Broadway so familiar today, including manifestations now processed as thoroughly "white." Given

> that hip-hop has been the mainstream for young Americans of all colors for at least 20 years, isn't this when we would expect Broadway music to come in for its next injection of, as it were, "flava" and evolve into a whole new direction?[27]

The aesthetic practices of jazz used during the Harlem Renaissance and the Black Arts Movement inspired theatrical innovations in poetry, writing, dance, theater, fine art, and music created by non-African American practitioners. Hip-hop continues in this same historical continuum of improvised aesthetics and has greatly influenced all of the aforementioned areas of cultural production, including American theater. In the above quote, McWhorter attempts to reconcile the consumption and absorption of Black popular music into mainstream pop cultural influences using African American vernacular terms such as "flava" to mock African American cultural influences on Broadway's normatively White and Eurocentric cultural aesthetic as well as its overall influence on American popular culture. McWhorter's assessment of Black influences on Broadway attempts to trivialize the influence of African American cultural production in the American mainstream and misses the opportunity to connect to the important contributions that Black American artists have made over time that have already transformed and continue to transform artistic practices in mainstream American theater as reflected in the phenomenal success of hip-hop-inspired cultural production.

Flava In Your Ear[28]

On the east coast, Danny Hoch's pioneering solo performances in plays such as *Some People* (1994) and *Jails, Hospitals & Hip-Hop* (1996) mark the beginning of the exploration of hip-hop by White theater artists, disrupting the normative associations of hip-hop and African American culture. By developing an artistic movement that could embody the contradictions of hip-hop's relationship to blackness and the multiculturalism imposed on it by the corporate mainstream, diverse racial and ethnic groups could lay claim to hip-hop's aesthetic syncretism—to which they were rightful contributors—and still borrow from Black performance practices. Hip-hop theater scholar Daniel Banks makes an important connection between hip-hop and Black ritual and cultural practices in his ground-breaking anthology *Say Word! Voices from Hip Hop Theater*. He notes that many hip-hop theater and performance artists engage in call-and-response, which is gleaned from the residuals of African griot storytelling traditions embedded in slave culture, as well as the Black church, and the ritual practices of hip-hop culture that include freestyling, braggadocio, poetic word play, signifyin', and other strategic movements of African American social and cultural commentary and critique.[29] Such improvisational impulses span the linguistic, visual, and embodied practices of hip-hop, allowing performers across racial lines to challenge the normative whiteness of mainstream theater-making and push audiences to interact with the shared community of hip-hop as a minority art form that has global aesthetic appeal.[30]

From the early to mid-2000s, a string of hip-hop-inspired works by African American and non-African American artists utilized the genre's improvised aesthetic to tell stories which began to decenter the normative White center of the American mainstream theater and performance scenes.[31] Many of these new hip-hop artists centered specific African American cultural and aesthetic samples to rearticulate their experiences. Founded in 2000, the Hip-Hop Theater Festival made the connection that hip-hop music and culture were directly influencing American theater practice. Artists across racial lines were creating new styles of performance using the hip-hop aesthetic. These works were both American and international with a shared connection to the hip-hop generation and a desire to connect to a historically underrepresented youth audience using the vernacular of hip-hop, which derives from African American language and culture.

The Hip-Hop Theater Festival began in New York City in 2000, founded by Danny Hoch, noted director and producer Kamilah Forbes, and playwright and activist Clyde Valentín, with spin-off festivals eventually emerging in Washington, D.C., Los Angeles, Chicago, and Oakland.[32] The festival was forged out of the founders' common interest and participation in hip-hop culture and provided audiences an opportunity to experience African American and non-African American artistic engagement with hip-hop and its influence on theater. The Hip-Hop Theater Festival has now existed for more than twenty years;

over those years it has created opportunities for performers across racial and national lines engaged with hip-hop performance to challenge the normative whiteness of American theater practices. The soldiers who do this work are a multiracial and ethnic amalgamation of artists and cultural theorists of inspired hip-hop theater and performance such as Kashi Johnson, Jonzi D (who is one of several artists credited with coining the term hip-hop theater), Holly Bass (who was one of the first artists to use the term hip-hop theater in print), Daniel Banks, Bryyon Bain, Eisa Davis, Kamilah Forbes, Danny Hoch, Baba Israel, Will Power, Kate Prince, Radha Blank, Sharrell Luckett, Rickerby Hinds, Marc Bamuthi Joseph, Joe Hernandez- Kolski, Jorge "Pop Master" Fabel Pabon, Daphne Sicre, Clyde Valentín, myself, and many others who not only have a history of performing variations of hip-hop-inspired theater and performance, but also teach hip-hop as it relates to theater and performance in academic and community institutions.[33]

In 2001, the popular HBO television series *Russell Simmons Presents Def Poetry Jam,* produced by African American hip-hop moguls Russell Simmons and Stan Lathan, featured a multiracial group of hip-hop-inspired performers and found critical success, revealing the links between spoken word and hip-hop theater. *Def Poetry Jam* was adapted to a Broadway play, *Russell Simmons Presents Def Poetry Jam* on Broadway, in 2002, and was one of the first Broadway plays to feature hip-hop-inspired works.[34] Even more theater and performance art spanning the early 2000s to the present exemplify hip-hop's influence on non-African American artists in American theater. To expand on the work of just one of these artists, in Sarah Jones's shows *Surface Transit* (2002), *Bridge & Tunnel* (2008), and most recently a sold-out off-Broadway run of *Sell/Buy/Date* (2017) being developed into a film Jones uses the solo-show format to explore experiences across race, ethnicity, and nationality using hip-hop aesthetics conflated with popular culture. The product of a multiracial family and community, Jones counts her background as an impetus for her to connect with people from diverse backgrounds. She was labeled by TED as "a one woman global village."[35]

Lin-Manuel Miranda's hip-hop-inspired *In the Heights* (2005) and *Hamilton* (2015) are two of the most successful musicals in Broadway history, having won numerous Tony Awards and a Pulitzer Prize. Miranda's knowledge of the White, Eurocentric Broadway musical form and hip-hop's dominant African American cultural cadences allowed him to remix African American and Latinx cultural experiences to make hip-hop-inspired theater legible for the masses. *In the Heights* chronicles Latinx perspectives and quests for the American Dream in Washington Heights, New York. The musical was presented in a workshop at the Hip-Hop Theater Festival in 2006. After a successful off-Broadway run, *In the Heights* moved to Broadway in 2008, and was nominated for thirteen Tony Awards, winning four of the nominations.[36] Miranda's exploration of the intersection of hip-hop with other Afro-Latinx inspired music and his challenging of dominant narratives of blackness that dominate hip-hop identities speak to the syncretism of hip-hop and the process of sampling.[37] *Hamilton*, a musical reimagining of the life of Alexander Hamilton based on the Ron Chernow biography, casts actors of color to tell Hamilton's immigration story. Using the bodies of oppressed minorities whose stories have yet to be heard on Broadway, this musical mash-up remixes hip-hop with other Black musical genres such as jazz, R&B, and pop, as well as traditional Broadway musical styles.

Hip-hop's influence on performance practices also extends to fine art, conceptual art, and dance. Many ex-graffiti artists shifted their skills from painting on public property to canvas and installation art in the late 1980s and early 1990s. Gallery owners across New York made pilgrimages to the Bronx and its environs to discover hip-hop street artists. African American artist Fab 5 Freddy, European American artist Keith Haring, and Haitian American artist Jean-Michel Basquiat were all street artists before crossing over to the gallery scene. Exhibits that explored the influence of hip-hop on contemporary art and performance began to surface in galleries in New York, Chicago, and Los Angeles in the late 1990s and early 2000s.[38] Korean conceptual artist Nikki S. Lee was one of the performance artists featured in the Bronx Museum's landmark hip-hop art exhibit entitled *One Planet Under a Groove:Hip-Hop and Contemporary Art* and curated by Lydia Yee and Fred Sirmans. Lee used her body as art to explore the intersection of blackness and Asianness in hip-hop's visual language. Her series of staged photographs, entitled *The Hip Hop Project* and *The Hispanic Project*, sampled dress, hairstyles, and skin color from African American and Latinx women in hip-hop culture in New York and suggested that the performance of racial identification can transgress racial boundaries. Solo artist Matt Sax and director

Eric Rosen's collaborations on the hip-hop solo play *Clay* (2009) and the dystopian rock/hip-hop musical *Venice* (2015) parallel the musical collaborations of old Broadway. Sax's plays are of millennial-generation hip-hop and have a very different understanding of the culture as not uniquely connected to African American blackness but a more distinctly universal form.

Internationally, British choreographer Jonzi D has been part of the hip-hop theater scene since the mid-1990s. Hip-hop theater in London is a hybrid form of dance and spoken word, and Jonzi D was one of the pioneering hip-hop theater artists in England. He was one of the first British theater artists to be showcased in the Hip Hop Theater Festival in New York the early 2000s, marking the transnational influence of hip-hop. Jonzi D is at the forefront of creating opportunities for European artists to connect hip-hop to physical theater and dance practice. These aforementioned hip-hop-inspired performances offer a snapshot of the wide range of work in underground, regional, and mainstream theater in America and the United Kingdom that is influenced by African American expressions of blackness. They challenge how stories about race are lived, told, and performed as they highlight which "American" experiences make it to the mainstream of theater and performance practice. African American theater scholar Harry Elam, Jr. links past and present American and European theater practices in American Theatre's 2004 analysis of hip-hop theater. Elam notes an overlap of African American cultural practices in hip-hop theater with classical American theater practices derived from European aesthetics:

> While Hip-hop theatre is a new form of cultural expression, it still retains, repeats, and revises the past as it pushes into the future. With its celebration of language, meter, poetic strictures, verbal play and display, it hearkens back to earlier traditions of oral expression in African-American culture, such as the spoken word of Gil Scott-Heron and the Last Poets, and even to classical theatrical conventions and the productive wordplay of William Shakespeare. Hip-hop theatre's inclusion of actual, live rap music and DJ scratching and sampling, its allowance for freestyle improvisation, its embrace of non-linearity and presentational direct address to the audience, breaks with conventional theatrical realism and reflects contemporary artistic directions.[39]

Highlighting many of the cultural practices of hip-hop discussed in *Sampling and Remixing Blackness*, such as verbal play and display, Elam notes that hip-hop theater's use of sampling and improvisational practices reflect its diversity as a new form of cultural expression indebted to African American oral expression and those European-derived practices that are imbedded in mainstream theater. Echoing Elam, Danny Hoch argues that hip-hop is indebted to African American culture, but is not dependent on it to survive: "The notion that Hip-hop is solely an African-American art form is erroneous. It is part of the African continuum, and if it were not for African Americans there would be no Hip-hop, but neither would Hip-hop exist if not for the polycultural social construct of New York in the 1970s."[40] Daniel Banks's claims about rituals in hip-hop theater provide a theoretical context to evaluate the redemptive aspects of cross- and intraracial performance that I propose in this book:

> For those audience members from the outside, Hip-hop Theater gives a glimpse into these inner workings—the culture's stories, core values, and ways of thinking and knowing. This is how any culturally specific theater functions, such as Noh theater, performances of the Hindu epic The Mahabharata, or Yiddish, Gaelic, and indigenous theater forms. These performances provide a cultural negotiation through expressive means for people both inside and outside of the work's cultural context. I propose, therefore, that Hip-hop theater is the ritual theater of Hip-hop culture.[41]

The inner workings and practices that Banks outlines may be more ritualistic than actually tied to any particular ritual recognized by the hip-hop community at large. Despite hip-hop's influence on theater practice, mainstream theater audiences and practitioners are still majority White, and the Black and Brown artists making theater are not really running around talking about making hip-hop theater. I don't know if anyone is. The moniker of hip-hop theater really identifies a non-Eurocentric approach to art-making that is inspired by hip-hop cultural practices which center Black creativity and consider self-taught Black and Brown people as important knowledge makers. When the commercial potential of Black art rises, the notion that the art remains "Black" is largely suspicious to White artists, producers, and consumers.

To that end, I offer a supplement to Banks's definition of hip-hop theater as ritual. If we think of hip-hop-inspired theater as a repetition of practices that are deeply connected to African American and African diasporic social and aesthetic codes, we can remix the idea of ritual as designating a practice that elevates experiences of oppression as central to art-making for social change which can be shared by those who live those oppressions and overcome them and those who don't.[42] Hip-hop's blackness finds shared community across racial and ethnic experiences. We are currently in the wake of a cultural shift where African American experiences of racial and ethnic identity in hip-hop are being borrowed and repurposed to forge new, self-fashioned experiences of racial identity, and those reconfigurations are being played out in hip-hop theater.

Time after Time[43]

My speculative timeline for mapping these artistic engagements with hip-hop's blackness in this book starts in 1995, at the beginning of hip-hop theater festivals in the United States, to 2017, the year that the hip-hop musical *Hamilton* began its international tour after one of the most successful Broadway runs in American history. This timeline also maps hip-hop's underground influence on theater, conceptual art, and dance in the mid-1990s, through its mainstream presence in the creative arts of the late twentieth and early twenty-first centuries. This timeline is not exhaustive and excludes many hip-hop-inspired theater performances. This book is not meant to be a history of hip-hop-inspired theater and performance at all, but seeks to identify the ways that samples of African American expressions of blackness in hip-hop have be used to shape the expressions of hip-hop in American (and, in one case European) theater spaces. I have selected representative, not comprehensive, works that challenge the normativity and stability of whiteness as a legitimizing social construct in the performing and fine art worlds. Though I read each work through the matrix of sampling and remixing, only a few of the artists who allowed me to interview them for this book acknowledged their sampling and remixing of expressions of blackness within United States and transnational contexts. Many artists whom I met and/or observed in performance struggled with labeling hip-hop as a Black aesthetic practice at all. The acts of sampling and remixing revealed in these works, coupled with the compelling, personal stories of how these artists came to hip-hop, demonstrate the connecting points of hybridity that construct and reproduce blackness and hip-hop anew in global contexts. Of the artists whose work is explored in this book, all create performance in the United States and/or England, locales that are heavily influenced by African American expressions of blackness in hip-hop. Their artistic work makes creative, theoretical interventions in current discussions about race, performance, and blackness because it reveals the socially constructed nature of race and our collective reliance on, and rejection of, socially imposed boundaries of racial identification.

In chapter 1, "Licensed to Ill: Performing Alternative White Masculinities in Danny Hoch's *Jails, Hospitals & Hip-Hop* and Matt Sax's *Clay*," I put Danny Hoch's critically acclaimed solo performance *Jails, Hospitals & Hip-Hop* (1996) in conversation with Matt Sax's one-man hip-hop musical *Clay* (2006). Hoch and Sax both use linguistic and embodied samples of African American expressions of blackness in hip-hop to construct and perform alternative White masculinities that challenge assertions of Black authenticity in hip-hop. Both Hoch and Sax create an alternative allied space of belonging through their fluency in hip-hop music and culture that challenges White youth to self-identify as antiracist, politically engaged members of the global hip-hop community.

In chapter 2, "Empire State of Mind: Performing Remixes of the Hip-Hop American Dream," I discuss the photographed performances of conceptual artist Nikki S. Lee in *The Hip Hop Project* (2001) and the performance of Sarah Jones's Broadway show *Bridge & Tunnel* (2009). Both Lee and Jones use their bodies and hip-hop as a site through which multiple racial identities are forged, transgressed, and remixed. Lee's performances in her conceptual art series entitled *The Hip Hop Project* and *The Hispanic Project* reference what Nicole Fleetwood calls "iconic figurations" of American blackness in hip-hop.[44] I read Lee's photographed performances as a series of theatrical reproductions of African American and Latina identities that overtake the narratives of blackness and hip-hop that they present. In Sarah Jones's solo show, *Bridge & Tunnel*, the actor uses her body as turntable to mix the samples of attire, language, and gesture of diverse racial groups under the umbrella of hip-hop culture.

Chapter 3, "One Nation Under a Groove: (Re)Membering Hip-Hop

Dance," explores the work of Afro-British hip-hop dance theater choreographer Jonzi D. I discuss the ways in which non-African American, hip-hop-inspired artists locate hip-hop in embodied gestures of African American hip-hop dance. Jonzi D's hip-hop theater performance *Tag: Me vs. The City* (2004) utilizes American hip-hop dance codes to narrate the story of a White, British, working-class graffiti artist. This play offers an opportunity to link transnational explorations of blackness and hip-hop through dance that enables social coalitions and embodies hip-hop across national lines.

Chapter 4, "Musical Mash-Ups of Americanness in Lin-Manuel Miranda's *In the Heights* and Matt Sax's *Venice*," discusses two works that remix notions of Americanness and hip-hop that challenge the Black–White binary to define what race is to us in the twenty-first century. A mash-up is a creative combination that fuses content from different sources in order to tell a story that has multiple (and often conflicting) stories playing at once. In most instances, the origins of the sample content are left in their original form, just repurposed in new relational contexts within new material. A theatrical mash-up, then, is one that samples and remixes indexes from diverse sonic, visual, and embodied sources and plays disparate and shared theatrical elements in new contexts. These two musicals mash up traditional Broadway formulas, hip-hop musical lyrics, and other Black and Latinx musical forms (such as R&B, rock, and reggaetón) to reflect the struggles of marginalized Americans who must negotiate the hyphens of their human experiences as they fight systemic inequality in quests to experience full citizenship. Hip-hop's blackness, as expressed in these two musical theater pieces that unsettle the normative whiteness of Broadway, is formed through its sampling of other cultural experiences. *Venice* pushes toward the future of hip-hop by presenting a dystopian view of race and ethnicity that attempts to deconstruct existing categories of racial identity. Miranda's *In the Heights* makes Latinx contributions to hip-hop visible and audible to challenge a dominant association of hip-hop with African American culture. In *Venice*, Matt Sax's hip-hop/rock mash-up musical collaboration with Eric Rosen offers a meditation on the demise of racial identification in the twenty-first century and the imminent rise of a post-racial society where current racial projects are reorganized anew. Focusing on a twenty-first-century civil war that takes place in a post-apocalyptic New Orleans, Sax and Rosen remix existing racial transcripts in a mash-up that samples and remixes how we read and interpret race.

Chapter 5, "*Hamilton: An American Musical*'s Ghosts: Digging up American History," explores how Lin-Manuel Miranda remixes American history in an attempt to challenge the dominant narrative of American history as told through the biography of Founding Father Alexander Hamilton. Using hip-hop and actors of color to narrate America's past in the present, Miranda's distorted reflection of America reveals the ghosts of slavery and oppression that were never presented in the musical, only referenced in the bodies of the performers of color and the sampled music of hip-hop. Chapter 6, "Arresting New Arrangements of Identity in Hip-Hop Performance," concludes the book and discusses the ways in which non-African American artists using hip-hop enable new understandings of identity and identifications with blackness that open opportunities for more empathetic connections with humanity.

Together, these artists and their works triangulate the Black–White binary to offer circuitous alternative engagements with hip-hop culture that spin from Jewish American, Asian, Latinx, and Black British artists and acknowledge the influence of African American cultural practice in hip-hop on popular culture as a place to reconsider what it means to be American and hip-hop. The pursuit of authenticity in performance does not have to aspire toward being perceived as real or essential. Alternate meanings of authenticity, such as those associated with particular identity formations, allow room for performers to abstract creatively from the so-called original lived experience by sampling from various indexes of identity to construct a performance. Performance studies scholar Richard Schechner argues against a limited definition of authenticity, instead opting for a harmony and mastery of disparate pieces, from research to rehearsal discoveries to actual experiences to full-out fantasy. All parts are necessary when a performer is scoring a character.[45] These scores that Schechner references can be read as indexes of racial transcripts that actors and performers identify to play a character. In cross-racial and intraracial performance, specific linguistic, embodied, and visual codes are essential to rendering a performance with depth and complexity. Building on Schechner, I argue that the artists in this book do not merely sample indexical markers of African American expressions of blackness verbatim in simple acts of mimicry or appropriation. Instead, they strategically sample and remix parts of Black cultural aesthetics as performed in language, styles of self-adornment, and embodied gestures, using their bodies and voices as spaces to theorize and critique the politics and contradictions of hip-hop in both transgressive and redemptive acts of racial and ethnic crossover.

African American poet, MC, and social activist Toni Blackman was selected as the U.S. hip-hop cultural ambassador to Senegal. Blackman is an innovator in hip-hop-inspired spoken word, theater, and performance. Applying the cipher, a circle of creativity used to inspire improvised social connection and artistry, Blackman worked with Black youth from Senegal to get them to positively identify with American expressions of blackness, not as a signifier of racial origins but as an iconic representation of dissent that could empower them to artistically respond to systems of oppression. Like Ellington, Blackman chose to use music—in her case, hip-hop—as a cultural form to tell the truth about strained race relations in the United States in the current millennium and to teach youth how to find a global community of self-empowerment using the positive aspects of the culture.[46] In a full-circle moment of cultural diplomacy, an African American woman used hip-hop, a musical form filled with African-derived aesthetics and devised by African migrants in the diaspora, to teach Black youth from Senegal about the power of hip-hop to transform self- and community perceptions. Blackman engaged the transnational legacy and language of hip-hop, which created synergy between the persistence of improvised struggles for equality by African Americans in the United States and the oppression of Black people in Dakar. As with any language, discursive or embodied, there are varying levels of fluency that often distort the intentions of the speaker. As performance studies scholar and theater historian Henry Bial notes:

> Rituals are based on repetition, and though most rituals change somewhat over time, we look to them as fixed points from which we measure the rest of our experience. Generally speaking, rituals exemplify and reinforce the values and beliefs of the group that performs them. Conversely, communities are defined by the rituals they share.[47]

The sampling and remixing of specific performative codes of blackness explored here are representative of the ritualistic points of connection that exist between performers engaged with hip-hop culture. Thus, the ritual of hip-hop is fluid and non-traditional. It is connected to the values of social justice, freedom of self-expression, and resistance to anti-Black racism. These are the values and beliefs that, even when contested or disrupted by acts that fall between appropriation and adoration, constitute how a new generation of artists measure possibility in relationship to hip-hop, and they are deeply shaping the way we understand how race is lived and performed in new, remixed imaginings of identity in theater and performance.

ONE

LICENSED TO ILL / Performing Alternative White Masculinities in Danny Hoch's *Jails, Hospitals & Hip-Hop* and Matt Sax's *Clay*

I remember the first time that I heard the music of the Beastie Boys. It was 1986 and I was riding with my brother Mack in his Volkswagen Rabbit. He played "No Sleep Til' Brooklyn" from his *Licensed to Ill* cassette. Mack was a rapper and an emerging b-boy in our predominantly White suburb in Marietta, Georgia, a suburb of Atlanta where we moved after leaving Dearborn, Michigan. I spent most of high school listening to John Hughes soundtracks, U2, and Prince records. This music, categorized as alternative and R&B in the case of John Hughes and Prince respectively, was respected as music in the mainstream. Hip-hop (I understood it then as "rap") was uniquely associated with Black culture in the 1980s. If you listened to hip-hop, you were actively engaged in Black culture. In my all-White high school, I wasn't strong or brave enough to be actively involved in listening to rap music, because to do so was to be ostracized from my White friends, and I wasn't strong enough to stand on my own.

A year and a half my junior, my brother was strong and unapologetically Black. He introduced me to hip-hop and helped me to understand its importance to the Black community. The Beastie Boys' sound was a remix of punk brashness and infectious hip-hop beats. Mack knew that this blend would be attractive to me. The lyrical content of the group focused on the social and cultural experiences of being White, Jewish party boys from New York. The Beastie Boys was one of the first non-African American hip-hop groups to find its place in hip-hop without having to hijack African American cultural aesthetics. Discovered by Def Jam Recording cofounders Rick Rubin and Russell Simmons, the "Beasties" cultivated an iconic sound that places them as one of a handful of non-African American hip-hop acts that have gained the respect of the African American hip-hop community in the United States. For my brother and me, the Beasties were a bridge between the two worlds we lived in: urban Black and suburban White—with a twist.

The Beasties are Jewish, and an understanding of systemic oppression and a shared commitment to fighting the powers of bigotry and prejudice may have come with that identity. When I listened to their music, I felt as if they respected that their version of hip-hop could only be White. From my perspective, they never attempted to act "Black," but instead chose what type of whiteness they wanted to represent. They lacked the culture associated with hip-hop, yet never aligned themselves with a whiteness that sought to demean hip-hop. Rather, they helped create space for a whiteness that appreciated the cultural contributions of African American, Latinx, and other artists of color in the hip-hop game. Despite the frivolity of the Beasties' raps, they were accused of being cultural appropriators, even by the very producer who helped to discover them, Russell Simmons. In an article in *Spin* in 1989 by Frank Owen, Simmons claimed that he had taught the Beasties what they needed to know so that they would be read as legitimate hip-hop artists and not as White men trying to be Black:

> "They had talent, but they came across as the worst sort of blackface band," he told *Spin* in 1989. "It was like they were making fun of black people. A lot of people thought they were racist, that they were putting down black culture. I taught them how to f—king walk and how to f—king talk; I convinced the black community that they were real."[1]

In the same article, Mike D of the Beastie Boys responds to Simmons's reduction of their work in the then-emergent hip-hop culture:

> The problem with Russell, [. . .] is that he likes to present himself as this Svengali with a master plan. Russell is like the great speech-maker. The raps he used to give you in interviews, he's practiced for days. But he's also extremely erratic.[2]

In this exchange of comments in Owens's interview, we see that the Beasties were very aware of their relationship with Simmons, and that it was their commercial appeal as White anomalies in hip-hop that Simmons was attracted to. They paid respect to the centrality of African American cultural contributions in hip-hop, even when they were ridiculed by African Americans with power over their careers.

Licensed to Ill, that first album, was as fun, raunchy, and misogynist as most hip-hop of the 1980s, with some unfortunate lyrics for which the band has since apologized numerous times. The album sits in a vexed place in hip-hop history. It personifies the hip-hop vernacular term from the 1980s, "ill," as much as the Beasties were "illin'" on the tracks. The term "illin," for the Beastie Boys, meant being the best of the best—the dopest. Being "licensed to ill" was being cool, street credible, woke—or self-aware. To be ill was to challenge the dominant culture and to legitimately engage hip-hop from a lived perspective, not through a mimicry of African American hip-hop artists from the United States. But for others watching White boys perform hip-hop, illin' could also mean appropriative, not conscious, not cool at all. Instead of creating an either/or binary, this chapter asks: Can White artists inspired by hip-hop make music or creative works inspired by that music, that appreciate and engage with the culture, without being accused of racial and cultural appropriation? In my work as an artist and scholar of hip-hop theater, I had difficulty finding clear-cut answers to these questions. I found myself needing a resource that could help me articulate to my White and non-White students alike that the phenomenon of hip-hop rose from a local movement that began in Black and Brown communities in New York in the 1970s, to a Black phenomenon in the 1980s, and to a national and international crossover genre in the 1990s. By the early 2000s, hip-hop had become one of the largest sites of cross-racial and ethnic exchange in the world. Many of these exchanges are not simply material swaps of the music and its ephemera, but are embodied engagements with hip-hop that make recognizable aspects of blackness transferable across racial lines. Accusations of cultural and racial appropriation arise when the complex and painful histories of racial oppression and subjugation addressed by African American (and other ethnically Black and Latinx) artists in hip-hop's oral history are sampled uniquely for artistic and/or commercial gain, while the history of Black freedom struggles is lost in the translation of the final performance. As non-African American artists remix their lived experiences with those borrowed from the Black music and culture of hip-hop, one must ask: How might the performance of racial identity change? My goal in this chapter is to examine the performance of White masculinity in the work of theater artist Danny Hoch and actor Matt Sax, seeking to understand the ways in which White masculinity and privilege are unsettled by and through hip-hop theater and the Jewishness of these artists. I analyze their work, looking for clues that identify the ways in which White allies in hip-hop pursue social justice in American theater practice. I focus on strategies that these artists employ to disassociate themselves from their White privilege in order to align themselves with social justice agendas that fight against racism and systemic inequality for artists of color in American theater.[3] Hip-hop music, and the theater it inspires, reveal strategies for teaching about White privilege and hip-hop in ways that can foster fruitful dialogues about coalition building and allyship in the twenty-first century.

White Privilege II[4]

In 2016, White indie rapper Macklemore released the single "White Privilege II," a searing manifesto in which the artist contemplates his White privilege by denouncing the cultural appropriation of blackness by White artists in hip-hop. The song gained immediate traction in the media and scrutiny from Black hip-hop artists and consumers, who critiqued Macklemore for ventriloquizing what Black people in the United States had been saying for decades about White artists trafficking in African American culture in hip-hop. Macklemore's intention was to draw attention to the social injustices against African Americans that persist in the United States in the wake of the Black Lives Matter Movement and the cultural appropriation of hip-hop by White artists; however, reception of his song was mixed. Though his goal was to position himself as a White ally of Black Lives Matter, his use of a Black art form to disavow his privilege made the artist appear more "White," privileged, and tone deaf than I am sure he ever expected. In her 2003 landmark book *Why Are All the Black Kids Sitting Together in the Cafeteria? And Other Conversations About Race*, Beverly Daniel Tatum outlines three identities available to White people: the overtly racist White person, the guilty White person, or the colorblind "I don't see race" White person.[5] Though White hip-hop artists are no longer anomalies in twenty-first-century American popular culture, in the early hip-hop history of the late twentieth century, White hip-hop artists riffed on the categories of White identity outlined by Tatum. Groups like the Beastie Boys or 3rd Bass were placed in a "woke" category of White artists who accepted their whiteness and rapped uniquely from a White heteronormative position, but were decidedly pro-Black in their social and political stances.[6] These artists stood in stark contrast to another hip-hop industry category of White rappers dubbed "wannabes." Artists such as Vanilla Ice, and more recently Iggy Azalea, presented faux gangster identities in order to align themselves with pseudo hardcore "Black-like" pasts to help them remix street credible bios that were supported by their fluency in hip-hop vernacular. But the line between hip-hop's vexed White past and its present has been subverted by the critical success of White rappers who occupy a fourth category of whiteness, one that is allied with the notion of anti-Black racism. Artists like Eminem, Post Malone, and Macklemore grew up with hip-hop music and present themselves as familiar with the culture, yet often experience slippages that reveal their White privilege in ways that undermine their intentions, as was the case with Macklemore's "White Privilege II." The historical negotiations of the color line in hip-hop have shifted, and so has the property line that separates intellectual and creative property. Allyship, as defined here, follows several phases of engagement that find kindship with the patterns in which White artists in this chapter engage. According to social psychologists Lisa Spanierman and Laura Smith, to be an ally, White contributors must:

> (a) demonstrate nuanced understanding of institutional racism and White privilege; [. . .] (b) enact a continual process of self-reflection about their own racism and positionality; [. . .] (c) express a sense of responsibility and commitment to using their racial privilege in ways that promote equity; [. . .] (d) engage in actions to disrupt racism and the status quo on micro and macro levels; (e) participate in coalition building and work in solidarity with people of color; and (f) encounter resistance from other White individuals [. . .].[7]

A new wave of White artists inspired by hip-hop music and culture have built on the mainstream acceptance of early White rappers, such as the Beastie Boys, and more recently Eminem, to construct an alternative White masculinity. As hip-hop music began to influence the creation of theater that challenged the normative whiteness and Eurocentricity of mainstream theater spaces in the late 1990s, White male artists in hip-hop theater began to gain critical respect and success in the underground theater world for developing works that challenged the White male status quo. These performers used the stage to call out White artists who simply mimicked African American culture and racial stereotypes in hip-hop. They presented their lived racial experiences as Whites in opposition to other Whites who have oppressed Black and other people of color in acts of solidarity. History books and popular culture do not teach us about White people who, throughout our history, have allied themselves with the struggle for anti-racism.[8] American history is full of White people who have skillfully and successfully fought racism, including those who fight racism by using hip-hop. Building on narratives of solidarity and community, these White artists personally identify with hip-hop as a dissident tool to challenge the status quo while using their fluency in the vernacular, sartorial styles, and cultural practices of the genre's blackness to inspire cross-racial coalitions and situate themselves as non-racist, hip-hop-inspired theater makers. To this end, this chapter interrogates the constructions of alternative White masculinities in hip-hop theater by White male solo artists—specifically Jewish American men. I place pioneering hip-hop theater artist Danny Hoch's 1996 solo play *Jails, Hospitals & Hip-Hop* in conversation with actor Matt Sax's 2015 solo performance *Clay*. These White artists navigate the vernacular and embodied histories of Black appropriation embedded in hip-hop's language. Hoch's and Sax's plays, spanning almost ten years of hip-hop theater history, sample cultural authenticity narratives in hip-hop and remix them with fictional experiences that reflect what they have lived as artists engaged with hip-hop culture. Instead of trying to legitimize their places in the music and culture through hip-hop's blackness, they center their own experiences within the culture as the basis of their stories. By sampling and remixing the linguistic and embodied vernaculars of hip-hop, they translate a new model of White hip-hop authenticity that allows hip-hop to remain Black, yet is intrinsically tied to forming alternative representations of White masculinity that seek to indict racist practices. Hoch and Sax forge an alternative space for White artists to claim hip-hop by using their work to draw attention to White appropriation of African American culture, while staking their own claims to a music and culture that advocate for racial and class equality through performance.

"It's Like That"[9]

Danny Hoch grew up in LeFrak City outside of New York at a time when hip-hop culture was considered decidedly Black, not only by the African American people who made it, but also by non-Black people who experienced the music as it seeped across the United States via mixtapes, radios, and MTV in the late 1980s. Many argue that hip-hop was a coalition of artists from multiple racial identifications in New York at the time: Puerto Rican and Dominican b-boys and b-girls; Jewish graffiti writers and producers; and Jamaican DJs—while Bruce Lee movies also shaped the culture. From that time to the present, when hip-hop is doing something great, it belongs to everyone; when hip-hop behaves badly, it becomes synonymous with African Americans. In the 1980s, a gesture, a word of slang, or an outfit associated with hip-hop all were read in mainstream society as performances of blackness. When Dan Quayle and Tipper Gore warned White suburban families about the dangers of rap music, White America subsequently criminalized hip-hop to target and criminalize Black youth. White men who have occupied hip-hop spaces over the course of its history are not targeted with the anti-Black violence that hip-hop chronicles. They can only comment on how bad it is, if they are so inclined.

Danny Hoch's *Jails, Hospitals & Hip-Hop* (1995) was birthed out of a late 1980s hip-hop that originated through African American cultural production and an early 1990s crossover hip-hop that shifted from being predominantly by African American MCs to a more racially diverse landscape of hip-hop artists. When I interviewed Hoch several years ago, he insisted that hip-hop would not exist without the complexity of the racial and ethnic configuration of a deindustrialized New York in the late 1970s and the aftermath of Reaganomics in the inner cities in the Bronx and Queens in the 1980s. Of course, he is right, but there is a catch. The delicate balance between hip-hop's blackness being configured by multiple samples from non-Black cultures and its core reliance upon very specific African American expressions of blackness has allowed the culture to sustain and reinvent itself for more than forty years of existence. Here is the point: hip-hop is syncretic and unapologetically Black at the same time. Performance scholar Meiling Cheng's theory of multicentricity offers a lens to see how such multiracial interactions of hip-hop can exist simultaneously in theater and performance, thus shifting the power hierarchies assumed between majority and minority cultures. Cheng contends that "multicentricity subverts the existing power structure which takes for granted the boundary between 'majority' and 'minority,' between 'dominant' cultures and 'marginal' others."[10] This is not to suggest that any racial, ethnic, or national group selectively performs its racial identities in one particular way, but there are codes associated with particular identity formations—in this case expressions of blackness by African Americans—that differentiate based on specific social and historical experiences. Understanding hip-hop as a multicentric construct in which the experiences of multiple racial and ethnic groups intersect and overlap allows us to see how non-African American artists sample from expressions of blackness in hip-hop in acts of creative solidarity that reflect the citational processes of being hip-hop without being Black. Danny Hoch is a committed social activist who has used hip-hop theater to help bring about social change in prisons, schools, workshops, and other community spaces around the world. Using improvisational methods to create and perform his work, he constructs a White masculinity that challenges status quo assumptions that White hip-hop artists are appropriators of Black American music genres and theater. Hoch uses his body as a site to sample from a wide array of ethnic and racial identities to perform characters across racial classifications that identify with U.S. hip-hop culture. Hoch specifically remixes any identarian claims to the music by making the hybridity of blackness visible to hip-hop audiences, giving small sonic and embodied pieces of hip-hop to each of his characters.

Matt Sax, a product of the suburbs of Westchester, New York, grew up with a worldview that was forged through hip-hop. Benefitting from the negotiations between Black and White identities of the hip-hop generation before him, Sax models his own constructions of masculinity and ways of knowing the world through cultural engagements with the works of African American hip-hop artists. He fashions a new language, comprising hip-hop, musical theater, and classic musical theater. Using his body and voice to create improvisations between so-called high and low cultures in *Clay*, Sax challenges simultaneously the normative whiteness and the linear form of mainstream theater. He remixes rags-to-riches stories of classic hip-hop MCs with riffs on Shakespeare and musical theater styles to create a storytelling form that reveals connections between seemingly disparate cultural experiences. For Hoch and Sax, *samples* of African American blackness in hip-hop are inextricably tied to class and constructions of White masculinity. Globally, White artists seeking social or political access to hip-hop have the capacity to pick and choose what aspects of blackness's historical dialogue with whiteness they want to utilize or ignore. Such editing allows White artists to recognize the cross-racial and cross-ethnic coalitions that helped to build hip-hop even as they cultivate alternative spaces of whiteness within it. These strategic moves are representative of an ongoing preoccupation with African American samples of blackness, wherein White practitioners of the genre may choose when to connect or disconnect their practice from Black life and its expressive forms. As Ian Maxwell reveals in his ethnographic study of White masculinity and hip-hop in Australia:

> The appropriation of black art forms by whites has a long global history, a history in which race tends to get erased, with a normative whiteness, making the claim that somehow, the use of those art forms is simply that: an unproblematic "use" in which the forms are divested of their embeddedness of lived struggles.[11]

Hoch and Sax attempt to move beyond such erasures of race to create alternative racial, ethnic, and national identifications that mark whiteness as visible. Claiming hip-hop feels safe for many non-Black and non-African American artists who consume the culture, while making claims to blackness does not, and for good reason. The long history of blackface minstrelsy and cultural appropriation that are tethered to all aspects of African American cultural production haunt White artists involved with hip-hop. For Hoch and Sax, these acts of transgression open opportunities to make real connections between racial and ethnic groups. But such risks come at a price.

The New Style[12]

African Americans often cosign on White musical artists who have shown deep cultural engagement with Black music forms (such as the blues, gospel, jazz, and hip-hop), and are less tolerant of White artists who appear to traffic in blackness merely for capital gains or pleasure. White blues artist Stevie Ray Vaughan, gospel artists Don Moen and Amy Grant, and jazz artists Peggy Lee and Diana Krall, for example, are representative examples of White artists in traditionally Black genres who, for the most part, are socially accepted, even though many still call them cultural appropriators. The acceptance/backlash cycle occurs when White artists such as the Beastie Boys are lauded by Black contemporaries and producers and then vilified by the same community for "trying too hard." Such is the case of Russell Simmons, who claimed all of the accolades for discovering and producing the Beastie Boys, and then in *Spin* magazine called them out as White rap artists in blackface. In some form or another, White appropriation of Black self-expression has been the essence of pop, from blackface minstrelsy to hip-hop. Like jazz music and culture in the early twentieth century, hip-hop has become a site whereby White artists around the world engage blackness, knowingly or not. Attacking White hip-hop artists for trying to act or talk Black leaves little room to consider how White artists may attempt to engage the subversive and emancipatory possibilities within the genre's aesthetic that are attractive across racial lines. Legendary White DJ and hip-hop producer J-Love addresses what he calls the "ethics" of Whites engaging in hip-hop culture without acknowledging its importance as a vehicle to express Black oppression:

> As simple as it may sound, it seems as if many white folks down with Hip-hop try to avoid the fact that they are white, at all costs. This must stop. Acknowledging your whiteness is an important step in recognizing that regardless of who you are as a person, we come from a lineage steeped in

> racism and white supremacy. [. . .] This is what we come from, and that we cannot change.[13]

Since the end of the 1990s, White artists have been flipping the script on White masculinity in hip-hop and remixing identifications of whiteness that accomplish exactly what J-Love prescribes: change. By acknowledging White privilege, denouncing acts of White supremacy and histories of blackface, and disavowing their relationship to historic Black appropriation in hip-hop's lineage, White artists are revising their historical positioning by proving their committed engagement with hip-hop. Successful White hip-hop artists of the twenty-first century owe a great debt to the White hip-hop artists of the past who fought to prove that they had a right to perform as rappers who could talk about their lived experiences, and not some contrived imagining of being "down" or "Black" in order to be taken seriously as hip-hop artists. Though the construction and performances of alternative White masculinities and femininities now incur fewer accusations that they are trying to act or talk Black, said performers still must prove the sincerity of their intentions, which are not always accepted. Iggy Azalea is a prime example; since her career began in 2011, the White Australian rapper has been under siege for appropriating the culture, despite her insistence that listening to African American female rappers while growing up changed her life and worldview.[14]

At the same time that these new discourses of White masculinity open opportunities to see positive identifications with blackness by White male artists, they still potentially undergird White male privilege and allow hip-hop to be disconnected from the lived experiences of the oppressed. White perceptions of African Americans engaged with hip-hop music across class lines are often shaped through the music itself, as Damien Arthur contends:

> Hip-hop shapes white perceptions of young, black men as objects of fear and fantasy, it also limits and determines the possibilities of racial and masculine identity for those individuals themselves, reinforcing the cultural narratives of deviance, misogyny and excess that perpetuate the abject position of inner city African Americans within American society.[15]

Understanding the intention of the artist is key to avoiding the wholesale dismissal of all these performances as new imaginings of minstrelsy. In some instances, White artists invoke the racism of blackface that mocked Black subjects, even when they make claims that any similarities between their work and those acts of the past are unintentional. In other performances, White artists work to critique and revise historical practices of blackface by delineating their political positions within whiteness and identifying with African American subjects in positive associations forged through a shared community of hip-hop.

In attempts to acknowledge the polycultural aspects of hip-hop culture, which includes White subjects as part of its historical narrative, White artists claim kinship by highlighting the value of class and experience narratives as core points of their identification. Many critics of White hip-hop artists challenge their racial authenticity by categorizing them as "wiggers, wannabees and wanksters," which poses challenging inconsistencies that this chapter attempts to untangle.[16] Many Whites have legitimate social claims to African American cultural practices, often attributing their fluency in hip-hop and African American culture to several factors, including growing up in predominantly Black communities engaged with the music and culture. Danny Hoch, for instance, grew up in urban New York in the 1980s with the same working-class status as many racial and ethnic groups from the community, including African Americans and other African diasporic subjects. I am particularly interested in the work of Hoch and Matt Sax because they both seek to expose the essentializing logic tethered to the hip-hop authenticity debates on both sides of the hip-hop crossover.

Tunnel Vision[17]

From the Harlem Renaissance through the Hip-Hop Arts Movement, the lines between Whites' Black cultural appropriation and their sincere engagement with Black cultural production have been vexed by ambivalences and anxieties based on perception and projection. What Fred Moten identifies as the "doubleness of blackness" highlights the tenuous relationship between blackness and whiteness that forces blackness to find its own space of being in attempts to disassociate itself from whiteness: "In the blackness of blackness, the doubleness of blackness, the fucked-up whiteness of the essence of blackness, there is an instantiation of a kind of dialog between knowledge of in/visibility and the absence of that knowledge. Between improvement and the vernacular."[18] For Moten, improvisational music provides a space to play with meanings, their inversions, and their doubled inversions. Hip-hop, then, becomes a site of performance where new constructions of identity can be formed. Within blackness, multiple narratives of subjectivity exist simultaneously and are shaped by different aspects of gender, sexuality, class, and nation. The unifying connection is their unbreakable link to un-freedom. In the case of hip-hop, American samples of blackness become spaces to theatrically improvise freedom's possibility in performance. In order to make sense of the politics of these representations of blackness in relationship to the construction of White masculinity, Hoch's and Sax's works must be read within the broader sociohistorical context of civil rights arts activism, the rise of feminism, the economic crisis in the early 1970s, and multiculturalism in the 1980s. Hip-hop is a direct response to these crises and builds on the performance activism of the Harlem Renaissance and the Black Arts Movement, in which similar attempts to construct anti-racist White masculinities took place, with White artists sampling Black performances of jazz. Hoch's and Sax's artistic practices link them to historical attempts by Jewish American artists to foster cross-racial and ethnic coalitions with African Americans through the adaption of, and immersion in, American Black music forms.

White Boy[19]

In his 1957 essay "The White Negro,"[20] novelist and cultural commentator Norman Mailer demonstrates how samples of blackness borrowed by Whites to express jazz music have the capacity to shape the collective consciousness of Whites and other racial groups. Mailer implies that White persecution of Blacks implicitly renders everyone powerless. He remarks that the lack of courage to resist social atrocities, coupled with White threats of violence, have material and psychical ramifications:

> Any Negro who wishes to live must live with danger from his first day, and no experience can ever be casual to him, no Negro can saunter down a street with any real certainty that violence will not visit him on his walk. The cameos of security for the average white: mother and the home, and the family, are not even a mockery to millions of Negroes; they are impossible. The Negro has the simplest of alternatives: live a life of constant humility or ever-threatening danger.[21]

For many critics, Mailer's "The White Negro" has come to signify the White male hipster who attempts to inhabit the discourse of African Americans through jazz culture. Much like the identification with hip-hop music and culture by White artists today, Mailer's identification with blackness and jazz is directly linked to the theatrical improvisation of racial identity. Black jazz artists such as Duke Ellington sampled the sights and sounds of freedom heard in music outside the United States to remix Black spaces that resembled what freedom could look and sound like for African Americans. Mailer's linguistic and social sampling from jazz culture allowed him to improvise particular narratives of Black subjectivity that supported his quest to construct an alternative White masculinity that could exist apart from dominant narratives of Jewish identity, White Jewish bodies, and the Holocaust. James Baldwin questioned Mailer's selective citations: "But *why* should it be necessary to borrow the Depression language of deprived Negroes, which eventually evolved into jive and bop talk, in order to justify such a grim system of delusions? Why malign the sorely menaced sexuality of Negroes in order to justify the white man's own sexual panic?"[22] These identifications with blackness represent Mailer's negation of particular narratives of whiteness and Jewishness. For Baldwin, these samples were highly charged because of their voyeuristic and fantastical identifications with Black masculinity that never really attempted to understand the expectation of violence that Black men, all women, and nonbinary people experience daily. Hoch and Sax differ from Mailer in that they attempt to construct something that lives at the line between Black and White, fully accepting the possibilities of crossover as their fluency in hip-hop spaces that allows them to resist notions of identarian politics assumed on both sides of the color line. By forging what Kimberly Chabot Davis calls "a transracial identity that is rarely explored in pop culture" from a

White perspective, they attempt to forge a new perspective of whiteness as a raced subject position in the present that has as many valences and specificities as blackness. Chabot Davis identified this moment of self-identification as one that inspires an opportunity for transracial coalition building through empathy with African American cultural experiences:

> Although white co-optation is an undeniably potent force in the present, the possibility remains for white audiences to do more than simply consume and copy black style, but to experience a perspective shift by being exposed to African-American ways of seeing and interpreting the world, including racist structures of power.[23]

Following Baldwin and Chabot Davis, it is the *privilege of whiteness* that offers many White hip-hop artists the agency to *choose* when and how their whiteness is made visible. People of color do not have the agency to disassociate their bodies from the mainstream stereotypes that attempt to define them. The flexibility of whiteness to double—in other words, to be defined in relationship to negative and positive versions of itself—is part of the revised racial scripts achieved through hip-hop performances by White artists. Hoch and Sax attempt to move beyond what literary scholar Susan Gubar calls "racial borderlands," or dwelling between Black and White spaces, by sampling from racial scripts of blackness embedded in hip-hop language, and remixing them with revised racial scripts of whiteness.[24] Hoch and Sax create discursive battlegrounds in which they work to disconnect themselves from past histories of White anti-Black racism, and they replace these narratives of whiteness with sincere attempts to use hip-hop music and culture to make a new type of whiteness that departs from anti-racist practice and a disavowal of toxic White privilege that seeks to center blackness as part of its artistic and theatrical practice.

In *Jails, Hospitals & Hip-Hop,* Hoch interrogates the borders of race, class, and gender and their relationship to hip-hop authenticity in the 1990s. Exploring the invisible spaces of hip-hop's influence—jails, hospitals, and hip-hop as an institution—Hoch flips mainstream hip-hop stereotypes while complicating and critiquing White masculinities engaged in hip-hop. He presents his own solo mixtape of hip-hop's consumers, who include Flip, a White teenager from the suburbs who attempts to pass as Black; Bronx, a racially ambiguous character from New York City; Sam, a White male in the hospital with a severe speech impediment due to his mother's drug use; Victor, a White victim of police brutality who walks with crutches; Peter, a Cuban student obsessed with Tupac Shakur who engages hip-hop in Spanish; and Emcee Enuff (Hoch's only African American character), a rapper who struggles with the contradiction of performing Black racial stereotypes for profit. Hoch's play constructs a multicentric blackness, which demonstrates the ways hip-hop's sampled references to African American culture are utilized by non-African American subjects in language, sartorial styles, and oral narratives of different historical moments.

Danny Hoch's play archives the crossover of hip-hop's blackness into White mainstream vernacular in the 1990s. He is fluent in hip-hop's changing language, learned as he was growing up in the wake of hip-hop's birth in the Bronx. As a result of his lived experiences engaging African American and African diasporic culture through hip-hop, Hoch is able to speak hip-hop, which allows him to navigate the racial tensions at play at the historical juncture where he performs his identity as a Jewish American. In the prologue to *Jails, Hospitals & Hip-Hop*, entitled "Message to the Bluntman," Hoch translates the crossover of Black discourse into American popular culture and hip-hop vernacular. Reading the language in the 2000s and seeing the dated phrases, icons, and experiences represented serves as a testimony to hip-hop's constant need to reinvent itself in order to remain relevant in the twenty-first century.

When I saw *Jails* live for the first time in July 2004, Hoch was participating in "Grand Performances," a Los Angeles initiative for the arts that took place in an open-air theater at the California Plaza.[25] As audience members bustled about to find any available seat in the standing-room-only performance space, Hoch entered the scene casually, making his way to center stage with a water bottle. He was dressed in loose-fitting jeans, sneakers, a baseball cap, and a hooded sweatshirt, demonstrating hip-hop style. Hoch found his mark center stage as a single spotlight hit him. He began rapping the prologue to his solo performance, personifying the White male establishment in a PSA-type warning:

> Forties, Blunts, Ho's. Glocks and Tecs You got your "X" cap but I got you powerless

Forties, Blunts, Ho's. Glocks and Tecs You got your Tommy Hil but I got you powerless
People be like shut the hell up when I talk
Like I shouldn't be talkin' "black," even though I'm from New York
But what's that? A color, a race or a state of mind?
A class of people? A culture, is it a rhyme?
If so, then what the hell am I you might be sayin'?
Well see if you could follow this flow, cause I ain't playin'
Ya' see I ain't ya' average 20-something grunge type of slacker
I'm not your herb flavor-of-the-month, I ain't no cracker
An actor? Come on now, you know you wanna ask me
I'll use my skin privileges to flag you down a taxi. [26]

Hoch automatically addresses his position of power as a White male and quickly makes claims to hip-hop as a native New Yorker. He establishes himself as a hip-hopper fluent in the sampling of African American blackness associated with original claims to hip-hop in the 1990s. Hoch has little interest in associating himself with any White liberal stereotypes. In the opening monologue, he unsettles mainstream associations of hip-hop with ontological ideas of blackness by critiquing himself: "People be like shut the hell up when I talk / Like I shouldn't be talkin' 'black.'" Blackness, as it relates to hip-hop, becomes a discursive formation that can be entered into and learned, although not necessarily lived. Hoch situates himself at the border between whiteness and blackness. Hip-hop is simultaneously Black and other—other than normatively White and appropriative.

By sampling familiar works that serve as markers of authenticity in hip-hop narratives, many of which now seem very dated in the 2020s, Hoch draws his audience's attention to images and destructive behaviors that are manipulated and objectified by hip-hop's commodification. Many people in the audience who recognized these codes and their relationship to hip-hop validated Hoch by cheering and talking back to him as he performed. They saw him as hip-hop, a person who spoke their language, not as a White guy trying to "act" Black. In the next part of the prologue, Hoch samples a reference to White American clothing designer Tommy Hilfiger ("Tommy Hil'"), a popular designer among African American male consumers in the 1990s.[27] Hoch uses this sample to mark the contradictions of excess materialism in hip-hop in the late 1990s that reached new heights of consumerism in the 2000s.[28] Hoch's knowledge of the urban hip-hop scripts surrounding the Tommy Hilfiger brand in the African American community during the late 1980s and early 1990s landed him a role in Spike Lee's *Bamboozled*, where he parodies the fashion mogul.[29] For Hoch, his "skin privilege" as a White man gives him the opportunity to critique the White status quo as a woke cultural ally and to distance himself from stereotypes of White men who appropriate blackness in hip-hop:

> An actor? Come on now, you know you wanna ask me
> I'll use my skin privileges to flag you down a taxi
> 'Cause that's my mission, profit in my pocket, I clock it
> I got billions invested in jails, you can't stop it . . .
> And I laugh at all these rap videos with these guns and ho's While you
> strike the rough neck pose, I pick my nose
> And flick it on ya, ya gonner, no need to warn ya
> Got mad seats in government from Bronx to California.[30]

Hoch makes it clear that his intention as an artist and social critic is to distance himself from Whites who exploit hip-hop in the way that he addresses the status quo's investment in keeping African Americans oppressed by rewarding only the negative representations of their experiences in mainstream music.

Similar questions of authenticity and stereotypes of White artists engaged with hip-hop are addressed in the 2002 film *8 Mile*. In the now-famous final battle scene of the film, the White character Jimmy "B-Rabbit" Smith (played by rapper Eminem), disarms his seemingly legitimate Black opponent, Papa Doc (played by Anthony Mackie), with a barrage of stereotypes about whiteness. Proving his fluency in historic discourses of whiteness, blackness, and hip-hop, B-Rabbit challenges the authenticity of Papa Doc because he is not from the "streets"—a title that would afford Papa Doc credibility in many hip-hop scenes—but a Black kid who goes to a predominantly White prep school and lives in the affluent suburbs of Detroit.

B-Rabbit's connection to poverty and his self-proclaimed "White trash" status allow him to construct an alternative whiteness that is firmly aligned with hip-hop's traditional rags-to-riches story, used by many Black MCs as evidence of street credibility, creating class kinship between Black and White masculinities. With this claim, B-Rabbit attempts to render his Black opponent inauthentic because of his middle-class status. Linking his own connection to living in poverty in the urban city of Detroit, Eminem as B-Rabbit legitimizes his access to hip-hop by connecting to shared histories of urban oppression that audiences across racial and class lines link to "real" hip-hop. Hoch's White characters employ strategies similar to those used by Eminem to suggest that blackness exceeds the limits of the Black body. Hoch's social and political perspectives of blackness as a state of mind—a state of hip-hop—are represented in the artist's representation of his knowledge of hip-hop culture. Hoch's naming of New York as a site that can authenticate his hip-hop pedigree speaks to identifications of place and purpose with perceived experiences of belonging.

Hoch's second transformation is his depiction of the character Bronx. He uses linguistic samples borrowed from hip-hop vernacular to present a racially ambiguous character who samples from African American Vernacular English (AAVE), yet is aware that his White skin—described as "light" skin—challenges how he is perceived by the police. Bronx, presumably a light-skinned Latino or White male, does not want to identify with a whiteness that represents privilege. He critiques advertisements of the American Dream by the media, citing TV commercials as falsely advertising to people from low-to-moderate-income communities. He narrates how his unlicensed selling of Bart Simpson t-shirts for profit as a street vendor resulted in his incarceration. Bronx's whiteness vacillates at the border of Black and White in a challenging dialogue that is filtered through the vernacular of hip-hop:

> So this cop . . . he has sunglasses, so when he looks at me in the car, I look darker. When he get out, he get confused, Cause if you put me next to the cop, I'm whiter than the cop . . . next thing he throw me down on the ground, he got his nightstick in my back. . . . He say'a What are you, what are you?! Are you Puerto Rican, are you Puerto Rican? I mean my color is white like Bill Clinton, but that's not good enough for him.[31]

The police officer cannot determine if Bronx's body is Black or White, and Bronx's use of hip-hop vernacular confuses the power dynamic between his self-perceived White body and the African American vernacular speech he uses in front of the police officer. Speaking about his prison sentence, Bronx states, "I been in here for a month I ain't had no hearing or nothing. This woman tried to assassinate me in the TV room and shit [. . .] I ain't here cause I'm a criminal I here because I'm poor, that's why I'm in here."[32] Bronx distances himself from the whiteness of the prison industrial complex, the whiteness associated with the police who profile his body, and the whiteness associated with the surveillance and punishment of bodies because they correctly or incorrectly perform a prescribed racial identity. The skin privileges afforded to Blacks and Whites based on lighter skin color are unsettled by Hoch's performance back and forth across the color line.

African American studies scholar K. Anthony Appiah suggests that such racial characteristics are what people use to shape their collective and individual identities. He argues that "collective identities, in short, provide what we might call scripts: narratives that people can use in shaping their life-plans and in telling their life stories."[33] Appiah submits that such notions "provide loose norms or models which play a role in shaping the life-plans of those who make collective identities central to their individual identities: of the identifications of those who fly under these banners."[34]

The play's title suggests the imagined community of hip-hop as a space to negotiate such loose norms. Here, hip-hop becomes a space potentially just as imprisoning as jails and hospitals. Hip-hop's referential whiteness also tells the stories of the residual effects of inequality in the same way that the nation's prison industrial complex and hospitals marginalize occupants based on race and class. Bronx sees himself as oppressed, and therefore the privilege of his light skin is something that he cannot benefit from within the context of how his body is read from the outside by police. Hoch's performance attempts to change the position of the racial seer from the outside to the inside of hip-hop, opening opportunities for the artist to play with the archive of Black and White racial scripts of masculinity in the late 1990s.

Another character Hoch performs is that of Flip. Flip is a young

Fig. 1. Danny Hoch in *Jails, Hospital & Hip-Hop*. Photo by James Hamilton.

White kid from the suburbs who wishes he were Black, which he believes would make him a better rapper. Representing White kids from the suburbs superficially crossing over into the blackness of hip-hop, Flip samples from thug and gangsta stereotypes in hip-hop to construct his persona. He dreams of leaving the luxuries of the suburbs to move into "some straight up thug-ass ghetto projects type shit"[35] in order to be read as hip-hop. Flip imagines himself as an African American guest on *The Tonight Show* :[36]

> I know what you're thinking Jay. You're thinkin' like "how is it that this white dude could be such a dope rapper?" Well the truth of the matter is Jay, is that I ain't white man, I'm really black. See, I went to the doctor Jay. This is between me and you Jay. And he told me that I got this rare skin disorder where I look white, but I'm really black. It's called like eosinophilic ionic . . . dermatitis.[37]

Hoch uses Flip to demonstrate how many White consumers of hip-hop believe that if they were racially Black, they would have more hip-hop authenticity. Yet, Flip's performance of blackness as hip-hop on *The Tonight Show* produces a disconnect between his improvised theatrical performance of blackness and his lived reality as a suburban White kid:

> My niggas in the front, while you be in the back
> Fuck bein' white, word up dude I'm black
> I'm only seventeen but my shit still thump
> And by the time I'm eighteen, I'll be chillin' with Donald Trump[38]

Flip's agency as a White male allows him to discursively negate his whiteness in order to combine his imagined Black, hip-hop, and White selves into one corporeal reality. His ambivalence in this transgression is marked as he uses the word "nigga."[39] In the 1990s, hip-hop's relationship to White youth, and their selective identification with selected parts of blackness in order to appear more "hip-hop," and a 1990s Donald Trump being represented within hip-hop narratives as an iconic figure of wealth-building, are all fraught relationships that predicted a very complicated present. In a twenty-first-century context, White youth no longer disavow with whiteness in order to claim hip-hop, they just take it, "the n-word," and all that hip-hop culture has to offer and occupy it as they see fit with very little regard for the trauma their acts of appropriation produce. At the time of this writing, Donald Trump is the forty-fifth president of the United States who may be historically remembered as one of the most openly racist presidents in modern history. He is no longer an aspirational icon for many African American rappers who aspire to acquire his wealth and privilege. American Studies scholar David Roediger argues that Hoch and other White performers who engage performative codes of blackness operate as "progressive minstrels."[40] However, in recalling histories of blackface minstrelsy, Roediger does not consider the performance by Hoch of Flip as a performance within a performance. Hoch is able to distance himself from labels of "White Negro," "wigga," and "minstrel" because he makes certain a character engaging in these practices as a critique of racial appropriation and mimicry by White artists is distinctly *separate* from his own identity as a White, Jewish artist. In his performance of a White guy playing a White guy appropriating blackness, Hoch recalls the histories of racial transgression that are generally projected onto most White males engaged with hip-hop by exaggerating what Dorinne Kondo identifies as "intonation, gesture, movement and accent."[41] Hoch's performance of racist characters who do not think they are racist samples historic performances of blackness by Whites that often trafficked in racial mimicry and cultural appropriation. Hoch teaches White audiences what *not* to do by drawing attention to the ignorant performances that undermine potential ally relationships between Blacks and Whites in hip-hop. Hoch's intention reflects John Jackson, Jr.'s observation that sincerity in racial performance privileges an "interiorized intent that decentralizes the racial seer (and the racial script) allowing for the possibility of performative ad-libbing and inevitable acceptance."[42] Hoch's sampling of hip-hop language, oral narratives, and stereotypes to unsettle normative constructions of White masculinity have placed him at the forefront of the Hip-Hop Arts Movement and enabled him to communicate hip-hop's connection to African American culture and the diverse cultural contributions within hip-hop that are often lost in translation. Black performance studies scholar E. Patrick Johnson urges us to consider the complexity of exchanges that are activated when White artists appropriate blackness:

> History demonstrates that cultural usurpation has been a common practice of white Americans and their relation to art forms not their own [. . .] thus when white-identified subjects perform "black" signifiers—normative or otherwise—the effect is always already entangled in the discourse of otherness; the historical weight of white skin privilege necessarily engenders a tense relationship with its Others.[43]

Hoch's intention to position himself as a White ally with Black struggles against anti-Black racism is clear. However, despite his efforts to disavow aspects of his White privilege, he is still responsible for constructing a particular representation of blackness that is dependent upon a White liberal analysis that can be obtained only by listening to him as a self-appointed translator for both sides of the color line.

Hoch's monologue "Danny's Trip to LA" is positioned as the central monologue of *Jails, Hospitals & Hip-Hop* and is the only space in his performance that allows the audience to see Hoch as himself, not playing any character. When Hoch performs this monologue, he stands stage right at a music stand with a script on it and begins to read to the audience. The script serves as the break between the fictional characters Hoch has already portrayed and his retelling of his lived experience as a White ally who struggles against anti-Black racism. He shares his experience of encountering racist writing and behavior in the television industry when he was offered the part of "Ramon—Pool Guy" on the American sitcom *Seinfeld* in the late 1990s. He tells the audience that he was flown first class to Los Angeles from New York for the table read. After reading the role straight, Hoch tells us that he was asked to perform the role of Ramon, described as a "pool guy with a Spanish accent," with a more generic, stereotypical representation of a Latino male. Hoch avoids a confrontation with the producers, but he respectfully informs them that their conflation of Spanish accents and pool labor with Latinx people is racist. Hoch also notes the geopolitical conflation of Spain, "Spanish" people, and Latinxs that is increasingly pervasive in American popular culture in the wake of twenty-first-century U.S. immigration reform, especially along border states such as Arizona and Texas, yet not new to the United States's history of bogus Americanization efforts sought to deracinate Latinx people from their language and culture. Hoch's refusal to do the role with the generic "Spanish" accent lost him a part on perhaps the most successful sitcom of all time. The comedian Jerry Seinfeld, the show's namesake, scolds Hoch in rehearsal, asking him, "But I don't get it. Is it derogatory? Is it derogatory? Aren't you an actor, isn't that your craft, isn't that what you do, you know . . . little accents?"[44] Hoch's response to Seinfeld positions him as an ally with Latinx people fighting for more equitable and inclusive representation in the entertainment industry: "Look, if you wanted a funny Spanish accent, you should have gotten a funny Spanish actor from Spain 'cause that's where Spanish people are from."[45]

Hoch was not willing to demean Latinxs in exchange for the opportunity to appear on a hit show. He tells the audience, "If they had paid me, I might not be telling this story right now."[46] Hoch uses this experience in the same way that he uses the prologue, to establish an alternative White masculinity that samples from White and Black hip-hop scripts. He also uses this monologue as a counterpoint to the problematic worldviews of the characters he portrays to distance himself from their ignorance and to align himself with the anti-racist agenda of hip-hop. This monologue renders Hoch's intentions in performance sincere and challenges default scripts of whiteness in hip-hop. Hoch's ability to identify the struggles of Latinx people in the United States and the conflation of all Spanish speakers with stereotypes of Latin identity is an attempt to create cross-racial and ethnic coalitions and to assert an alternative whiteness.

For Hoch, alternative whiteness signifies a conscious acknowledgement of shared oppression through various modalities of being, such as race, ethnicity, gender, class, sexuality, ability, and nation. Phil Cohen sees this alternative construction of White masculinity as a sign of an alternative whiteness that was constructed in the aftermath of the civil rights movement and proceeded from "a critical reflection on the particular history of slavery, settler colonialism, White European immigration, and Black segregation that constitutes the trajectory of White supremacism in North America."[47] Sampling performative codes of identity from Latinx and African Americans, Hoch enlivens paternalistic scripts of the White guy who "gave voice" to the Other, but also resists such simplistic readings of his work. In my discussions with Hoch, I asked him if he thought it was easier for audiences to accept cross-racial performances by Black performers such as Sarah Jones, Anna Deavere Smith, or even Eddie Murphy. Hoch posited:

> Yes, I think it is. Again, this is simply because of American history. However, it is a projection of liberal racism to infer that people of color (actually just black folks) have the "right," the "ability," the "sole talent" to play others, because it is assumed that they have suffered the worst and therefore are the biggest victims and the biggest victims get to play everybody. This liberalist victimization only bolsters racism and misunderstanding.[48]

Hoch's correction of his use of "people of color" and replacing it with "Black folks" reinforces the ways in which other minoritized groups are racialized within a Black–White binary. Playing "White" in this case is also an act of playing another alternative White perspective: his own. Hoch's expression of White victimization reifies the privilege that he works to dismantle. Yet, in order to sustain an alternative White masculinity, White artists must continuously sample and remix their relationship to blackness and otherness as indexical markers that make the privilege of whiteness visible and variable over time. For Hoch, intentions and actions are key to determining hip-hop's realness.

The only African American character in Hoch's play, Emcee Enuff, appears at the end of his show. The play's script describes Emcee Enuff as "a famous and successful rapper in a baseball cap, gold teeth and Versace shades [who] makes his first appearance on *The Late Show with David Letterman*."[49] Hoch makes a choice to separate the way the character speaks in the fictional interview with Letterman from the character he performs for his fans in order to highlight the conscious decision that many Black artists make to perform minstrel-like characters in order to succeed as rappers in American popular culture. When the fictional David Letterman asks Emcee Enuff about the misogyny and violence in his music, Hoch, playing the African American rapper, responds:

> You know I started rappin' about "Stay off crack, stay in school, don't do drugs, organize" et cetera . . . but to be honest Dave, the shit wasn't sellin'. And I had to pay my rent, man. I had house payments. I had people in my studio on salary. I mean what? I'm supposed to just fire fifteen people? That's un-American.[50]

Hoch offers Emcee Enuff as a commentary on the mainstream's inability to see the characters rappers create as constructions of Black masculinity. He also takes Black rappers to task for their stereotypical constructions of blackness. Many African American rappers create characters to capitalize on the hypermasculine imagery that the mainstream sells to the world as representative of hip-hop. The subversive part of Enuff's performance is that he is aware that he can use this money to employ fifteen people and enable them to live the promises of the American Dream, at least materially. By profiting from the popularity of gangsta rap stereotypes, he makes it possible for himself and his employees to live better lives. Hoch's early engagement with these racial scripts in the late 1990s opens opportunities for more complex critiques of hip-hop culture in the present. Old debates of racial authenticity and sincerity are echoed in my interview with Hoch in which he stated his position on hip-hop's aesthetic:

> Because Hip-hop's forms screamed of their Caribbean-African Diaspora based roots, they always got associated with Black & Puerto Rican [sic]. More

> so, it served the ruling class structure (and the underclass structure too) to put Hip-hop in the Black/Latino box. It served the ruling class because Hip-hop had created forms of cultural resistance to urban poverty, and it served the underclass (or so they thought) because when urban poverty became chic in the early 80's, authenticity or "down-ness" became synonymous with race/class, thereby creating a sense of power by self-determination. No one ever even made the distinction between Jamaican, Dominican, Puerto Rican [sic], Cuban, and Ecuadorian. Nor did they make the distinction between Black class structures, White class structure, Latino class structure. Class was virtually illegal to discuss in the 80's. You were either Black or Latino (poor and cool), or you were White (rich and uncool). You had better not be white and poor or Black/Latino and middle class or you were "unauthentic" and therefore useless to either side's struggle.[51]

Hoch is able to create a theatrical improvisation of whiteness that departs from simple positive or negative identifications with Black samples to mobilize different racial and class positions that mirror negotiations of authenticity within hip-hop. Though Hoch sacrifices moments where he reinscribes stereotypes to accomplish this task, his engagement with hip-hop is largely told from his lived and witnessed experiences. Hoch takes Black and White artists to task for remaining tethered to the very institutions and commodity culture that oppress Black people at the intersections, poles, and margins of hip-hop. Ironically, by remixing his own version of White privilege, he creates a critique that can be easily read as paternalistic of Blacks and other minorities simply because Hoch can never escape the historic racial and ethnic scripts of anti-blackness that are mapped onto his body. Hoch's alternative White masculinity critiques the exploitation of hip-hop as a commodity in the 1990s, thus challenging identarian claims to blackness or whiteness in hip-hop that remain relevant today.

Fight for Your Right[52]

More than ten years after Hoch's show opened opportunities for White performers to move beyond defending their authentic engagements with hip-hop music and its intersectional relationship to African American culture, Matt Sax's solo performance *Clay* (2008) constructed hip-hop identities that unapologetically center African American samples as a central force of self-definition. Building on Hoch's work, Sax's sampling of African American language and styles of self-adornment in the twenty-first century—more than fourteen years after hip-hop theater became a genre of performance—allows for hip-hop's African American cultural production to become the foundation of any artistic work informed by hip-hop aesthetic practices. Sax's strategies of improvisation, freestyling, live remixing on stage, sampling, and call-and-response incorporate the ritualistic components of hip-hop theater that the millennial generation understand as the fundamental qualities of hip-hop performance. Sax is not as interested in proving lineage to hip-hop; for him, hip-hop has become a way of knowing the world. Sax is a young Jewish American theater artist from New York; he is a trained actor, self-taught rapper, beat boxer, and composer. He grew up in the era of hip-hop when Dr. Dre endorsed the biggest White rapper of all time, Eminem, and in a culture where accusing White rappers of blackface was a thing of the past. Because he was born and raised in Manhattan, Sax's worldview was greatly shaped by hip-hop, Shakespeare, and musical theater. *Clay* began as a student project at Northwestern University, where Sax trained as an actor. He was tired of not getting cast in roles that truly engaged his talent as the proverbial triple threat: actor, singer, dancer. Following the emerging hip-hop theater scene in New York started by Hoch in 2000, Sax decided to construct a play that could demonstrate his versatility as a theater artist who grew up on hip-hop. He even submitted his work to the Hip-Hop Theater Festival started by Danny Hoch, Kamilah Forbes, and Clyde Valentín in 2000, although it was ultimately rejected. With the help of some dedicated friends and producers, Sax took the show to the Edinburgh Fringe Festival in 2004. After great reviews in Edinburgh, he began to showcase the piece, catching the attention of then About Face Theater company producer and director Eric Rosen. The partnership that was born between Sax and Rosen inspired a new vision for *Clay*, the story of a young Jewish rapper on a pilgrimage to learn how to rap from an African American hip-hop head who owns a bookstore that sells radical works. In an interview with the *New Yorker*, Sax discusses his capacity to see connections across cultural experiences:

> Rap isn't all drugs and shooting people. I was born in Manhattan, moved to Mamaroneck when I was eight. My parents still live in the same house. My

> father is a wealth manager. My grandfather is a psychoanalyst; his wife is a food critic. When I was sixteen, they took me to London and to the Royal Shakespeare to see *Henry IV, Parts One and Two*, in one day—eight hours.[53]

In a magazine with a predominantly White, upper-class readership, Sax attempts to reevaluate hip-hop's stereotypical associations with Black male gangsters, drugs, and violence to connect it to a revered Shakespeare play, which is riddled with its own dysfunction. Moreover, Sax's narrative of how he came to theater reveals the White privilege that has empowered him to make connections between two seemingly opposed genres of performance. Sampling from *Henry IV*, hip-hop rags-to-riches narratives, reality TV-style White suburban dysfunction, and the latest hip-hop vernacular, Sax remixes a semi-autobiographical tale of a White male coming of age in *Clay*. The plot twist is that this young White male is also Jewish, thus embodying histories of both privilege and systemic oppression from which he creates a remixed social identification that aligns his persona with the historically oppressed status of Jews in the United States and the perpetual dismantling of Black hip-hop stereotypes.

Escape from Westchester

Clay centers on the character of Clifford, an awkward suburban kid from Westchester, New York, who is seeking an escape from a father who has chosen business over family, a mother who killed herself because she couldn't live up to the suburban mom myth, and a restless stepmother with whom he is sexually engaged. Sampling back and forth between the past and the present, Sax constructs a story of family secrets, playing back the pain of growing up with less than the ideal family. Sax plays all of the characters in Clay's story, transforming his body into a veritable turntable. Clifford (who transforms into Clay over the course of the musical) is facing adulthood burdened with the destruction of his family structure. Though on the outside he is living the American Dream projected in commercials, part of a perfect, White nuclear family in suburbia with two cars and two kids, Clifford's life is less than perfect. Flashing back to his childhood, we see samples of his father forcing Clifford to choose him over his mother in a custody battle. We watch Clifford

Fig. 2. Matt Sax in *Clay*. Photo by Don Ipock.

grapple with the loss of his nuclear family. Leaving his mom, he lives with his father, who remarries and chooses his job over his son. Restless with young angst, Clifford grows up with an absentee father, a depressed mother who drops out of his life, and a stepmother, Jackie, who is just as restless and lonely as Clifford. Time passes. Jackie's sexual appetite and Clifford's budding sexuality converge in a secret affair.

Working to escape his pain in suburbia, Clifford commutes every week to take rap lessons from his Black hip-hop guru, Sir John, who owns an underground bookstore in Brooklyn. Building on Hoch's work, Matt Sax presents a new hip-hop story of a millennial-generation White boy growing up in a world where hip-hop is the language of dissent for both the marginalized and the privileged on both sides of the color line. The play opens with a rap that introduces the arrival of Clay, a newly birthed rapper à la Eminem. The play operates in flashback, scratching parts of Clay's past into the present to give the audience insight into the history that shaped his identity as an MC. Sax enters the stage in virtual darkness, with a spotlight on his White face shrouded in a Black hoodie—a hoodie that is now a doubly coded symbol that archives hip-hop sartorial styles from the 1980s, which have become synonymous with urban Black masculinity and current histories of violence against Black males.

The stage is covered with books to indicate the open-mic space within Sir John's bookstore, where Clifford is transformed over the course of the play. We discover that the end of the play is remixed to the beginning, which Clay will play backwards for the audience. At the top of the musical, we meet Clifford, who has become Clay, a skilled rapper whom the crowd has come to see. Sir John has been waiting for Clay to arrive at the packed concert space in which he will perform. Clay shows up with blood all over his face and is too panicked to do the show. Sir John tells him to get himself together backstage after he learns that Clifford has had a run-in with his father. Sir John stalls the crowd and begins the narrative of Clifford's story on stage:

> **SIR JOHN**
> Yes, yes y'all. To the beat y'all. (etc.)
>
> Ladies and Gentlemen how y'all feel out there? I go by the name of Sir John and I'll be your host for this evening. My man Clay is 'bout to come out but before he does I need to put you on to something . . .
>
> Now ever since I was a youngin'/ comin'/ straight out the womb / the urban jungle spoke and my mind was consumed / by this love affair with Hip-hop / a flower in bloom / with powerful views / an art that refuses to lose / and in that context I mean to now dissect / the soul of a boy / but a boy you don't expect / and a boy who does possess / the lyrical rhyme ability of a well-seasoned vet / plus the story may reflect / and don't forget that the struggle remains / universal in the hurt recognized as pain / and while some Hip-hop be talking cars and chains / the truth remains / in the stories on this stage / so perk up your ears / yeah this story's got some gravity / and at first glance / you may view it as a tragedy / but that's a fallacy / cause in reality / the boy comes of age using Hip-hop's theatricality.[54]

Sax, as Sir John, becomes Falstaff to Clifford's Hal as the everyman, the person with whom the audience can identify on the journey. When Sax plays Sir John he puts his hood up; to play the role of Clifford he takes it down. Operating as a hip-hop griot, sampling "yes yes y'all, to the best y'all" from Common's classic hip-hop track "I Used to Love H.E.R.," Sax, as Sir John, gains the trust of the hip-hop community within the play and demonstrates his skills and knowledge as a hip-hop MC. Sir John educates his audience about hip-hop, telling them that the White boy whom they are about to see is not what they expect in a rapper. Clifford's (i.e., Clay's) apprenticeship with a Black MC works to authenticate Clifford as a White rapper, similar to the way that Dr. Dre's endorsement of Eminem introduced him as a legitimate rapper in the predominantly African American hip-hop community in the United States. But now the play backtracks to the moment that Sir John sees Clay at the concert, when Clay has shown up on the scene with blood on his face. The moment before Sir John hits the stage to stall the crowd, he and Clay share this exchange:

SIR JOHN
Why you got that blood on your face boy? Why you got that blood on your face?

CLIFFORD
Something bad happened. Something really bad happened.

SIR JOHN
I can see that. We got an audience out there Clay. This is your show, this is your concert.[55]

Sir John, depicted as an African American man through Sax's use of intonation and gesture to indicate African American/hip-hop vernacular speech, steps in to rescue Clay, taking on the role of a father figure. Clay shifts the Black–White binary by devaluing White masculinity as representative of refuge, protection, and comfort and projects these qualities onto Sir John who, as a Black male, would stereotypically be depicted as a violent, threatening individual from whom there could be no expectation of protection. Flipping mainstream stereotypes of Black males in hip-hop as dysfunctional fathers, Sax creates a sense of family for Clay that is directly connected to the mythologies of extended families that are embedded in hip-hop. Sampling from narratives by Black men in hip-hop about dysfunctional fathers, Sax creates a connection across class lines to connect Black and White male experiences of paternal rejection. Going back further into the story, Sax plays three characters interchangeably: a younger version of Clifford (i.e., Clay); his father, Geoffrey; and his mother, Nancy. They are at the dinner table as the parents break the news of their divorce to their young child:

NANCY

(*Surprised and self-conscious, she puts out cigarette. Stumblingly, she tries to continue the conversation.*) Umm, your father and I have decided . . .

GEOFFREY

Jesus Nancy, get on with it.

NANCY

. . . have decided that we are going to get a divorce.

GEOFFREY

(*Reacts with some disgust.*) Ahh! (*A beat.*) This doesn't mean . . . I still love . . . I mean *we* still really love you.

CLIFFORD

So what you guys aren't gonna be together anymore?

NANCY

No, but I think it's for the best.

CLIFFORD

So what's gonna happen to me?

NANCY

Oh Cliff . . .

GEOFFREY

You're right I'll figure it out. (*A beat.*) I gotta get down to the office but I'm glad we had this talk. I'll see you later. I love you. Clifford, who's my little man? You are.

(He exits.)[56]

As he plays all of the characters in *Clay*, Sax uses distinct language to mark the differences in their race, class, and gender. Using alternating rhyme and prose schemes for the voices of Clay and Sir John, and vulnerable vocal inflection to play the mother, Sax makes efforts to mark hip-hop experiences as far distanced from the whiteness of the suburbs and Clifford's family. Echoing Shakespeare's use of prose and verse to distinguish the statuses of his characters, Sax transforms Clifford into Clay by relying on multiple samples of identity that he remixes live before the audience. The audience feels, sees, and hears the indexical shifts Sax makes vocally and physically to indicate the different characters and their social positions. Young Clifford's line "So what's gonna happen to me?" becomes the key line of the play at this defining moment of his identity. Will he choose to repeat the cycles of abuse of his father? Will he choose an alternative representation of masculinity that will allow him to be more than his dysfunction? Sax reveals to the audience that everything is not what it seems inside the walls of suburbia, or within the urban landscape of hip-hop, and children experience dysfunction and pain equally across the lines of color and class.

You Must Learn[57]

When I saw *Clay* for the first time in Kansas City in 2008, it was making its way from the underground theater scene to mainstream regional theaters. After successful workshops at Northwestern, *Clay* premiered at the About Face Theater in 2006, directed by Sax's collaborator Eric Rosen and coproduced with the Lookingglass Theatre in Chicago.[58] The show toured to Los Angeles and Kansas City before it left to launch Lincoln Center's LCT3 new artist series in 2008. The Kansas City Repertory Theater's subscriber base mirrors the upper-middle-class White subscriber base of most regional theaters in the United States, and Sax's in-your-face approach to storytelling and his capacity to disrupt the stereotypes of hip-hop that play in the national imagination sent visceral shocks throughout the audience. When I talked with Sax about his concept for *Clay* and what he hoped to achieve with the piece, he expressed his intention:

> In 2004 the culture was different. Eminem was the lone figurehead of white people in Hip-hop at that time. Beasties were there. 3rd Bass was there. There were other white people in the business, more specifically Jewish people like me in the business. It's not just performers, it's producers and collaborators, all levels of the business, etc. In terms of being a rapper and a white artist—it's been asked of me so many times. *Clay* is about Hip-hop. It's about my particular history with Hip-hop. The story is not entirely autographical but what is biographical is an artist struggling to find his voice and he finds it in an unlikely space. To a large extent this is where I'm from and what I'm about. This idea that I could take place and be a part [sic] of this culture isn't something I just stepped into. It didn't happen overnight. I started beat boxing first thinking that I could acceptingly do that. I started making beats and then I finally came up with enough courage to start rapping. The marriage between the storytelling capacity of Hip-hop lyricism in particular, was very similar to the way in which I grew up studying Shakespeare and I grew up studying musical theater they didn't seem that far apart.[59]

Sax put himself through the same self-reflexive mentorship in hip-hop that he gives to his character Clifford. Understanding his body's relationship in the theater space, the predominantly White audience, and the history of Jews in blackface performance, Sax works in the break between overlapping spaces of whiteness, blackness, and Jewishness to remix an alternative representation of White masculinity that identifies as both hip-hop and Jewish. Connecting past histories of marginalization and oppression with transgression and appropriation, Sax creates an open dialogue about the embodied contradictions that are enabled through hip-hop performance. Sax faces the uncomfortable parts of those intersecting histories head-on. Flipping the historically paternalistic master–slave relationship between White and Black men, Clifford heeds Sir John's guidance—Clifford is the pupil and Sir John is the mentor.

Sir John tests Clifford's intention as an artist, challenging him to learn the culture and practices of hip-hop from technical and historical standpoints before he can even begin to learn to rap. After forty years of hip-hop music, there is still no formal school that an artist can attend to learn any of the elements of emceeing, breaking, DJing, or graffiti.[60] Formal and informal apprentice programs that existed during the Harlem Renaissance and Black Arts Movement offered new artists opportunities to learn from watching and following more established artists. Hip-hop MCs follow in this tradition in the United States and around the world today by listening to the music, watching videos, and absorbing the culture through the consumption of its products and influences. In *Clay*, Sax samples hip-hop oral histories of young MCs apprenticing with experienced rappers to chart Clifford's transformation into Clay, and to demonstrate his own knowledge of hip-hop culture and implied cultural ethics. Playing the two characters engaged in dialogue by switching his hood on and off, Sax performs Clifford's first challenge to earn membership into the hip-hop community. Clifford approaches Sir John after watching him rap, hoping for admittance:

SIR JOHN
Clifford. How old are you Clifford?

CLIFFORD
I'll be seventeen next month.

SIR JOHN
What's a white kid like you doing down here on Flatbush Ave. at 12 o'clock at night?

CLIFFORD
I saw your show . . . and . . . I . . . really liked it.

SIR JOHN
Thank you, much appreciated, peace.

CLIFFORD
Wait! I wanna learn how.

SIR JOHN
You wanna learn this? What you wanna do? You wanna make music? You wanna rap?

CLIFFORD
Rap.

SIR JOHN
You want to learn how to rap? Shit that can be arranged. See if you can vibe with these words little man.

Speak the speech I pray you / trippingly on the tongue / don't let the fact that you are young / impact yourself to come undone / beget a temperance / of excellence / while showing off your prevalence / appreciate all elements / of Hip-hop at its essences / What you know about music huh? You know anything about Hip-hop?

CLIFFORD
Yeah. I know plenty.

SIR JOHN
Okay. Well then let's do a little music survey.[61]

Sax depicts Sir John as an educated, clever Black man with great lyrical prowess, and Clifford as a clueless White boy who sincerely wants to change his stars. Sir John samples and remixes Hamlet's speech in Act 3 Scene 2 of *Hamlet*, engaging the poetics and language of Shakespeare to test not only Clifford's knowledge of African American culture and hip-hop, but also his broader sense of the world. The citation of the line "speak the speech, I pray you, as I pronounced it to you, trippingly on the tongue; but if you mouth it, as many of your players do, I had as lief the town-crier spoke my lines."[62] is a test to make certain that Clifford is not a cultural tourist, a White boy from the suburbs slumming it in Brooklyn to escape his reality.[63] Sir John informs Clifford that hip-hop is more than it appears to be in the pop realm. His line "appreciate all the elements / of hip-hop at its essences" samples from the underground edicts of authenticity; real hip-hoppers know that "real" hip-hop history cannot be learned on MTV and reality television. Sax places stereotypes on both sides of the color line in direct conversation within the scope of the play.

Sir John moves into a series of hip-hop history tests, beatboxing sonic references to underground hip-hop in Wu-Tang Clan, pop crossover of Michael Jackson, and suburban pop princess Britney Spears in order to test Clifford's knowledge of hip-hop and popular culture. Three times Clifford tries to recognize the music, carefully working to mimic Sir John's styles, but each time he fails miserably. Still, he is encouraged by Sir John to "come back tomorrow." By knocking three times at the door of hip-hop, Clifford can prove his sincere desire to learn the culture and can be converted from outsider to insider.

In Jewish culture, the tradition of turning the seeker of Judaism away three times is based on the biblical book of Ruth. Sax's surface sampling and scratching of Jewish religious rituals and remixing them with hip-hop here allows him to begin to remix Clifford's self-identification as more Jewish and hip-hop than generically White and suburban. Ironically, Clay's dysfunctional personal tales, the very suburban tales of excess that inform narratives of excess materialism in hip-hop, launch him into the stratosphere of success.

Rap School

The opening rap school sequences set the scene for the partnership between Sir John and Clifford. Filling the void of the father-son relationship lost between Clay and his father Geoffrey, Sir John takes the opportunity to show Clifford the power of charting his own destiny by rapping, or speaking truth to the dysfunction in his life. Sir John's own promising rap career was derailed after he was horribly disfigured in a car accident which also resulted in the death of his mother, a fellow passenger. He and Clifford share this loss of the maternal figure. Clifford becomes the hope for success that Sir John had abandoned and the son that he never had. In turn, Clifford begins to model his masculinity on a blueprint sampled from Sir John and hip-hop. Schooling him on the elements and culture of hip-hop, Sir John teaches Clifford—soon to take the stage name Clay—that the foundation of the music and culture is built on finding truth. In the confines of the bookstore, Clifford and Sir John engage in deep discussions about the "real" hip-hop and the truth of the culture—its capacity to be the repository of what is wrong and right with society:

SIR JOHN

Know the difference between tameness and smoothness / tutored by discretion / but your mentality must be ruthless / the fewest are those who choose to find out what the truth is / most end up talking pimps and chicks and cars and looking foolish / show virtue her own feature / by becoming your own teacher / I beseech you—don't overstep the modesty of nature / if you want to rap and rhyme boy / make sure it's something you can relate to / but show the pitiful ambition of the fool—and they will hate you / the underground will scoff at you if your shit is unsteady / and pop culture will chew you up if your shit is too heady / and if you feel what I'm saying.[64]

By sampling again from *Hamlet*—the phrase "pitiful ambition of the fool" occurs in Hamlet's instructions to the players who are to perform for the court—Sir John reveals that part of his Black masculinity and worldview is sampled and remixed with other cultural experiences. Riffing on Shakespeare's coming-of-age story in *Hamlet* and the mentoring relationship between Falstaff and Prince Hal in *Henry IV Part 1*, Sax connects Shakespeare and hip-hop to everyman. As an old-school hip-hopper, Sir John has seen the past and present of hip-hop and knows the inauthentic from the real. Discouraging Clifford from the misogynist rap narrative, he prompts the boy to rap for the first time, only to find recycled samples from gangster rap in this powerful exchange:

CLIFFORD

So whatever Hip-hop means to me? Aight. I can do this. Bitches and hoes and bitches hoes. And titties. Yo titties. I got mad titties in this bitch.[65]

Sir John challenges Clifford's misogyny:

SIR JOHN

You ever met a prostitute before?[66]

Feeling the insincerity in Clifford's rap, Sir John forces him to face his transgression and his dysfunction and to give himself to the *craft* of hip-hop. By showing him that his forced narratives (mirroring those constructed by Flip in *Jails*) reflect the same misogynist lyrics of the many

Black MCs who create commodified hip-hop that perpetuates stereotypes, Sir John holds Clifford accountable to himself and his personal history by challenging him to write stories from his personal truth, not copied from Black MCs whose cultural experiences he cannot inhabit.

Sir John continues his tutelage with Clifford, who travels back and forth from Westchester to the Brooklyn bookstore on the subway as his home environment continues to implode. One afternoon, Clifford has a breakthrough in his rapping session in which he reveals his relationship with his stepmother to Sir John:

> **CLAY**
> The game's over / it's taken hold of/ my body / my thoughts / and everything that I control / I stick my middle finger up at the ordained / I have gone insane / this shit is racking my brain / they tell me left from right / they tell me right from wrong / they are narrowing my sight / till eventually she's gone / how to justify my needs / is something that I cannot see / knowing she will have me—confirms enough / but knowing she will love me—it'll be tough / why's that? / because there's something that I haven't mentioned / something that might cause some tension / something that is looked upon as worse than getting school detention / the reason that I'm struggling / and the reason it might be wrong / is cause the woman that I love—is my step mom.[67]

Shocked, yet compelled by the honesty of Clifford's narrative, Sir John prompts him to leave the dysfunction behind and to move to Brooklyn to begin his rap career. Despite this warning, Clifford, convinced he is in love with Jackie, returns home and is caught having sex with her by Geoffrey. Their relationship is forever changed, and Clifford leaves his biological father to live with his new surrogate father, Sir John. Clifford realizes that his relationship with his father's wife was a pathetic attempt to be seen and heard after years of stifling his feelings of abandonment and grief over his family dynamic. He funnels all of this emotion into heartfelt raps that earn him Sir John's respect and admiration as a truth teller. Sir John's teaching pays off so fruitfully in Clifford's lyrical prowess that it pushes him to dig deeper into his own losses to find more material for storytelling in his raps.

Two years pass and Clifford is on the road to rap stardom. He works at the bookstore, acquiring the knowledge he needs to construct an alternative image of whiteness that is deeply engaged with hip-hop's positive message, commitment to truth, expressions of lived subjectivity, and equality. He is confronted with the possibility of the racism implied by his father's White masculinity in the mainstream. His father visits Clifford at the Brooklyn bookstore after being invited several times by his son to see what he does as a hip-hop artist:

SIR JOHN
Your father ain't your father / I'm your father let's ride through /
Your father ain't your father / let my wisdom guide you

GEOFFREY
His father is his father, who the fuck are you?
Have you seen my son—what are you a black Jew?
Or maybe you're a homie / homie / want to get to know me homie?
/
Clifford this is what the fuck you wanted to show me?[68]

Geoffrey attempts to speak in hip-hop vernacular to mock Sir John and Clifford. Calling Sir John a "black Jew" is Sax's clever connection of hip-hop to Black Jewish populations in Brooklyn engaged with hip-hop culture and also works to establish a patrilineal connection between Jewishness and masculinity. For Clifford's father, his son's engagement with Black culture in hip-hop is an embarrassment to his whiteness and Jewishness. He expresses his fears of blackness by admonishing Clifford to leave this Black hip-hop life and to come home:

CLAY
Whoa! Dad, you're overstepping your bounds
I don't like how this sounds.

GEOFFREY
Cliff let's go, you're fucking coming with me
Leave this nigger he's not your family

CLAY
No.[69]

Remixing transcripts of White Jewish male identity and its relationship to blackness in the United States, Sax performs two representations of White masculinity, back to back, so that the audience can see the different perspectives. Shifting from Geoffrey to Clay, Sax comments on the simultaneity that White Jewish artists often feel balancing expectations of Jewish authenticity and sincerity with whiteness and privilege. Geoffrey worked to give everything material to his son so that he would not have to struggle, yet Clifford chooses struggle and a loving father figure in Sir John instead of the comfort of his White suburban home and feelings of emotional abandonment. By calling Sir John a "nigger," Geoffrey marks his body as Black and hip-hop, hoping to draw a line that highlights what he sees as the impossibility of John, as a Black man, being a role model for Clifford. Geoffrey marks the discursive differences between whiteness and blackness that Clifford has ignored between himself and Sir John because of hip-hop's capacity to unify different racial identities. Clay's alternative White masculinity is formed in the break between the negation and affirmation of blackness between father and son. Negating the word "nigger" that his father used to devalue blackness and hip-hop, while accepting the racism of his lineage, Clay denounces his father's construction of whiteness to stand with his new father, Sir John, allowing his identification with hip-hop to double anew; he scratches out his old White identity and remixes his Jewishness with the blackness of his experiences to forge something different.

GEOFFREY
Who the fuck you think you are?

SIR JOHN
I'm the nigga who's turning your son into a star.[70]

This is the moment in the play where Sir John dubs Clifford "Clay," renaming him with his MC name and claiming his role as a father figure who will guide Clifford and protect him from harm. This naming can also be read as a hip-hop rite of passage: the claiming of an MC name. Sir

John affirms his blackness much as he affirms his connection to Shakespeare and the hipster literati scene of Brooklyn. By shifting the word "nigger" to "nigga," Sir John stands in as model of Black masculinity who allows Clifford's whiteness to be remixed, thus covering and authenticating his relationship to indexes of blackness in hip-hop. In claiming Clay as a hip-hop son, Sir John also acknowledges the color line between them. They are not the same. They don't share the same burdens. They relate deeply to one another, but Clay can never fully understand what it's like to live on the lesser side of the color line. Thus, Clifford can be hip-hop, but he can never be Black.

The play ends where it begins, with Clay racing to the concert after the fight with his father, who has confronted him for rapping about their family drama in a hit single. Clifford flees the whiteness of his family to find comfort with his new Black father figure, Sir John. With blood on his face, Clifford truly begins to embrace his new identity as Clay, telling Sir John that he almost killed his father:

SIR JOHN
What happened. You didn't kill him?

CLIFFORD
No.

SIR JOHN
You didn't kill him?

CLIFFORD
No. I looked at him and he wasn't worth it.

SIR JOHN
Well goddamn boy . . . you have far exceeded all of my expectations. That's your song . . . you ready to go rock that crowd?[71]

Hoch and Sax have written and performed alternative references of whiteness that did not exist in the American theater archive prior to hip-hop. Creating a call-and-response with the past, and with the audiences for whom they perform, they challenge the protocols, structures, and language of the mainstream theater in innovative ways, but still have the luxury of having White bodies with which to do it. They are painfully aware of this and work diligently to sincerely address their privileged identities in their theatrical intentions and practices. Through hip-hop, Hoch and Sax will never be able to sample the full threat of death, imprisonment, daily racial profiling, denied employment, family structures destroyed by slavery, or the socially imposed threat their bodies offer society. They can identify with the injustices and threats that these structures enact but will never feel the full physical and material impact on their everyday lives. They must fight to make their alternative White masculinity visible at all times in order to counter racism and social inequality. The theater space allows these artists to counter the assumed racial scripts projected onto their White bodies.

Conclusion

Performance artist and cultural critic Carl Hancock Rux argues that Black people are forced to embody an oppressed identity performance that "relies upon a collective agreement informed by a historical narrative that either supports the validity of, or opposes the construct of, these identities."[72] White artists engaged in hip-hop are assumed to embody an identity of privilege, despite the class, religious, cultural, ethnic, and social orientations that could also link them to an oppressed status. However, just as Black artists cannot disentangle themselves from embodied identities, White artists must also claim the problems of racist and appropriative histories that are inseparable from constructions of alternative whiteness. While Black people around the world have to grapple with stereotypical associations with blackness that are defined by their particular national and ethnic location, conflations with hip-hop, minstrel imagery, and racial stereotypes and language, regardless of their association with the music and culture; so must Whites negotiate their bodies being constant reminders of White supremacy, blackface, systemic inequality, and global oppression.

Alternative performances of White masculinities make steps forward to remix and perform alternative racial constructions that reveal the overlapping histories of the burdens of blackness and whiteness, but we still have a long way to go. As Harry Elam, Jr. contends, "Definitions of race, like the process of theater, fundamentally depends on the relationship between the seen and the unseen, the visibly marked and unmarked, between the 'real' and the illusionary."[73] Hoch and Sax can disconnect themselves from historical narratives of oppression and inequality of whiteness in order to be down with hip-hop. Still, their performances do not require a deep recognition that the life left behind, the White life that does not require a conscious acknowledgement of oppression, nor an emotional connection to the tragic histories of Jewish identity, can always be lived unmarked. In the case of Emcee Enuff in Hoch's *Jails*, or Sir John in *Clay*, both characters' desire to be "be" hip-hop is the hope of denouncing their negative relationship to whiteness.

The performances of the particular African American blackness associated with hip-hop that Sax and Hoch sample to remix their alternative White masculinities is only one part of the whole of blackness. In order for us to move beyond understandings of particular expressions of blackness as unique unto themselves, we must interrogate the new constructions of identity, both positive and negative, that hip-hop holistically enables for non-Black artists and consumers. Such examinations will allow us to understand blackness and hip-hop as mutually constitutive sites of human identity negotiations that inspire non-Black racial and ethnic groups to rethink the legacy of their subject positions. Reducing all performances of hip-hop by White artists to acts of racial and cultural appropriation forecloses open conversations about the potential of these performances to be read as acts of allyship that have the capacity to challenge stereotypical depictions of whiteness as always anti-Black in the American racial imaginary.

TWO

EMPIRE STATE OF MIND / Performing Remixes of the Hip-Hop American Dream in Nikki S. Lee's *The Hip Hop Project* and Sarah Jones's *Bridge & Tunnel*

As a child, I knew that if I could get to New York City, I could be anything I wanted to be. That's what all of the television shows told me (even though the shows were talking to White youth, I inserted myself) and I believed it. I watched Debbie Allen play the dance teacher Ms. Grant on the television show *Fame* and I knew that one day I would be a director like her. I would be able to act like her. I would be able to inspire others like her. Allen embodied multiple slashes of identity as an actress, director, producer, and dancer who seemed to have it all despite all of the odds stacked against her. Another woman who inspired me with her experience in New York was my Aunt Roberta. I idolized her. It was in New York that she beat the odds of living in the inner city of Detroit, where I was from. My aunt was a first-generation college graduate. The daughter of a mother born only half a century removed from slavery. The daughter of an immigrant father from Algeria. When my aunt returned home for the holidays to Detroit, she told me stories of her editing job at McGraw-Hill, where she worked with famous authors like Toni Morrison. She told me about the museums and Broadway theater, the symphony, the discos, and the jazz clubs. She was an independent African American woman living an American Dream narrative that was constructed by her, for her. Her dream was realized despite the fact that she was from a low-income Black family with little education. Her story would never appear in Norman Rockwell paintings as symbolic of the American Dream, nor would stories about her life shape the lyrics of songs about American patriotism.

My aunt's belief that she could be anything she wanted to be, despite institutional and systemic inequality based on her race, gender, and class status, inspired me to visit New York at a young age. The city became a symbolic location of becoming in my pursuit of my own dreams, which I knew worked against the American Dream narratives that told me my choices as a young Black woman would be limited. Like my aunt, I had to cultivate a different state of mind to realize all of my "slashes." My slashes comprise the complexity of my identity. My particular blackness, my mixed-ness, my class, my being an artist who doesn't want to sell out. My being an academic who wants to do work that helps my community and who has no desire to comply with the hierarchies that determine my "excellence" within the academy. I had to see myself differently than society saw me, in stereotypical images and possibilities. According to Jay-Z, having an "Empire State" of mind flips the age-old adage that anything is possible with hard work and determination to consider the ways that American Dream narratives are racialized and classed. In his song "Empire State of Mind," Jay-Z subtly critiques the White picket fence, White family, two-car garage myth to imagine the concrete streets of New York as inspiring success against the odds in America:

> In New York,
> Concrete jungle where dreams are made of
> There's nothin' you can't do
> Now you're in New York
> These streets will make you feel brand new
> Big lights will inspire you[1]

Jay-Z creates a sonic landscape that maps his journey from being a drug dealer on the streets of Brooklyn to his current reality of living as a Black billionaire and one of the most famous celebrities in the world. Jay-Z's New York is an Oz of sorts, where immigrants, both forced and selective, can spin a rags-to-riches story into inspiration for the American Dream. I made my first trip to New York at sixteen and the city lived up to my expectations. I saw people of different races, ethnicities, nationalities. People dressed how they wanted. Talked like they wanted. My core belief that theater and fine art were cultural sites for artists to rehearse and perform possibilities for change were affirmed by my experiences there over the ensuing years. New York has become a place that I go to help me restore my faith in humanity in the face of social inequality and anti-Black violence. Returning to the streets of Harlem, where W. E. B. Du Bois created a little theater company called the Krigwa Players, who performed in the basement of a New York Public Library that is now the home of the Schomburg Center for Research in Black Culture, affirms our humanity and our struggles as a Black community to be legible within a nation that continues to fetishize our art and our politics. Riding through the Bronx on the subway, imagining what it must have been like to see hip-hop rise from the wreckage of a deindustrialized New York, inspires me and people around the world to fight the good fight against racism and institutional inequality.

Two artists whom I discuss in this chapter, Nikki S. Lee and Sarah Jones, are hip-hop-inspired conceptual and theater artists whose work I discovered in New York. These women made significant impacts in the theater and art scenes in the late 1990s and early 2000s, using their bodies to challenge the boundaries of race, ethnicity, and gender through multicharacter performances. Both create work that is in conversation with Jay-Z's perspective narrated in "'Empire State of Mind" in that they create art and theater that challenge American Dream narratives sustained through systemic racism and institutional inequality in vexed reflections on their experiences through observation, characters created for performance in their respective genres and personal narratives. By pointing out whose stories are omitted from the implicit whiteness of mainstream narratives of the American Dream, Lee and Jones activate what sociologist Maxine Greene calls the imaginary sphere:

> The American Dream exists in the imaginary sphere. The real world is its foundation; but the dream reaches beyond what is to what is not—, perhaps, to what is not yet. We might say that it refers to future possibility, the idea of which arises out of what we feel to be lacking in the "now."[2]

Green outlines the structures of such an imaginary space that leaves room for many everyday citizens to ignore the fact that promises of life, liberty, and the pursuit of happiness, explicit tenets of the American Dream narrative and the U.S. Constitution, have long been forgotten promises for many minoritized Americans. She continues:

> That, of course, was part of the creed, of the American promise: the view that each living human being, no matter what his origin, is equal to every other. In almost all cases, at least until the mid-20th century that person was white and male; and, for many blacks and many women "equality" was a name for an unkept promise, or for the freedom of rights of which they were deprived.[3]

Nikki S. Lee and Sarah Jones are linked to a legacy of unkept promises for people of Asian and African descent in pursuit of the American Dream. The two artists approach their self-identifications within the United States and social critiques of American Dream narratives from very different standpoints. Lee, born Lee Seun-Hee, is a Korean conceptual artist working in New York. In Lee's series of American identity explorations called *Projects*, created between 1997 and 2001, the artist plays with the malleability and contextual specificity of race and the ways that her body can be manipulated in particular social and cultural contexts. Performing African American, White, Latina, elderly, punk, and a host of other American "subcultures," Lee attempts to assume the identities of these various groups by sampling parts of their aesthetic identities (styles of dress, hair, skin color, etc.) and interpreting them through performances that are captured in photographs. She has been compared to Adrian Piper and Cindy Sherman, two celebrated conceptual artists in the United States who also explore the confines of identity formation.[4] I read images from one of Lee's explorations in the *Project* series entitled *The Hip Hop Project* as her interrogation of American identities in hip-hop as a Korean national. In *The Hip Hop Project*, the artist uses her body and instant cameras as technologies to create reproductions of blackness that result in commodities of American hip-hop that are disconnected from histories of anti-Black racism, specifically blackface. I then turn to Sarah Jones, a Tony award-winning actress and solo performer best known for her multicharacter solo performances that explore race, ethnicity, gender, and citizenship. Jones is a self-identified Black woman of Caribbean and European descent who positions herself as both Black and multiracial. American theater critics read Sarah

Jones as a multicultural artist who embodies quests for the American Dream. Similar to Lee, Jones uses the blackness of her body to play back the voices, gestures, and languages of a myriad of American characters in performance acts that attempt to bridge connections between racial and ethnic groups in the pursuit of legible citizenship. I saw Jones perform her play *Bridge & Tunnel* at the Helen Hayes Theater on Broadway in 2006, offering a compelling solo performance. Jones's unifying setting in *Bridge & Tunnel* is a hip-hop-inspired, spoken word, open mic night, which serves as the center platform from which a diverse group of American immigrants and nationals share their stories about being and becoming American. Former *New York Times* theater critic Charles Isherwood describes *Bridge & Tunnel* as a "valentine" to the city of New York:

> "Bridge & Tunnel" is Ms. Jones's sweet-spirited valentine to New York City, its polyglot citizens and the larger notion of an all-inclusive America, that ideal place where concepts like liberty, equality and opportunity have concrete meaning and are not just boilerplate phrases slapped around in stump speeches and news conferences.[5]

For Isherwood, and many other critics, Jones's play performs possibilities of an American Dream that includes equal rights and privileges for all. Isherwood, who set the culturally deaf tone for many White, male mainstream theater critics, departs from a standpoint that privileges Jones's virtuosic abilities, choosing to categorize her work with a colorblind lens. Isherwood, along with many other White critics of theater by people of color, refuses to see how Jones's Black body and hip-hop become sites through which social critiques of the American Dream perform. Her body, a Black woman's body, become a vehicle for a solo performance about difference that suggests possibilities for "an all-inclusive America." I read Jones's performance as a mixtape of American immigrant voices that compiles a series of footnotes and addendums to the dreams promised to so many Americans, which have been only partially realized.

Together, Nikki S. Lee's and Sarah Jones's works ask audiences to examine their beliefs about what the American Dream means for countless non-White citizens who pursue the myth with no guarantees or expectations of protection. Lee, a first-generation immigrant to the United States, asks audiences to process how her particular Asian body fits into the existing categories of racial identity formation in the United States. Jones challenges the conflation of all Blacks in the United States with African American ethnicity, identifying as a multiracial Black woman whose history of blackness departs from a Caribbean (and thus, non-African American perspective), asks why her blackness and vexed relationship to hip-hop are defining characteristics of her work. Both artists sample language, styles of dress, and embodied gestures of diverse racial and ethnic groups to perform their identities beyond the confines of their own bodies, thus demonstrating the ways in which racial identities are produced in relationship to one another.

This is America[6]

The first time I saw Nikki S. Lee's photographs, I was doing research on hip-hop's influence on African American art at the Bronx Museum of Art's 2002 exhibition *One Planet Under a Groove: Hip-Hop and Contemporary Art*, curated by Franklin Sirmans and Lydia Yee. This was one of the first exhibits to document the ways that hip-hop aesthetics moved beyond literal representations of the four elements of hip-hop music and culture—DJing, emceeing, breaking, and graffiti—to influence fine and conceptual arts that reflected a hip-hop America. Walking through the exhibit, I arrived at a series of photographs entitled *The Hip Hop Project*, which consisted of pictures of an African American woman in various hip-hop spaces in New York. In one of the photos, the woman posed with Mobb Deep, a successful 1990s African American rap duo from Queens.

As I continued to walk through the exhibit photographs, I noticed that the woman changed her look dramatically in each image. I never questioned the validity of the woman's blackness upon first look at the images. African American women change their hairstyles and clothing in hip-hop culture all the time. Our complexions vary, as do our hair textures and styles. Moreover, there are many Black women of mixed African and Asian ancestry.

Fig. 3. From Nikki S. Lee's *The Hip Hop Project.* Artwork © Nikki S. Lee, courtesy of Sikkema Jenkins & Co., New York.

Eventually I realized the artist credit for the photographs was "Nikki S. Lee," and that Lee was also the woman who appeared in each image, posed as a "Black" woman. I learned that Lee achieved her convincing (albeit at first glance) physical appearance by sampling the varied looks of African American women and altering her skin tone and hair texture. Lee's performance immediately brought to mind the practice of blackface. But as a Korean artist, Lee did not fit easily into the specificity of blackface and yellowface performances in the United States. This particular performance was not created with the intent to mock African American people. Lee had darkened her skin to appear more "hip-hop," and this performance was achieved by the use of tanning beds, which are socially accepted technologies of skin darkening used most often, but not exclusively, by people of European descent.

For Lee, hip-hop's Americanness was specifically linked to Black Americans. She could have easily created images of Latina, White, or Asian women in hip-hop. She also could have sampled different fashion styles and poses to create the desired hip-hop "look" without the physical changes of her skin color and physical appearance. The still images document her performance as they suggest a few sets of relationships. Firstly, Lee's tanned Asian body summons a commentary between past histories of Whites mimicking Blacks in acts that perform the oppressive power dynamics that have existed between Whites and Blacks in the United States since slavery. Secondly, the photographs map the ways Asian people (both immigrants and American-born Asians of various ethnicities) are racialized within the Black–White binary or as a monolithic group in the United States. As a Korean woman, Lee is not Black or White, but she is racialized in relationship to both racial groups and their respective relationships to histories of oppression in the United States. Thirdly, the photo captures a haunting presence of diverse Asian influences embedded in hip-hop's aesthetic by the use of Pan-Asian samples in hip-hop's sonic and embodied landscape from its inception to the present. Though Lee may not be intentionally commenting on her racialization in the United States, as a self-identified Korean immigrant who sees herself in a Korean national context, her body performatively excavates histories of the U.S. racialization processes. Curators Lydia Yee and Franklin Sirmans seemed to ask their audience the questions "What are the limits of hip-hop's cultural and aesthetic appropriation? Is there any space for other racial and ethnic groups to be inside hip-hop without appropriating culture?" The possibility of Lee offending minoritized groups in the United States with her work is greatly reduced by the fact that, like many theater audiences, the audiences at venues in which Lee's works are presented are mainly White and upper middle class.

Lee's photos circulate as representative of Black women in hip-hop, yet the Black women who pose with her in most of the photos are not credited as co-artists, nor are their voices heard in her description of the performance process. In her reading of stills of Shakespeare's plays, the late theater historian Barbara Hodgdon observes the duality of the theatrical still and its capacity to inspire the onlooker to imagine the past event of the performance, as it documents only a partial account of the event. These comments are useful in interpreting Lee's work:

> The theatrical still has a double history. Before and during the run of the performance, it takes life as a commodity, teaser, or provocation; only when

> the performance is no longer "up" does the photograph reach the archive, where signifying the death of the theatrical event, its materiality is less factual than textual, closer to written imagery than painting.[7]

Hodgdon's insight into the potential of a theatrical still to serve multiple purposes is important. *The Hip Hop Project* samples styles of self-adornment, hairstyles, and Lee's adaptation of the varied skin colors of African American women. By sampling from parts of these identities and then repurposing them as artistic performance, the artist turns these styles into commodities that she samples and remixes in repetitive acts of being hip-hop. Lee manipulates how her body can be read as both Black and hip-hop, depending who is looking. The images capture the partial presence of the improvised practice of "being" hip-hop. As provocation, the images suggest to the viewer that what they see—Lee as an African American woman dressed in hip-hop styles—is real. Theater and performance studies scholar Philip Auslander identifies theatrical documentation in two forms: documentary and theatrical. The requirements for the documentary still are as follows:

> The documentary represents the traditional way in which the relationship between performance art and its documentation is conceived. It is assumed that the documentation of the performance event provides both a record through which it can be reconstructed though, as Kathy O'Dell points out, the reconstruction is bound to be fragmentary and incomplete and evidence that it actually occurred.[8]

> The theatrical category includes cases in which performances were staged solely to be photographed or filmed and had no meaningful prior existence as autonomous events presented to audiences. The space of the document (whether visual or audiovisual) thus becomes the only space in which the performance occurs.[9]

Auslander's observation finds synergy with Kathy O'Dell's assertion that documentation cannot completely capture the ephemerality of performance. In his commentary on theatrical documentation, Auslander references the work of Nikki S. Lee to highlight the performative possibilities of photographs and the intention behind the process of their creation for documentary or theatrical purposes. The photograph, for Lee, is both documentation *of* performance and *is itself* a performance that is enlivened with each new audience that encounters the image. Performance studies scholar Rebecca Schneider asserts that the photo allows the act of reenactment to exist simultaneously within the theatrical still. Referencing the work of Lee and other artists who use the photograph to capture live performance work, she contends:

> Photo-performance "re-enactment" is evident in the work of Sherrie Levine, Yasumasa Morimura, Gregory Crewdson, Eleanor Antin, Yika Shonibare, Nikki S. Lee, Lorna Simpson, Jeff Wall, Bill Viola, Tina Barney and many others (whether they receive the appellation "reenactment" or not) in which work is staged, with evident theatricality, creating photographs that both document theatricality (the posing subject) and are theatrical (the photograph is the performance).[10]

Schneider suggests that the relationship between the pose and the photograph can never be separated. They are grafted together in potential success or failure through the intention of the artist to create such a performance. Schneider's anticipation that the documentation and theatrical capture of performance provide a limited frame in which to account for the intention of the performer is highlighted in her connection of the photograph to the actor's capacity to pass/fail as the person he/she wishes to enact using his/her/their body and voice. Schneider's critique of Jens Hoffman's work creates a connection between the photograph and the actor's capacity to conceal and/or make visible that which they need to enact. This analysis is useful in connecting Lee's desire to play with the limits of her body and status categorized in a U.S. context as a Korean woman:

> The photograph, like an actor for hire, is not the thing itself, but that very fact—the fact that it/he/she/passes and cannot quite pass—is an ambivalence that seems to get something right by getting something wrong.[11]

Lee's sampling from African American feminine aesthetics used in hip-hop (hairstyles, styles of self-adornment) as well as her attempt to make her skin color look "Black" underscores the ways in which Americanness and hip-hop are entangled. Moreover, Lee's use of the still to perform an ambivalent relationship to the racialized sociopolitical histories of Black people surrounding hip-hop suggests that the process of remixing can manipulate the boundaries of race and flatten history in a way that makes it comfortable for mass consumption without the consequences of the trauma that Black people face daily. Though Lee may enter into the practice of emulation as an act of imitation, the photograph can be interesting independent of the artist. The photo can be read as an object that attempts to equalize the disparities between Blacks and Whites and Blacks and Asians within hip-hop's past and present history. Many artists engaging with hip-hop outside of a U.S. context attempt to translate hip-hop from its point of reception without careful consideration of the pretext and context of hip-hop's complex connection to histories of Black subjugation.

No Matter What They Say[12]

Conceptual art is broadly defined as art that derives an idea or concept of an artist's process from a particular goal or disseminating a message using those concepts or ideas.[13] Many conceptual artists challenge conventional criteria of what counts as art. The improvised changes that Lee makes to her body are based on aesthetic understandings of her subjects that most often reduce their identities to phenotype, hair texture, and sartorial style. These are the principal codes of racial identification for many people: markers of identity that many people use to make sense of race, no matter how problematic. Lee's work highlights the disconnects that exist between social constructionist and biological understandings of race that trickle down and persist respectively in our society. Her unique focus on the corporeality of her subjects ultimately leaves little room for the artist to demonstrate sincere intentions for her artistic samples outside of using the images and likenesses for her own self-exploration. Lee's lack of interest in what her subjects think and her lack of desire to make a connection between her experiences and those of her subjects brings an etic quality of artifice to her performance, yet it is impossible to understand how and why she wants to make the work that she makes. As an artist, she is entitled to explore her body in relationship to other racial, ethnic, and cultural experiences. However, there are several parts of Lee's process that function to manipulate her audience's perceptions about who she is and what she does. Much of the illusiveness about Lee's intentions as an artist is admittedly personal. She reports that she tells people right away that she is an artist, but that they soon forget her disclosures. She never talks about the people whom she performs with as individuals in themselves, but more as people who help her by participating in her self-study. Lee spends approximately three months with the group she is performing for each study, two months to gather information and one month to socialize and meet the people she wants to appear in the image with her. How she meets the people that she decides to include in her photos is arbitrary. Nikki S. Lee explains in an interview for the Creators Project website in 2010:

> I like to work with the idea of identity and my views toward it. I think the other people were important for me to identify my own identity within the relationships with those people. In Buddhism there's a saying that goes something like "I can be someone else and that someone else can be me as well." Thoughts like this one—thoughts that cause you to view yourself in other people's shoes—were my main focus, so the people play a significant role.[14]

When Lee is ready to capture the photograph of her performance, usually in a public venue, she asks someone she has befriended in the group to take a photograph with a disposable camera that she provides. Lee's *Projects* predates the digital selfie era of photography, yet foreshadows the popularity of self-documentation that launched via Facebook in the early 2000s, shortly after she created the series. In an interview on a Korean talk show called *INNERview* on Arirang Television Korea, Lee discusses (in English) the time she spends to capture her photos for each group:

> I spend one month for actually taking photos. After one month I didn't feel. I feel like this fake [*sic*]. It felt too real. It's a ridiculous process to think one month is fake and one month is real, but that's my process. I go there to make a friend. I spend time with them and I go back home to watch Korea drama at night. People don't understand each other if culture is different

> [*sic*]. Western. Eastern. Emotion is the same. Like sad and laugh [*sic*]. You know? But the concept of life is different for each culture [*sic*]. Each culture has similarity.[15]

Lee, unlike the women whose identities she explores in *The Hip Hop Project*, has the agency to remove the aesthetic characteristics of blackness she puts on and the sociopolitical framing that accompanies the life experiences of living while Black she assumes for the performance. The Black women who are featured in the photographs with her live as Black women in a society that marginalizes them on a daily basis. Lee profits from the performance of the physicality of their identities. The images of these Black women are forever captured in the photographs and displayed in various galleries and museums around the world. Based on a brief conversation with Lee at a dinner, I was able to ask her about consent forms. She never truly responded, but implied that she "just asks the people to take a picture" with her. In other words, she does not necessarily go through the channels of consent that would involve review from her human subjects or other ethically responsible measures.[16]

After Lee's performances, she returns to her original look as a Korean woman without penalty or accusations of racial transgression. Though Lee's description of her process attempts to articulate her desire to identify the emotional connections between cultures, her statement also eschews responsibility for the feelings of "not rightness" she has difficulty articulating. Because Lee frames her intentional process as one of self-exploration (despite her formal disclosure, her body is still disguised), her projects are largely championed as innovative. Few critics have commented on her multiple acts of racial and ethnic borrowing, instead using Lee's Korean nationality as a protective cloak from the histories of U.S. racism and imperialism of African American and Asian American subjects. Most of the critics who examine Lee's work are White. Lee's refusal to identify with the ways in which she is categorized and/or viewed as a person of color in the United States complicates the frame of her performances. Following the artistic trajectories of conceptual artists such as Cindy Sherman, who is European American, and Adrian Piper, who is African American, Lee has her work circulated in galleries and museums all over the world.[17] The difference, however, is that Sherman and Piper intentionally explore the malleability of social categories of race, ethnicity, and gender to make larger social commentaries and connections about inequality. Lee intentionally ignores the connections that occur between her acts of self-reflection and histories of inequity and racism, as she refuses to admit the ways in which she circulates stereotypes of identity. For all practical purposes, Lee refuses her own historic and present oppressions. Asian American social activist Chisun Lee identifies Nikki S. Lee as an artist of color who provides novelty for curators in major museums and galleries around the world. Chisun Lee observes:

> As with so many cultural producers of color, Lee's work is defined by the mainstream's frame of reference. In the universe of Chelsea art galleries and world-famous museums, that frame is moneyed, genteel, and white. Hence, the voyeuristic astonishment over her blending in to these "subcultures"—threatening, bizarre underworlds to these viewers. Plus, Lee's youth and facility with clothes and makeup suggest a hipness, a certain "getting it," that those who don't get it must covet and envy.[18]

As an Asian American critic, Chisun Lee recognizes the ways in which Lee manipulates her "outsider" status as a Korean-born artist working in a U.S. context. Lee resists any analysis of her work as a process of interrogating racial, ethnic, and gender identities. In fact, the only category that the artist strongly identifies with is her national identity as a Korean subject. Lee refuses to identify with the category "Asian American," instead choosing to identify as "Korean, Korean."[19] Her refusal to understand that her body is read in this country in multiple transnational contexts contributes to the mystique of her performance. Once we realize that Lee is a Korean woman, we can see that she is manipulating transnational perspectives to claim projection of hip-hop as it is received in Korea as an "American" product, without the racial signifier of African American. Lee's public presentation of her understanding of hip-hop firmly situates it as an American product that "sees no color." Lee self-presents as ignorant of the histories of blackface and yellowface in American popular culture. She grew up in Korea, associating the United States and all things American with American cultural products such as McDonald's and Mickey Mouse:

> Kids in Korea grow up watching Hollywood movies, listening to foreign pop songs and eating McDonald's hamburgers. I never feel uncomfortable or embarrassed when in an exotic atmosphere since I feel like I grew up in a foreign culture myself.[20]

Lee's recollection of her childhood is shaped by her consumption of American products as a process of learning to be more American. For Lee, Americanness is a commodity that you can put on or consume. Korean pop groups sample from a broad range of representations of American blackness that range from nineteenth-century blackface makeup; to sonic samples from R&B vocal styles; to contemporary, late-twentieth-century and twenty-first-century hip-hop music, dance, and fashions.[21] Despite the fact that samples of American blackness are remixed by Korean consumers and artists as American products, Lee's sampling of African American female identities in hip-hop as "American" strategically ignores the social environment of African American women living in New York when she created the images. Lee's photographs make visible the dreams attached to the powerful products and culture that the United States exports as American without notifying consumers abroad that it also excludes African Americans from full citizenship rights. Hip-hop's blackness, then, is consumed via its sampled markers, yet still works to challenge American Dream narratives that ignore the importance of African American cultural products in shaping such ideals of success and belonging that exist as fantasies both inside and outside the United States.

Just the Way You Are[22]

Lee's concept of changing her Korean identity in order to blend into the various communities that she identifies as subcultures of American identity is the unifying idea in all of her photographs. Her artistic practice is vested in locating and translating obvious performative samples of self-adornment that traffic in recognizable stereotypes of Black women and remixing them to challenge the boundaries of her self-presentation as a Korean woman. Because Lee's photographs are all that remain of the performances, the sense of the live performances are only partially captured in the images. The superficial aesthetic of Lee's concept reinvests the minstrel image and histories of yellowface performance in American popular culture more than it redresses or subverts these histories.[23] African American women in hip-hop continue to work within and outside of the contradictory space of hip-hop culture and manipulate the ways that their bodies are read within larger social and historical contexts of oppression in the United States. As Harry Elam, Jr. observes, the performance of blackness can occur "in acts of personal survival as well as reaffirmations and renegotiations of cultural identity."[24] Black women have to renegotiate their images in acts of survival as their styles of self-adornment are constantly sampled and remixed in non-Black embodied contexts in White mainstream culture in ways that often render invisible Black women's performances as cultural innovators and trendsetters.

The photographs create representations of the theatrical performances that we cannot see. Lee's sampling of African American female looks as hip-hop attempts to mask the codes of her Korean ethnicity. However, there are indicators of Lee's race and ethnicity that escape the theatrical still that have the capacity to undermine her performance of blackness as hip-hop. For example, Lee has a pronounced Korean accent when speaking English. This marker of Korean identity extends beyond the realm of the photograph. Lee's work manipulates fluidity of racial categories, in that she can identify and translate enough samples of self-adornment of African American women in hip-hop to transgress her Asian identity to be read as Black, depending on who reads the photographs. Roland Barthes makes an abstract connection between photography and theater in *Camera Lucida*:

> Photography seems to me closer to the Theater, it is by way of a singular intermediary . . . by way of Death. . . . [H]owever lifelike we strive to make it (and this frenzy to be lifelike can only be our mythic denial of an apprehension of death), Photography is a kind of primitive theater, a kind of Tableau Vivant, a figuration of the motionless and made-up face beneath which we see the dead.[25]

Perhaps to some Asian, Asian American, and African American communities, Lee's "made-up face" is more obvious. The fact that Lee is accepted into the African American hip-hop circles she used to pose with her in the images indicates that she has successfully blurred the lines between her Asianness and those samples she uses to project a specific African American expression of blackness. Lee's work troubles how we "see" Americanness, hip-hop, and race more broadly. She challenges the ways in which we incorporate particular stereotypes of blackness and other racial minorities as the social norm even as oppressed minorities (and, in some cases, White allies) fight against these stereotypes. Lee's commentary on racial injustice and stereotypes can be read as deflective: "I am not Korean American so I don't have all the problems and issues about race that other Americans do."[26]

Lee's so-called ignorance of blackface is difficult to believe for me, yet she could be oblivious to the history. Art critic and blogger Eusong Kim takes Lee to task for her historic amnesia about the history of blackface minstrelsy in the United States, quoting Lee as stating:

> "I'm not Korean-American, which means I don't have issues about race. . . . But I'm really happy that people talk a lot about different things from my work." Good to know Lee believes Koreans in the US and Koreans overall don't have "race" problems.[27]

Even in Korea, Koreans using blackface is well documented. Korean musicians and consumers of hip-hop and R&B music have performed their versions of these American music genres created by African Americans by donning Black makeup; perming their hair to appear more "Black"; and learning to vocally imitate Black American singers, rappers, and dancers.[28] The obvious coalitions that Lee had the opportunity to build between histories of oppression of other African American, Asian, or Asian American women are lost in translation. Her self-identification as a "Korean, Korean" woman is a strategy that she uses to absolve herself from any artistic responsibility for acknowledging the ways that women of color are racialized and stereotyped in the United States, and how those acts play out in Black women's quests for the American Dream inside and outside of hip-hop culture.

Reading Lee's photographs in relationship to one another and in the context of Lee's process as a conceptual artist offers the viewer more information to negotiate between what is staged and what is performed by Lee in her acts of reproductive remix. The lived experiences of the African American women who pose with her are lost as their bodies and voices become what African American studies scholar Nicole Fleetwood calls "excess flesh" that serve as props for Lee:

> Excess flesh performance in mass culture produces a sharper lens to see the operations of the discourse of captivity and capital that frames the black body in the field of vision. The visible black body is interpreted through the discourse of commodification and the simultaneous punishment of circum-Atlantic trades in the flesh and the structures of racialization that emerges through these practices.[29]

Lee's performances rely on remixing and performing her version of Black women's bodies, rendering the commodified "parts" sampled hyper visible. She does not consider what she does as commodification or appropriation. Her narrative about her conceptual practice always focuses on herself. She has the opportunity to allow the Black women in her projects to determine how their bodies are depicted and circulated in the photographs, yet she focuses on depicting hip-hop culture as an American phenomenon that is disconnected from the music's history of contesting racism, White appropriation, and the marginalization of Black women. In the current age of selfie culture, nearly twenty years since Lee used a disposable film camera to capture her various "looks," Black women's bodies in hip-hop culture are still objectified and animated as objects of sexual fantasy and desire. Not only do Black men in hip-hop videos and Instagram posts use Black women's bodies as enticement for followers, likes, and reposts that have direct monetary returns for their brands, but Black women also recuperate the excess of their bodies as profitable commodities that can be used to critique their simultaneous exploitation and empowerment in sex-positive performances. As Black women decide how to possess themselves, they also engage in strategic reproductions of themselves by Black and non-Black subjects as they pursue their versions of an American Dream narrative that resists and consumes Black female identity and sexuality that are produced in relationship to whiteness and American Dream narratives that dictate that White is what is beautiful. Lee's body stands in for notions of White femininity that shape the notion of excess flesh. She wears a low-cut top to reveal her cleavage and a gold chain, reflecting her knowledge of popular styles worn by women in hip-hop in the late 1990s. Revealing clothing is often associated with the "video vixen" stereotypes that hypersexualize women across racial lines in hip-hop, while expensive jewelry is a code of self-adornment used by African American men and women in hip-hop to indicate class status. Lee's skin is only "tan" when read through the discourse of White European beauty standards. In African American discourse on physical blackness, Lee's skin tone would be read as light brown or light-skinned. By positioning herself next to another Black woman of a lighter skin tone, and framing their centered position with darker-skinned Black women, Lee creates a frame that values the women's skin tones from dark to light from a central perspective. She holds a glass of cognac, an older hip-hop symbol of excess.[30] Her proficiency in translating both physical and social samples of blackness in hip-hop addresses her ability to take what she observes to lend sincerity to her performance. Lee adds commodity value to her Asianness within the U.S. visual field when the viewer of the photograph discovers that Lee's blackness is reproduced and circulated in galleries and museums around the world. Hip-hop culture's connection to what Nicole Fleetwood calls "circum-Atlantic" trades in the flesh is important here.[31] Lee's body remixes routes of trade through the sampling of specific Black African American racial codes with her non-Black body to create a reproduction of blackness. Her analog captures of Black women with a cheap disposable camera allows her to hold their images and likenesses hostage in the photographs. However, what does Lee's work show us about the "excess" of blackness and hip-hop that makes us feel so uncomfortable? Lee's performance of hip-hop as Black and female does reveal the ways in which hip-hop's mainstream American Dream narratives are wrapped-up representations of rags-to-riches stories that center hyper-materialistic and hypermasculine narratives that perpetuate Black male and female stereotypes. Then how might we look at what Lee's performances are doing that illuminate those conflations? Lee uses her body to play back how the Asian body is triangulated within the White hegemonic discourse that determines the commodity value of bodies and trades in human flesh along the axis of the Black–White binary in the United States. From Lee's perspective, these ideas of transgression and deception are constructions to which she does not prescribe. She does not translate her cross-racial performances in this way. In an interview in *Paper* magazine in 2003, Lee contended:

> I come from a homogenized country . . . so I don't frame myself as Asian or Korean American. A lot of the issues that arise from my work aren't necessarily by design. Most of the projects I choose because I personally like those given groups of people.[32]

Lee's reproductions of Black women in her hip-hop series of photographs highlights the silencing of the wide range of expression of Black women globally who create hip-hop-inspired art, yet inevitably have to fight to have access to the same elite performance spaces, galleries, and museums that contain reproductions of their likenesses as rendered in Lee's *The Hip Hop Project*. Black women in the United States who create conceptual art and hip-hop have to fight for the right to show their work in prestigious White venues that become the validation places of Black cultural producers in the art world.

After several unsuccessful attempts to contact Lee to interview her about race and her representation of African American women in *The Hip Hop Project*, I was invited to an artist talk with Lee at the University of Southern California by art historian Richard Meyer in March 2007.[33] After the talk, I was invited to attend the dinner for Lee organized by Richard Meyer and David Román. Román was my professor and he knew that I had a very difficult time gaining access to Lee because my project was about race. (Lee and her gallery had declined to talk to me previously because I described my project as addressing racial performance.) When I went to the post-talk dinner in a group that included Lee, I was able have an informal discussion with her about the race and gender dynamics of her work. Lee was very reluctant to talk about the subject of race. I had only a few questions that I could ask her. For Lee, the word *race* was automatically conflated with blackness and she did not want to talk about it. Shifting gears, I attempted to change the focus of the conversation to the process of how she becomes the characters she portrays. Attempting to move away from her engagement with blackness and hip-hop in her performance art, I mentioned another series of images in the *Projects* series: *The Hispanic Project*, in which Lee conflates "Hispanic" identity with the styles of Puerto Rican women in

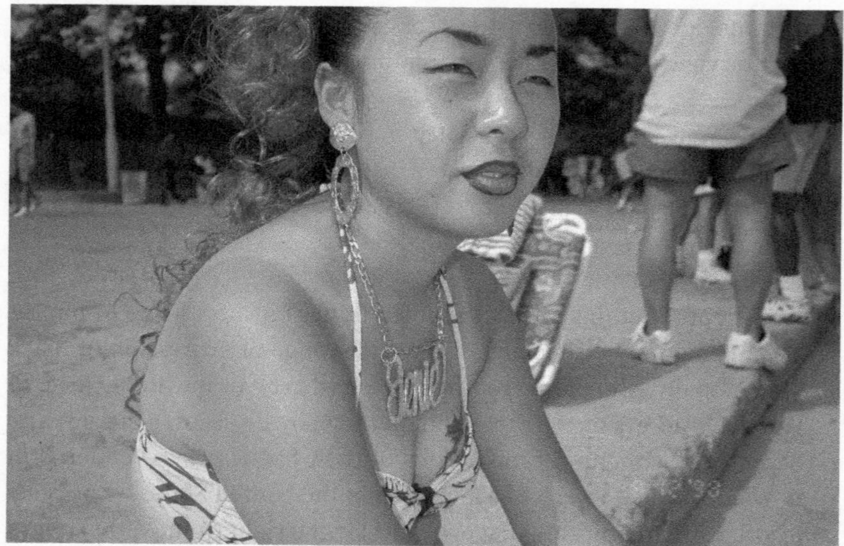

Fig. 4. Nikki S. Lee in *The Hispanic Project*. Artwork © Nikki S. Lee, courtesy of Sikkema Jenkins & Co., New York.

the Puerto Rican Day parade in New York. Lee also refused to qualify why she changes her skin color to sample looks of Puerto Rican women despite the wide range of complexions extant in the Latinx community, some of which correspond with Lee's own skin color. Lee's conceptual conflation of Hispanic and Puerto Rican identities (see *Hispanic Project* image) allows the bodies of Latina women to become the excess flesh props that help Lee's self-exploration at the expense of transgressive exploitation of Black and Brown women. Lee never goes beneath the surface projections of identity. Despite her interactions with these various groups, Lee has yet to speak out about specific connections between herself and them. She simply focuses on themes of changing.

I asked Lee at dinner if she saw opportunities to make connections between her experiences as an Asian woman and those of African American or Latina women. Lee admitted to me that after several years of living in the United States, she was becoming more aware that her body was being read as a "minority body." Her recognition of this fact alone suggests that her newfound awareness of her "otherness" in a U.S.

context positions her as knowledgeable enough about U.S. race relations to further investigate how her work is read within different national contexts. When I asked Lee about her social responsibility for potentially offending the groups whose identities she performs, she responded, "I am not responsible for people's feelings. I am responsible for myself. People can think what they want to think."[34]

There was always the possibility for Lee to explore hip-hop music and culture in New York as a Korean woman, yet she makes a conscious choice to mask her Asian identity under performances of blackness associated with hip-hop. Moreover, Lee's sampling of Puerto Rican women's codes of self-adornment speaks to the ways in which American minorities' cultural products are grafted onto hip-hop to create a virtual "body" that stands in for specific racial and ethnic identifications. Despite Lee's sociopolitical self-positioning as an Asian woman, she has shared histories of subjugation with Black and Latina women around the world. In the eighteen years that the *Projects* images have existed, there is still little discussion about Lee's remixing of racial samples and the tremendous financial profits she has gained from sampling Black and Latina women's identities and remixing them with her public persona as Nikki S. Lee.

Lee plays on the assumed authenticity—the realness—of photographs (both print images and digital photos) in popular culture. By remixing images that document both fabricated and lived experiences of African American women, Lee creates a connection between the cult value of African American women's bodies and the exhibition value, avoiding what she calls "Western preoccupations with race" to explore her own personal engagement with changing:

> People are always bringing up the question of identity. I don't care if people call me a chameleon—it's cliché and people are too lazy to invent new words. But I forgive them. Changing me is part of my identity. That's never changed. I'm just playing with forms of changing.[35]

Mainstream curators, gallery owners, and critics choose to laud the artist for her seeming capacity to transform herself. But if you look closely at Lee's photographs, the lines of demarcation between what is sampled as real and what remixed as a fake representation of blackness and hip-hop is always already subjective. D. Robert Okada and Z. Samual Podolski challenge reads of Lee's work that position her as a cultural appropriator. Lee's depiction of hip-hop as part of American culture that is open for consumption by all highlights the fact that the American Dream narrative does not see all women, men, and nonbinary citizens as created equal. Okada and Podolski note:

> Lee is not stereotyping and marginalizing her subjects, but rather indicting those stereotypes, exhibiting the fluency with which we can shed and assume any of them we like. She doesn't objectify the person; she objectifies the ideas we all have about minority identities. She shows her audience the extent to which they stereotype—and marginalize—themselves. In this way, Lee achieves two biting critiques in one fell swoop—cutting at both the stereotyped and the stereotype. We identify others and ourselves in purely visual terms. If Nikki Lee's "Projects" seems at first ridiculous, then, that's the whole point. They are ridiculous, and so are we.[36]

The fact remains that Lee's performances of hip-hop transgress boundaries that alert us to our collective responsibility to challenge the consumption of Black women's aesthetic production as well as the erasure of the creative labor that they contribute to challenge the dominant masculinity that define the parameters of hip-hop's aesthetic framings. I now turn to the work of African American actress and solo artist Sarah Jones. Jones creates solo performance pieces for theater that address issues of race, gender, and ethnicity in relationship to the American Dream.

It Was All A Dream[37]

As a celebrated solo performer, Sarah Jones has access to prestigious theater venues; funding from major foundations; and support from established artists, directors, and producers.[38] Her theatrical works initiate conversation about race and ethnicity, as well as the multicentricity of blackness. Yet Jones, unlike Danny Hoch and Matt Sax, is invested in narratives of multiculturalism rather than in any social activist stances about the unifying power of hip-hop.

Before Jones's *Bridge & Tunnel* performance became popular in the underground New York theater scene in 2002, Jones provided a critique of hip-hop in a spoken word/rap performance entitled "Your Revolution" that took Black male hip-hop artists to task for marginalizing Black women as sexual objects. She received international attention as a performer when her poem was banned from radio play by the Federal Communications Commission.[39] Ironically, Jones's critique of hip-hop from a Black woman's perspective helped further her career. Before the media attention in 2002 that launched her as an internationally recognized performance artist, she performed her first full-length solo performance, *Surface Transit*, as part of the Hip-Hop Theater Festival in New York in 2000. Many of the characters in *Surface Transit* became stock characters for Jones that would travel with her to other performances throughout her career. In *Bridge & Tunnel*, many parts of those early characters become fully realized. Jones explores a diverse group of characters' relationships to hip-hop, from a bigoted Jewish woman named Lorraine to a hip-hop-addicted African American rapper named Rashid. Using a hip-hop-inspired spoken word poetry night as the link between characters, Jones uses her body and voice to sample from a wide range of performative codes of identity in order to illustrate how differences in race, ethnicity, sexuality, and class have shaped their journeys toward American citizenship. When I saw the show at the Helen Hayes Theater on Broadway in August 2006, the audience was a cross-racial and cross-ethnic mix of people of all ages. I sat next to a group of lively, well dressed, seventy-something White women who kept asking one another, "So she is going to play all of the people? Amazing . . ." Nearly every billboard in front of the theater attested to Jones's ability to transcend her blackness in order to represent the "multicultural" qualities of New York.[40] Directed by Tony Taccone, the play focuses on immigrants to New York City and the ways that race and ethnicity have shaped their struggles to identify as Americans.[41]

The preshow offers an eclectic mix of hip-hop and techno music. The two-level stage is set with a microphone stand down center stage, a multipronged coatrack holding various garments upstage left, and a staircase leading up to a door with an opaque window that indicates an office. The lighting is dim, creating the ambiance of a 1960s poetry reading. A few tables and chairs stand stage right. Jones enters the scene from behind the audience, making her way down the aisle from the entrance of the theater to the stage. Dressed as a homeless woman, burdened

Fig. 5. Sarah Jones as Rashid in *Bridge & Tunnel*. Photo courtesy Paul Kolnik.

with bags and extra clothing, Jones delivers a prologue that announces to the audience that they are about to witness a poetry jam. Instead of an usher making the announcement about no cell phones, pagers, and candy wrappers which usually precedes Broadway shows, Jones makes all of the announcements to the audience. As she saunters to the stage, she takes off the sweaters and bags worn by the homeless woman, places them on stage, and grabs a dark blazer from the coatrack to become a Pakistani poet/accountant named Mohammed Ali. The audience now understands that the coatrack holds all of the costume changes Jones will use to portray her characters.

The poetry night takes place in a coffee shop in Queens, which hosts a weekly poetry jam for immigrants entitled "I. Am. A. Poet. Too." This is an acronym that is used to describe the group, which consists of "Immigrant and Multiculturalist American Poets or Enthusiasts Traveling Toward Optimistic Openness." Mirroring Jones's own experiences as a former "hip-hop poet," the actress uses poetry as a platform for new immigrants who want to learn English. The spoken word venue imagines poetry as a site that facilitates new imaginings, translations, and interpretations of the American Dream. As hip-hop music blares from the speakers, Mohammed Ali tells the audience to "make some noise," using Hip Hop Nation Language to excite the crowd. The hip-hop poetry "jam" provides a space where poets of all racial, ethnic, and gender identities can imagine themselves as American.

Jones creates fourteen characters, each with a distinct voice. Yet some are caricatures of various racial and ethnic groups. Jones's performances of Black characters from throughout the African diaspora reveals the multicentricity of blackness re-articulating a wide array of "blacknesses" experienced by Black women from the United States, Jamaica, Haiti, London, and the Dominican Republic. Jones appears to strongly identify with these characters, perhaps because their experiences have something in common with her own experiences as a Black woman. I make this assertion simply because these characters are very strong in her performance; however, connections to Jones's position as a Black woman can also be identified in other characters in the show. When Jones samples from other performative codes of identity, including a Chinese mother of a lesbian daughter, a young Russian Jewish grandmother, or a smart-mouthed Latina, she offers a way for the audience to connect to diverse immigrant experiences. Yet many of these samples echo racial and ethnic stereotypes. However, Jones uses these stereotypes as a bait-and-switch tactic that allows the audience to quickly identify with the race or ethnicity of a character. Her performances work to incite a larger understanding of how particular immigrant groups are marginalized in the United States based on being read as "foreign." Jones asks, "Who has the right to claim the 'American' Dream?" Using hip-hop's aesthetics to shape the poetry slam (hip-hop music playing, unique characters taking on the gestures of rap performances, etc.) allows Jones to create a most complex critique of the American Dream. Jones indicts American Dream rhetoric that promises equal opportunities to all with no mention of the institutional and systemic racism that limits opportunities for historically underrepresented minorities and other marginalized immigrant communities to achieve these promises. The characters' varying degrees of English fluency suggest language as a depository of intersecting cultures. Such intersection of language allows us to see the connections between "group differentiated vulnerabilities"[42] that are separated by a bridge between inequality and equal opportunity in the United States.

Mohammed Ali, the Pakistani host of the poetry event, uses hip-hop-inflected poetry to recount his experiences as a Pakistani male who is often mistaken for a terrorist in the United States because of his style of dress and his physical appearance. Ali is dressed in a tight-fitting blazer and introduces each immigrant poet as he or she steps up to the microphone. He uses newly learned hip-hop language to show his "hip-ness" in English, mirroring immigrants' attempts to forge an "American" identity by adapting popular American vernacular, which often finds its source in hip-hop vernacular. Mocking himself and his heavily accented use of hip-hop terms such as "hype" and "dope," Ali manipulates American stereotypes and misunderstandings of Pakistani and Arab identity. He reminds the audiences that he is not a terrorist and that he "pays his taxes" and has heard all of the jokes about the "other" Mohammed Ali. He has learned about American identity and the rules with which he must he must comply to be regarded as an American citizen. By paying his taxes, distancing himself from racist performatives associated with "terrorists" (i.e., those people who may "look" of Middle Eastern or North African descent—or who physically present as "Muslim," drawing on American stereotypes), and speaking English, Ali feels he should have access to the American Dream. However, by naming her Pakistani character Mohammed Ali, a spelling variation of the chosen moniker (Muhammad Ali) of the late African American boxer formerly known as Cassius Clay, Jones makes a commentary on the relationship between Muslim identity and its stereotypical associations with dissident behavior that seemingly threatens American democracy.

Another hip-hop-inspired character in *Bridge & Tunnel* is Rashid, a male African American rapper from Brooklyn who also appeared in Jones's first hip-hop-inspired solo play, *Surface Transit.* Like Danny Hoch's White wannabe rapper Flip and his African American rapper Emcee Enuff characters, Jones's Rashid uses hip-hop language and gestures to embody the b-boy stereotype. He wears a baseball cap and parka jacket, looks worn by many African American rappers in New York in 1990s hip-hop. Rashid has his own analysis of immigrants in New York and comes to the poetry slam presenting his perspective as an African

American "immigrant." He argues: "'Cause no what tam sayin, like, aiight, black people, we got imported, y'all get deported, you feel me?"[43] Here, Jones uses Rashid to connect the experiences of African Americans to those of several immigrant communities explored in the show. By analyzing the experiences of African Americans as forced immigrants to the United States, Rashid underscores the impact of the transatlantic slave trade on the social identities of African Americans. Black people, for Rashid, are uniquely African Americans. His simplistic identification with Black immigrants from other countries facilitates discussions about how African Americans see themselves through blackness before they identify as Americans. He critiques the American government and generic promises of the American Dream that are deferred for many poor African American men, who often feel as if they have more chances of incarceration than education and social advancement. Rashid pleads his case before the microphone as an African American male who has been denied access to rights, compensation, and social liberty as the descendant of an African American slave. He wants to know why so many other racial and ethnic immigrant groups have received help in realizing their potential as American citizens because of their elective choice to come to the United States. Rashid cannot understand why the influx of immigrants in New York leaves him with fewer opportunities as an African American male. He identifies with the immigrant experience in the United States and wants his particular Black voice to be heard. He wants to connect with his audience to show them how his experiences relate to their own.

Hip-hop also enters Jones's show through the life of a Russian Jewish immigrant character, Lorraine Levine, who also appeared in Jones's *Surface Transit.* Lorraine is a poet from Long Island who learned poetry at a senior center workshop. Jones peppers Lorraine's speech with Yiddish words, wears gaudy clothing, and sports large 1970s-style eyeglasses reminiscent of parodies of Jewish women performed by the late improv comedienne Gilda Radner on *Saturday Night Live* in the 1980s. Lorraine's link to hip-hop is through her grandson, a kid who worships African American hip-hop mogul P-Diddy (Sean Combs). Lorraine writes and performs a protest poem entitled "Please, Don't Get Up" that narrates her experiences with young people who have no respect for the elderly. Through her encounter with hip-hop and blackness, Lorraine

Fig. 6. Sarah Jones as Lorraine Levine in *Bridge & Tunnel*. Photo courtesy Paul Kolnik.

finds community and "unity" within the difference of hip-hop. Her experiences now become relevant to her grandson, because she samples from hip-hop in order to communicate with him. Jones's commentary here also addresses how hip-hop serves as a bridge between racial and ethnic groups as well as different generations. The fact that a young Jewish kid can have an African American role model speaks to hip-hop's ability to inspire cross-racial and cross-ethnic coalitions.

In *Bridge & Tunnel*, Jones's performance disrupts conflations of blackness with African American identity as she plays several Black characters from throughout the African diaspora, yet only two are African American. Despite the fact that many of Jones's characters are of African descent, most of the media attention Jones receives is about her ability to play characters who are not Black or American. Critics, and Jones herself, seem to reserve the term "Black" for African Americans, as all other Black groups are identified by national origin. In fact, most critics focus on her ability to embody notions of the "multicultural," perhaps because of her identity as an African American woman of mixed racial and ethnic backgrounds (her mother is European-Caribbean, and her father is African American). Jones's attempt to use hip-hop to universalize experiences across categories of difference often diminishes the social, economic, and material disparities that limit the quality of life expectations for people of color both nationally and internationally. Connecting to earlier discussions of coalition building, Danny Hoch's and Matt Sax's whiteness often foreclose opportunities for audiences to see their performances of other racial and ethnic groups as positive efforts to incite dialogue about racial inequality. Jones's blackness and her ability to seemingly transcend it in performance is most often the focus of critics, who often forget that Jones is not exempt from creating characterizations that may also reinforce existing racial and ethnic stereotypes. In my correspondence with Jones, the actress offered her perspectives on her work. She considers her personal racial and gender identifications as part of her artistic practice:

> As an African American woman who came of age in "post-post-Civil Rights," "post-feminist" America in a multicultural family and community, I have long been acutely, sometimes painfully aware of the complex layers of discrimination and injustice endured by women of African descent worldwide. I am interested in how we cope and create space for our own self-determination, self-expression, self-love, no matter what economic, health, social, sexual, and other issues we face. I know this resistance, in both overt and subtle forms, is taking place in London flats, on the streets of Kingston, on unpaved roads from Port-au-Prince to Panama to Pretoria, and that regardless of our nationality or worldview our struggles—while very specific because of the dual impact of race and gender—represent the universality of all people's struggles for human rights.[44]

Jones's perspectives as a Black woman who perceives herself as "multicultural" draws our attention to the ways that conceptions of multiculturalism often disavow racial and ethnic differences in favor of a fabricated notion of universal "cultural" identity that is seemingly not impacted by racial, ethnic, class, and gender differences. Though Jones's performances, like Hoch's, Sax's, and Lee's, offer opportunities to create cross-racial and cross-ethnic collaborations in performance by presenting seemingly "universal" experiences, these experiences often become "universal" because a Black or White person playing other racial and ethnic groups presents them. By embodying and voicing the experiences of other racial and ethnic groups, the artists using hip-hop in theater whom I have discussed thus far can often absorb the ways that race and ethnicity specifically shape the painful parts of their experiences and present them as "universal" experiences that happen to everyone.

Jones offers both superficial and complex perspectives on immigrant identity, specifically in her performative engagement of blackness as a multicentric possibility that can be experienced by non-Black people and non-African Americans. Like Hoch, Jones is guilty of creating characters that remain based in stereotype, even if for effect. Both Hoch and Jones evoke Stuart Hall's question, "Under what conditions can a connection be formed or made in processes of articulation and re-articulation?" As described in chapter 1, in my discussions with Hoch I asked if he thought it was easier for audiences to accept performances by Black performers such as Sarah Jones, Anna Deavere Smith, or even Eddie Murphy to engage in cross-racial performance. Hoch posited:

> Yes, I think it is. Again, this is simply because of American history. However, it is a projection of liberal racism to infer that people of color (actually just black folks) have the "right," the "ability," the "sole talent" to play others, because it is assumed that they have suffered the worst and therefore are the biggest victims and the biggest victims get to play everybody. This liberalist victimization only bolsters racism and misunderstanding.[45]

Hoch's correction of his use of "people of color," replacing it with "Black folks," reinforces the how the Black–White binary is used to racialize who has access and privilege to play the "other" in performance. "People of color" is a politically correct term that is used to refer to African Americans and other racial and ethnic minorities. It is also used to generalize the particular histories of each group as interchangeable in relationship to whiteness in the United States. Hoch's problematic reference to slavery as the norm of African Americans being understood as the "biggest victims" reifies existing polemical discussions between African American and Jewish Americans about suffering. Perhaps Blacks and other racially marginalized groups in the United States are more open to watching minorities perform other minorities, because there is an implied empathy or shared struggle between minorities that is often missing when White performers take on the performative codes of non-White racial identity (i.e., Blackness, Latinxness, etc.). Because Hoch is marked as "White," his Jewish ethnic and/or religious identification is often absorbed by his White privilege. Though Hoch attempts to be clever and sarcastic in his response, these sensitive issues between African Americans and Jewish Americans should not be taken lightly and might be used to illustrate the coalitions between these groups because of similar histories of struggle and persecution, yet completely different experiences of freedom and racism.

Jones's attempts to foster cross-racial and cross-ethnic coalitions have the same potential to reify racial stereotypes as those of any White artist. Jones's representations are not necessarily rendered more "Black" or "authentic" because she is racially Black. Nor does Jones's blackness make her more "authentically" hip-hop. Jones's embodied blackness does provide a *text* for the audience that imparts larger social histories of oppression of Black people generally, and Black women specifically, that may serve as a point of perceived empathy with the experiences of other racial and ethnic groups. Jones remains a woman of color whose image is always already compared against existing racial and gender stereotypes of Black women inside and outside hip-hop culture's intersection with African American life. Danny Hoch's and Matt Sax's ability to perform blackness through hip-hop does not threaten their White privilege; in fact, it often gives them more access because they can maintain their White privilege and perform blackness in ways that give other Whites access to it and to hip-hop without the threat of the presence of the Black body. As a Korean artist, Nikki S. Lee can perform hip-hop as American and use blackness as a prop to convey the ways that blackness is always already a part of hip-hop expression and then return to being an Asian woman. Jones can never escape her Black racial identity in her performances.

The three characters discussed in *Bridge & Tunnel* who directly engage hip-hop music—the Pakistani immigrant, Mohammed Ali; the African American rapper, Rashid; and the Jewish female character, Lorraine—are characters created through Jones's use of hip-hop language and stereotype. In my interview with Jones, I asked her if she believed that her characters were engaging with blackness and she told me that she did not. However, in addition to Rashid and Lorraine, many of her other characters in the show, including a young Vietnamese immigrant who creates a spoken word piece about being perceived as a "model minority," use the spoken word platform and hip-hop vernacular to speak to how race, ethnicity, class, and gender shape citizenship in the United States.[46] One reason Jones may not want to focus on "blackness" and "hip-hop" is because she wants to be perceived as an actress and not just an "African American" actress. The way that Black actresses' racial identity is used to qualify the types of work they should be allowed to perform is problematic, and is addressed by Jones's desire to resist labels that pigeonhole her capacities as a performer uniquely because of race.

The hip-hop platform in Jones's show cannot be denied and is used by all of her characters in some way to underline that race and ethnicity have enabled and foreclosed their opportunities for social and economic success in the United States. Jones's desire to be read as an actress and not an African American actress can stand in for the hopes of most marginalized people, who want to have the same opportunities White performers have the ability in theater to inhabit various roles without racial signifiers. Danny Hoch has the privilege of being an actor, not a "White" actor. Jones is read through the "global" and "multicultural" labels that mainstream White theater critics use to describe her. White critics rarely mention her blackness, which seemingly allows her more flexibility to break down socially imposed barriers based on race. Yet do these racial barriers really break down? Roberta Uno, a hip-hop theater studies scholar and one of the first producers to program hip-hop theater, alerts us to the ways in which mainstream White critics may identify hip-hop theater artists as token representatives of multiculturalism, even when the artists themselves resist such labels:

> Still other artists, raised in the hip-hop era, acknowledge its influences but they are concerned that hip-hop's hegemony produces formulaic work rather than encouraging an expansive definition. The worry is that producers, presenters and those who are external to the hip-hop culture will recognize its presence only if marked by the most obvious characteristic of

> the four elements, narrowing innovations, subtleties and original points of departure. Rather than grapple with their complexities, the theatre, many hip-hop artists feel, the theater has tended to relegate hip-hop to audience-development/"audience of tomorrow" slots, to second-stage outreach and education slots, or to token "minority"/ "multicultural"/"diversity"/"artist of color"" "kill-two-birds-with-one-stone–if it's a woman too" programming slots. The concern is that *hip-hop theatre* will become the latest, and even more restrictive, buzz word for the multicultural box.[47]

The institutional inequalities that make it so that qualifiers have to be used to separate White performers from the experiences of people of color speak to the racist practices embedded in mainstream theater that segregate experiences of Americanness based on racial identity. *Bridge & Tunnel* may be read by theater critics and Jones as a multicultural work, yet a closer analysis reveals that Jones may be more in tune with the complex predicaments that race, ethnicity, gender, and class impose on being perceived as "American" inside and outside the theater. While Jones is recognized in the hip-hop community because her works appear in reputedly "high" art places such as Broadway and documentary films, she is often associated with "multicultural" and/or White mainstream media. In the African American community, Jones is referenced in the context of "Black" and/or African American theater, usually by scholars rather than the mainstream media. She has been an "it" girl of the social activist, foundation, and nonprofit set, and is invited all over the United States and abroad to perform excerpts from her work as examples of racial and ethnic harmony. Jones is clever at critique, but understands the limits of what she can do when commissioned by foundations and other nonprofit groups. Though Jones's diverse depictions of blackness are complex and reveal the multicentricity of blackness throughout the African diaspora, these critiques are never the focus of her critics, who see her as embodying the multicultural rhetoric of the American Dream. Nor are they the focus for Jones, for that matter, who makes it clear in her press materials and show descriptions that she is in the theater world to bring people together. She is most interested in identifying as an American bridge builder, not as an African American. Of course, this interest is fundamental to most African Americans or people of African descent around the world, who want to be identified by their interests and what they do in life, not by their race. On Sarah Jones's website she describes her work and background in the following way:

> Renowned as "a one-woman global village," she has also given multiple main-stage TED Talks garnering nearly six million views, performed at The White House and United State of Women Summit for President and First Lady Obama, and given an historic performance at The World Economic Forum in Davos, Switzerland. The daughter of two physicians, Sarah was educated at The United Nations School and Bryn Mawr College, all of which contributed to her becoming a vocal advocate for the empowerment of women and girls globally. In her role as a UNICEF Goodwill Ambassador, she has performed for audiences around the world, and raised awareness of issues including ethnic, racial, and economic disparities in the United States.[48]

Jones's website description of her history and her work specifically aligns with the multicultural ideas of White upper middle class concerns of liberal humanist ideals. She resists categorizations based on race. Jones works in predominantly White theater spaces that encourage mythologies of multiculturalism and colorblindness. And goodwill, without an in-depth explanation or exploration of the structures of inequality that produce those perspectives, protect the power interests of those White theater spaces. The White fragility of mainstream White producers cannot handle the work of artists that are in constant critique without a happy ending. Jones's work traffics in hope and promise for a better tomorrow, yet rarely addresses the dark side of systemic inequality and anti-Black racism that can't be used to galvanize a White audience to shame or reconciliation.

For non-Black artists, association with hip-hop can make them anomalies and attractive to casting directors and producers, who want to discover a connection to hip-hop that supports the idea of hip-hop as a multicultural art form, not one that reinforces its connections to African Americanness. Jones's association with hip-hop is something she dismisses, as she wants to be seen as an American actress; not a "Black" performer or a "hip-hop" performer. When I asked Jones about her artistic identification with Black and hip-hop, she observed:

As for "Hip-hop theater," this was a descriptor which was affixed by others to my work and which I resisted at first. At the time (summer of 2000) it felt like a marketing strategy that I didn't think I needed, and even though I certainly count myself a member of the Hip-hop generation, I was concerned about my work being categorized too narrowly—I believe I said something like "nobody calls Eric Bogosian's work 'rock and roll theater!'" One of my aims was not to be labeled or have my work prejudged one way or another because of assumptions about my race, gender, or one of the various styles of music and culture that influenced my sensibility. However, I greatly respect the Hip-hop theater movement and its goal of reaching people of color, young people, and other underserved communities and reflecting all our stories using the four elements and their now multi-generational, international influence.[49]

Jones's Black body can perform that labor within the context of the theater, but when it comes to HBO specials, television sitcoms, and films, she becomes another Black actress standing in line waiting for a role to come along. This is the double standard and systemic racism in the entertainment industry that continues to marginalize the talent of Black women. Jones does not want to be labeled "hip-hop" because ultimately the music and culture are conflated with a particular low-to-moderate income vernacular of African American hip-hop artists and stereotypical behaviors in Hollywood's limited translation of what blackness is and can become. As she notes, such specific labeling will ultimately limit her opportunities to be read as simply an "actress." Her desire to be recognized for her talent and not her race, ethnicity, or gender is the desire of many actors of the global majority whose life chances have been diminished because of their racial, ethnic, gender, sexuality, and/or ability. Jones has had supporting in films such as Spike Lee's *Bamboozled* (2000), and several television pilots she has developed have yet to be green-lighted by any major or cable network or streaming platform, such as Netflix or Hulu. One of her pilots/films listed on IMDB, *The Sarah Jones Show* (2005), was a one-hour special produced by Bravo right after Jones's Off-Broadway run with *Bridge & Tunnel* that promised to be a "Tracey Ullman meets *Carol Burnett Show*" type format. The show featured many characters developed in *Bridge & Tunnel*, yet was not picked up as an ongoing series by the network. In 2006, Jones made a brief appearance speaking to issues of violence and misogyny in hip-hop music in the documentary *Hip-Hop Beyond Beats and Rhymes*. In 2008, Jones went on hiatus to develop new work. She did various public performances for conferences, such as TED talks, appearances at the White House under the Obama administration, and an appearance in comedian Chris Rock's film *Good Hair* (2008), a documentary about the hair care politics of African American women in the United States. Jones resurfaced in 2011 to workshop new and old theater pieces at Nuyorican Poets Café center in New York under the title "New Year, Nuyorican!" The Nuyorican Poets Café is the same venue that featured Jones as a spoken word artist and early hip-hop theater performer who staged work for Hoch's Hip-Hop Theater Festival. In 2017, she had a guest starring role on comedian Jessica James's Netflix show *The Incredible Jessica James* and launched a new one-woman show entitled *Buy/Sell/Date* in which she performed nineteen different characters and ran off Broadway in 2018. Jones's most recent work was a supporting role in Noah Baumbach's Oscar winning film *Marriage Story* (2019) and a series regular world in the television streaming series *On the Verge* (2020). If you could compare the sheer level of cultural content and career trajectory of Sarah Jones in comparison to her White female peers such as Amy Schumer, Tina Fey, and many others, one notices a disparity of material reward for White actresses with similar talents and prolific creative output.

Jones has found her own space in the entertainment market working as a cultural bridge builder between racial groups and a translator about marginalized experience to largely White audiences. She is not necessarily waiting for a television sitcom deal or film role to define the success of her career, but in a moment when actors of all races and ethnicities, especially African American actors, are out of work, these lucrative opportunities would most likely be welcomed.

Ironically, when I asked Jones about performing blackness in her show, the only character she identified as "Black" was the African American rapper, Rashid. Despite the fact that her characters Mohammed, Rashid, and Lorraine engage hip-hop, and despite Jones's performances of Black Dominican, British, and Jamaican characters in the show, only Rashid was identified as Black. Jones explains her views on blackness:

> For me, the label "blackness" is more about a set of progressive political ideas than it is about particular kinds of behavior, speech, style of dress or cultural sensibility. That said, I perform one character who is a rapper and whose identity is rooted in a Hip-hop style, so since Hip-hop is certainly an art form and culture with origins in blackness, it's fair to say I perform blackness in that way.[50]

Jones's comments reflect the ways that blackness is conflated with African Americans and hip-hop in the American racial imaginary by Blacks and Whites. Jones does not consider the multiple engagements with African diasporic representations of blackness she has presented in her performance. Jones's translation of blackness is limited to its articulation in the context of the United States. She disregards the multicentric possibilities of blackness as articulated by the Black people portrayed in her show who are not originally from the United States. Despite Jones's view of her work and blackness, her show's use of hip-hop—from the spoken word platform, preshow music (fragments of hip-hop and techno music designed by Chris Meade and DJ Rekha), and graffiti-inspired set (created by Blake Lethem)—offered opportunities to see how other racial, ethnic, and national groups identify with hip-hop's blackness as a multicentric space to negotiate their subjectivity. Jones's conflation of blackness with a "set of progressive political ideas" underscores my analysis of why non-African American artists may be attracted to hip-hop. Her attempt to represent the pursuit of the American Dream as conforming to American rhetoric of multiculturalism is often undone by the text of the performance.

Conclusion

Bridge & Tunnel was a phenomenal success and attracted a wide array of racial and ethnic audience members. Images of Jones outside the theater showed the actress with her head opened up to reveal all of the "people inside her head." She was represented more as a novelty performer instead of the talented and extremely intelligent woman she is, who joins an artistic genealogy that includes other African American performers such as Whoopi Goldberg in presenting one of the most successful one-person shows in Broadway history. Jones follows celebrated African American women performers such as Pearl Bailey (*Hello Dolly!* [1967]) and Lena Horne (*Lena Horne: The Lady and Her Music* [1981]) as the third African American woman to receive a Special Tony award, which she won for her performance in the show in 2006. *Bridge & Tunnel* was produced by a multiracial group of producers of the Culture Project in New York, a nonprofit theater production company dedicated to developing new voices in American theater.[51] Indeed, *Bridge & Tunnel* helped Jones reveal the contradictions, promises, and dangers of the American Dream, narratives that don't include the voices of the oppressed. However, she is admittedly still striving for some version of it that can help sustain her as an artist. The marketing of *Bridge & Tunnel* clearly attempted to disarticulate Jones's "blackness" from her ability to embody racially and ethnically diverse characters. Her play was marketed as a "multicultural" play that was used to describe the "diversity" of New York. Such strategies sought to distance Jones from the types of "urban" labels that often follow hip-hop when it is connected to Black bodies. When hip-hop is connected to White, or non-African American, performers, it becomes legitimized by its new cultural container and context. Jones needed the ethnic and national identities of the characters she plays to be read as "differently" Black than the African American blackness associated with hip-hop that carries with it Black racial stereotypes and histories of anti-Black racism as much as it does survival and Black genius. Jones identifies as African American, but she makes specific references to the cultural and ethnic specificity of her Caribbeanness and multicultural background as a self-identification that is different from hip-hop produced through an African American standpoint. Hip-hop's risky, unapologetically Black blackness occurs through practice and doing, not just performance. There is a distinct difference between performing blackness and doing blackness. The former is reliant upon whiteness and the hierarchies of power it produces to contain Black people and their art. The latter creates art and music as an expression of a life lived through the being and living of blackness, which cannot be mimicked or sampled or remixed. Eventually, the truth prevails. I argue Jones's work is somewhere between performing and doing.

One of the biggest interventions of *Bridge & Tunnel* is that it depicts an ideal of a "multicultural" New York City, not necessarily one that engages its racial and ethnic difference with any specificity, cultural context, and/or engagement with anti-racist sentiment and systemic inequality that people of color in New York experience. This fictional New York presented by Jones is definitely more reflective of its inhabitants and their experiences than the whitewashed versions of New York that have become commonplace in popular theater, television, and film depictions of the city, which edit people of color out of the visual and sonic landscape of the city. At least Jones says out loud that New York is not simply "White." The city comprises a multicentric, ethnic, and racial group of people who depart from different cultural positions, yet their lives intersect and overlap daily. It is a terrible injustice that Jones's plays have not been published. She has not reaped the material reward of selling them for profit and possible reproduction so that her blueprint for diverse representation on stage can actually be played by the people of different racial and ethnic groups that she highlights in her solo performances. Jones is asked to speak and perform all over the world, but despite her tremendous success as an actress, she joins the ranks of thousands of underemployed Black female performers in the United States. Jones stays relevant in the off-Broadway set of American theater. She has created five solo shows—*Surface Transit* (2000), *Women Can't Wait* (2000), *A Right to Care* (2005), *Bridge & Tunnel* (2006), and the previously mentioned *Sell/Buy/Date* (2017)—along with several commissioned works on various topics, from healthcare to women's rights. She must constantly generate product to maintain her position as a working actress, who is Black, in a market that is technically incapable of seeing the multiplicity of Black female subject positions, ethnicities, and nationalities discussed by Jones in her play. The undocumented physical, emotional, and intellectual labor and styles of Black women are used to fuel popular culture, politics, fantasy, and entertainment with little regard for the struggles Black women face daily, as their aesthetic and intellectual property is sampled by non-Black people as a commodity. In 2009, quality roles for African American female actresses in theater, film, and television reached an all-time low (Barrois 2009).[52] As of 2021, the roles for African American women in progressive roles that speak to the social advances of African American women have doubled, yet are not the norm of how Black women are read by any means. Though Sarah Jones may avoid some of the most direct engagements with the particularity of African American blackness in her work, similar to Nikki S. Lee, she used hip-hop early in her career as a bait-and-switch tactic to get her audiences to think about the intersectional and multicentric facets of Black identities and the connections that their journeys to American citizenship have in common with those of other racial and ethnic groups. She never disavowed African American cultural production of blackness, but more so challenges the ways in which blackness, African American culture, and hip-hop are conflated in reductive and problematic ways by the mainstream media. She also could have been performing other racial and ethnic identities using hip-hop and spoken word as a connecting thematic as a long-term audition for bigger things. Demonstrating her capacity to play across ethnicities and nationalities using the multi-character solo show format allowed Sarah Jones to showcase her wide-ranging talents and to undermine notions of a monolithic Black experience.

Nikki S. Lee is a keen businesswoman who realized that the cross-racial performances in her *Projects* series would incite a polemic that would launch her into the center of American conceptual art in the late 1990s and early 2000s. Lee's use of her body to implicitly challenge notions of Americanness marks her Korean Asianness as something distinctly different from Asian American and African American identities. Her use of hip-hop to strategically disrupt constructed boundaries of race and ethnicity and default depictions of hip-hop as both American and Black attempts to disidentify with notions of racial particularity. Lee's critique of American popular culture signifies America's racial past in the present as it highlights the commodity value of hip-hop as a cultural expression that can be disarticulated from Black life in the United States. Reading Lee's photographs as stills that document her performance of Black women's styles of self-adornment and skin color grafted onto her Asian body through performance reveals the multitiered usages of Black women's labor. Though Lee's intention was to explore the malleability of her identity, her refusal to acknowledge the histories of racism and exploitation of Black women in hip-hop ultimately works to further marginalize Black and Asian women as commodities within mainstream American Dream narratives. Black and Asian women are subject to racial and gender stereotypes in both hip-hop and American culture writ large. Lee's success in *The Hip Hop Project* was earned through two strategic moves that are important to my analysis of her conceptual performance. First, she understood the ways in which American Dream narratives in hip-hop narrated by many African American artists exploit the rags-to-riches story as much as they critique its exclusionary and racist practices. However, Lee's practice of avoiding the racial polemic that her work evokes for people of color is cultural and more specific to her Koreanness than she led me to believe in our dinner conversation years ago. In 2018, in the newspaper *China Morning Post*, journalist Crystal Tai took many Asian pop stars to task for sampling from African American expressions of blackness in hip-hop and R&B music. She contends:

> Unfortunately, embodiments of Hip-hop and perceptions of African-American culture are more reflective of stereotypes and diversity in countries like China, South Korea and Japan, where widespread discrimination and negative stereotypes about people with darker skin continue to exist. In Korea, music and street fashion have definitely been influenced by African-American culture.[53]

For many Asian people living in countries like China, Japan, and South Korea, hip-hop and other Black American music genres' connection to the Black specificity of African American culture is inseparable. The mimicking of blackness and the constant sampling of African American and other African diasporic styles of self-adornment, language, and cultural practices, by Japanese and Korean hip-hop artists, even when framed as an homage, completely injures Black people because it enlivens past histories of blackface and reduces African American people to their expressive culture. Lee's evasive discussion in the United States about having little knowledge of racism and American race relations is a strategy of omission. South Korean "K-Pop" (Korean pop music) artists' use of blackface, vocal mimicking of R&B and hip-hop styles, and sampling of styles of self-adornment is pervasive in the twenty-first century and has been circulating since the mid- to late 1990s, very close to the creation date of Lee's *Projects* series. That Lee took advantage of the fact that few Americans read Korean and Chinese newspapers or listened to and monitored Korean pop music aesthetics in the late 1990s to early 2000s is apparent. By 2006 and the rise of Facebook, Instagram, and Twitter, Korean sampling of hip-hop's blackness through styles of self-adornment, dance, voice, and overall aesthetic can be found as foundation elements of the K-Pop scene that has exploded in twenty-first-century popular culture. Today, Lee's work performatively indicts African American hip-hop for its lack of acknowledgment of its Asian influences and orientalist history, but Lee does not do this work herself, nor is she engaged in this conversation. Her work also affirms the international commodification of African American blackness as public consumable number one with American popular entertainment and pleasure industries. This profit and pleasure comes at a price that few Black people can afford to pay. Black bodies, American Dreams, presents, and futures are pushed into what African American director Jordan Peele calls the "Sunken Place," which Peele cinematically draws in *Get Out* (2017) as an underworld of sorts that captures the liminal spaces that Black people must wade in between White hegemony and self-possession as Black people living in the African diaspora. I analyze Peele's "Sunken Place" as an ideological and metaphysical metaphor for the places where the abyss of Black trauma, pain, and suffering collide with the air of anti-Black racism and systemic inequality. The "Sunken Place" is an overlapping and suffocating vortex where the Black past and present collide with the consumption of blackness by Whites. In this vortex, the need for the embodied presence of Black people and our art are canceled out. When other historically underrepresented minorities believe that it is okay to occupy blackness without any regard to the particularity and specificity of its multiple histories in the United States and the rest of the African diaspora and the African continent, for that matter, the message to Black people is that their bodies and their lives matter as long as they are producing content for consumption and reproduction. Hip-hop becomes a malleable and inhabitable state of identity that can be used to make White people feel less fragile, culpable, accountable, and implicit in bystander politics. Hip-hop's global popularity and capacity to sample from other cultures and to rearticulate those parts as blackness is not necessarily a free pass for theater and performance artists who clearly create offensive work and claims about hip-hop under the protective cloak of anti-essentialist analysis. People get upset about binaries, but those very binaries structure thought and can be undone only by engaging them, by bending the line that runs between the poles that reify stereotypes about Black men, Black women, and American culture, and connecting it on the other side to the White fragility and commodification of blackness that must rely on whiteness to act up in order to be legible at all. Being unapologetically Black means to say to hell with White referential expressions of blackness. Black people are sick and tired of being sick and tired, to paraphrase Ntozake Shange, with people "walking away with all of their stuff."[54] Greg Tate's 2003 anthology *Everything but the Burden* began a conversation about Black resentment of the contradictions of Black cultural appropriation. Nearly two decades years later, no matter how post-soul, Afro-futurist, biopolitically conscious we are—I'm asking us to think about how naked and bare African Americans have to become, until we are culturally unrecognizable as anything but inauthentic reproductions of ourselves. Jones's and Lee's attempts to position themselves within a multicultural lens without any connection to their particular or shared histories of racial subjugation works only as a temporary strategy. To live and create art without racial or national signifiers in order to achieve the American Dream can take an artist of color only so far in the United States. Both Lee's and Jones's sampling of racial and ethnic codes of identity to appeal to the predominantly White audiences that frequent the galleries and off-Broadway and Broadway venues in which the artists present their works last only as long as the artists' works find favor with critics who write about their very insular parts of the art world. In fact, most of the most celebrated African American actresses in theater, film, and television are often out of work. Similarly, Asian American actresses have even more challenging employment odds to face in the entertainment and fine arts industries. Nikki S. Lee has gone on to produce several more conceptual art series in addition to *Projects* that explore her identity as a Korean artist. *Parts* (2002–2005) explores Lee's connection to other identities in and around New York City, yet features only "parts" of their identities captured in photographs, with the heads, arms, and bodies of the people she poses with cut out of the image. *Layers* (2007) is a drawing-on-paper piece in which Lee traveled around the world asking street artists to draw her. She then created a palimpsest of herself, layering the drawings on top of one another in a painting that merges all of the different interpretations of herself. She also has directed and produced a documentary, *AKA Nikki S. Lee* (2006), in which she challenged audiences to guess what part of her identity was real or fabricated. The film was screened at several venues across the nation, including the Museum of Modern Art, in 2006. As of 2018, Lee's works have mostly been featured as retrospectives in smaller museums across the United States, including her most recent show at the gallery Various Small Fires in Los Angeles, California in 2019. This show, entitled *Parts and Scenes: Nikki S. Lee,* showcased a retrospective of Lee's work as well as unseen video works completed in 2014. It was one of the first exhibitions of the *Parts* series in the United States in almost ten years. The show also presented *Scenes* (2014), which is a series of short videos that were not shared prior to this exhibit. According to the Various Small Fires catalog of the show, "'Parts and Scenes' both feature the artist in tableaux of her own design; her visage is the constant that nonetheless changes in the contexts of the various photographs and videos. Parts and Scenes have much in common with Projects (1997–2001)."[55] One must ask how Lee's sensational representations of Black, Asian, and Asian American women might be read as a larger palimpsest of the failure of the entertainment and fine arts worlds to recognize and reward the creative genius of Black and Asian women at the same rate of White women in both industries.

In the case of hip-hop theater and performance in the United States, both Jones's and Lee's critiques in their solo performances have worked to complicate the conflation of hip-hop and blackness in the mainstream. Jones and her non-Black creative peers, including Lee, embody the multicentric struggles of identifying spaces to occupy hip-hop as an American art form and as an expression of racial and ethnic identity. Despite the intentions of many artists, Black and non-Black, who want to use hip-hop as a site of social critique, cross-racial and cross-ethnic coalitions cannot be successful forged unless the Black and Brown bodies and voices that are sampled and remixed into neat packages to sell Americana can also tell the stories of racial oppression and subjugation that artists may not feel comfortable sharing as they pursue their art and their versions of the American Dream. Hip-hop-inspired theater and performance, such as Sarah Jones's *Bridge & Tunnel* and Nikki S. Lee's *Projects,* open opportunities for us to imagine the dangerous stakes of reimagining and romanticizing how much we don't need racial identification in the name of coalition building. It allows artists to dream out loud on stage, leaving clues for how we might acknowledge the sights, sounds, and pains of the past that are remixed into blueprints that may help us perform new futures in the present. My discussion of Lee and Jones in this chapter, although it works to disrupt discussions of Black people in the United States and their rights to claim hip-hop as Black music and culture, does not have to suggest that I am reinforcing binaries. My discussion can just be what it is. I, and many other hip-hop listeners, cultural producers, and artists inspired by hip-hop, have a real problem with both non-Black people and Black people from around the world entering into the culture on layover to take them where they want to go, which usually is a place that has nothing to do with African American people and their needs, fears, wants, and desires for safety and freedom. The possibility of blackness, of course, is not limited to African American particularity as expressed in hip-hop. Black-derived art forms are rarely given the title of "universal" unless they prescribe to European derived art standards. As non-Black and non-African American Black artists sample from hip-hop to create art that is presented in the mainstream as universal, they are responsible not only for the joy but also the sadness embedded in these samples. Hip-hop was created as a creative outlet for Black and Brown people in the United States to heal, to protest, to rage, to signify, to challenge, to create, to love, and to dream. Without the struggle of hip-hop's history, the sampled content is only breaking the surface of what the music and culture of hip-hop really is.

THREE

ONE NATION UNDER A GROOVE / (Re)Membering Hip-Hop Dance in Jonzi D's *TAG* and Rennie Harris's *Rome & Jewels*

Here's a chance to dance our way out of our constrictions
—Parliament Funkadelic (1978)

Another thing to share about my brother Mack is that he was a b-boy in Marietta, Georgia, a predominantly White suburb of Atlanta where we moved after leaving Dearborn, Michigan. Marietta was where I discovered not only the Beastie Boys, but also other components of hip-hop culture. Our family moves to different cities were not great for my siblings and me. My divorced single mother told us that she moved us to Georgia to give us a better quality of life and to find work. I think that we left to save my brother from the increased violence that young Black men were being subjected to in Detroit. My sister Heather and I seemed to adjust to suburbs a little more easily. We were cheerleaders. My sister played soccer. We morphed into the life of being "one of the only" Black kids, but because we were read as "mixed." Our skin privilege as light-skinned Black girls allowed us to be "accepted" into the popular fray. I think we both suffered differently because of this. Speaking for myself, I was afraid to love hip-hop openly. I feared that if I was actively engaged in Black culture in the "multicultural" microcosm of Marietta, an upper-middle-class suburban enclave that was a TV show version of the "MTV generation," that my friends at my predominantly White high school would ostracize me. I wasn't strong enough nor knew myself well enough to stand on my own. I lead a "multicultural" life because even after we moved to the suburbs of Michigan, my brother was attracted to life outside the so-called safety bubble. So, once again, we left Black spaces, where we were part of a majority, to move to Marietta, Georgia to become Black anomalies in White spaces. My brother learned to channel his frustrations of "living while Black" in the suburbs of Georgia into breaking. I saw the joy he experienced. He found a community of African American dancers that made Black space for him within a White community that, on most days, found some interesting way to exclude him. Just as Black and Latinx dancers in New York created hip-hop dance out of a need to express their frustrations about racism, anti-Black violence, and the lack of socioeconomic opportunity, so too did my brother need b-boying (*breaking* was the term we used at the time, not realizing the term was resisted by many b-boys and b-girls in New York) to stay alive to himself physically, emotionally, and spiritually. The culture, which my brother learned intuitively, and the moves he shared and invented with fellow dancers, helped him to express his identity as a young Black man coming of age during the late 1980s. In the 1980s, hip-hop and breaking were definitively viewed as *Black* dance. We are now over twenty years into the 2000s and the dance form continues to transform as a transnational dance language that challenges the way we see and experience blackness.

Popular dance-based television shows in the twenty-first century such as *So You Think You Can Dance?* and *World of Dance* offer pop culture projections of hip-hop dance that differ greatly from the African American and Latinx dancers of hip-hop movies and MTV videos that I saw growing up. Today, hip-hop dancers are from diverse racial, ethnic, gender, class, and national identifications, and they perform hip-hop dance with a level of fluency that communicates an embodied connection to African American culture, which may not necessarily be the case. How is a Black dance form so closely associated with Black cultural production now packaged to almost completely disconnect it from any reference to African American culture? Instead it is presented as a generic "American" culture that shrouds hip-hop's contentious relationship to exclusive notions of Americanness. Hip-hop dancers who perform movements rooted in African American dance idioms—such as breaking, popping, and locking, as well as traces of the Charleston, lindy hop, and juba—speak a corporeal language that resonates with audiences through acts of embodied communication. But what are these dancers saying to us about race and blackness? To the naked eye, the dances are just exciting entertainment; to those who speak hip-hop dance language, the gestures have definitive meanings that link them to a rich cultural history of African American dance practice.

Intentionally or unintentionally, hip-hop dancers are communicating a specific Black American history through their bodies. The same dance form that allowed my brother in Marietta and other young African American and Latinx youth in the Bronx to avoid gang culture or to negotiate their way out of social, economic, and political constrictions is now a commercial dance genre that performs blackness with or without the African American and Latinx people who created hip-hop in its entirety: breaking, graffiti, emceeing, and DJ-ing. All culture is shaped by race, ethnicity, class, and gender. In dance, the cultural particularity of gesture is important. The fact that African American culture dominates hip-hop dance language is an important part of understanding its meaning. Just as we understand that the dance language of ballet connects its gestures to its Italian and French heritage, we must understand hip-hop culture as a fluid set of practices shaped by the differences of the people who created it. A process of embodied translation must take place when one body enacts the racial, ethnic, gender, and national specificities of another through gestures or dance moves. The history of the gesture can never be separated from its performance. The groove of the music situates the dancer within a specific sociocultural frame that tells the audience a bit about what the dancer is saying and meaning with his/her/their body. Similarly, a hip-hop dance gesture associated with a so-called thug stereotype is always already racialized as Black in the context of hip-hop. When a non-Black person performs the same move, the gesture is re-racialized accordingly. However, if the dancer neither is connected to what it means to be Black in America nor understands how the projections of racial stereotypes in hip-hop impede Black living, they must improvise an imagined history to relate to the performance of the gesture that may not have anything to do with living Black lives. Without any links to the social context in which the gestures are produced, much of the social and political urgency of hip-hop dance is lost in physical translation. Such assumptions of belonging and cultural fluency cannot be uniquely achieved through performance.

If we could flash back to the Bronx in the 1970s, we would witness

Black and Brown youth frustrated with the social and economic inequalities imposed from above. These young people danced in the streets to improvise a language of embodied, non-violent protest for social change. Sampling from African, African diasporic, Latinx, and Asian influences, hip-hop dance was corporeally translated as a "Black thing" that concerned all who were oppressed and wanted to influence change. Blackness became bigger than skin color, cultural heritage, and racial or ethnic origin. As expressed in hip-hop dance, blackness represents a power that diverse participants can harness with their bodies to contest White hegemony. Black performance studies and dance scholar Thomas F. DeFrantz highlights the subversive stance of hip-hop dance that fuels its power in local and global contexts:

> Hip-hop dances [also] gain power from their subversive [black] stance outside the moral law of [white] America. The black body in America has long been legislated and controlled by political systems both legal and customary. In social dance, the black body achieves a freedom from traditional American strictures defining legitimate corporeality. The dancing black body, responding to and provoking the drumbeat, acts performatively against the common American law of black abjection. "Speaking well" in terms of black social dance defies—temporarily—systematized oppression.[1]

Hip-hop dance language reveals the music and culture as a multicentric historical movement across time and space. The power of regeneration in hip-hop dance language is fueled by its connections to Black American cultural production, histories of abjection, and radical Black historical movements for social justice. The "Black thing" that we see when hip-hop dance is performed (especially when it is performed by non-Black or non-African American Black people) is absorbed by the encompassing rubric of hip-hop that tends to obscure its origins. As Tricia Rose notes:

> For many cultural critics, once a black cultural practice takes a prominent place inside the commodity system, it is no longer considered a black practice—it is instead a "popular" practice whose black cultural priorities and distinctively black approaches are either taken for granted as a "point of origin," an isolated "technique," or rendered invisible.[2]

This chapter explores hip-hop's dance theater practice in London and the embodied translation of popular hip-hop dance language. It inquires: How can hip-hop's specific translation as an African American dance form help us to understand intra- and interracial identifications with specific African American expressions of blackness? I argue that embodied translations of hip-hop's specific African American blackness by non-African American performers (both Black and non-Black) can both facilitate transnational coalitions and reinscribe ideologies of inequality that particularly devalue Black American cultural production. I read Black British choreographer and dancer Jonzi D's hip-hop theater piece *TAG . . . Me vs. The City*, a hip-hop dance performance I saw in the spring of 2006 at the Peacock Theater in London, as a site of embodied translation of blackness. I then place Jonzi D's production in conversation with African American choreographer Rennie Harris's production of *Rome and Jewels*, a remix of Shakespeare's *Romeo and Juliet* performed at Jacob's Pillow, a dance center located in Massachusetts, in 2000. Jonzi D's and Rennie Harris's hip-hop theater works address the specificities and generalities of blackness by using dancers with different corporeal histories to suggest the ways in which blackness samples from itself as well as non-Black sources in remembered acts of embodied translation. As Black and non-Black British dancers and choreographers create hip-hop dance in London, they acknowledge the impact of African American hip-hop and its influence on American dance traditions. Because hip-hop is viewed outside the United States as "American," often without the signifier *African*, these dancers also acknowledge the important impact of African American cultural practices on British and global popular culture.[3]

Conversely, by including work by an African American artist who samples from British expressions of whiteness via Shakespeare to articulate African American experiences, I demonstrate that dance vocabularies—like verbal languages—contain idiomatic phrases and ideas that cannot be translated word-for-word or experience-for-experience across cultural lines. If we understand "culture" as a fluid set of practices shaped by the differences of the people who produce it, then a process of embodied translation can be read as the process of one body translating the racial, ethnic, gender, and national specificities that exist within a gesture or dance move and performing them with his or her own interpretation in a dance performance.

Jonzi D's hip-hop dance theater piece *TAG . . . Me vs. The City* is a site to explore these acts of embodied language immersion and translation. *TAG* is the story of a White graffiti artist from London whose life has been shaped by hip-hop music and culture. Jonzi D chronicles the story of his White protagonist, Banxsy,[4] using a cast of dancers from diverse racial and ethnic backgrounds, all of whom perform moves specifically linked to African American translations of hip-hop. He uses this multiracial group of dancers to indicate a multicentric blackness within the genre. The diversity of the dancers speaks to the wide range of cultural influences that constitute hip-hop music and culture, as well as the possibilities of other racial and ethnic groups to indicate the "Black body" associated with African American hip-hop through dance.[5] Jonzi D is able to act as a hip-hop DJ who uses the dancers' racial and ethnic differences, nationalities, and genders to suggest hip-hop's sampling from diverse cultural practices to constitute its aesthetic. *TAG* reflects hip-hop's ability to incorporate many overlapping centers of influence within blackness as well as the other cultural samples within hip-hop. The dance also shows the successes and failures of embodied translation.

As British dancers and choreographers have created hip-hop dance in London, they have acknowledged the transnational impact of African American expressions of hip-hop and its influence on European dance traditions. Because hip-hop is viewed outside the United States as "American," they also acknowledge the importance of African American cultural practices on global popular culture, as African Americans are always already subsumed under the term "American."

Hip-hop's development within a particular historical moment in New York in the late 1970s and early 1980s—when Black and Brown people were faced with devastating conditions of poverty, unemployment, and institutional corruption—allowed it to become a response to and material denouncement of the effects of White capitalism. One would assume that a rebellion against White capitalism would mean that Black and Brown youth distance themselves from the commercial aspects of hip-hop materialism and consumerism, which often glamorize images of the "ghetto" and "gangsta" life with little consideration for the ways these stereotypes impact the life chances of urban youth. In our current moment, hip-hop's commodification of the title "urban" has incorporated blackness and its relationship to the racial and cultural identities of African Americans as more representative of a "style" than a racial and/or cultural identity. While many "underground" hip-hop artists and dancers are committed to debunking the social stereotypes of rappers in Black communities, they are often undercut by hip-hop artists and producers of all races and ethnicities—including African American—who profit from these contradictions.

Literature in cultural studies in the early 2000s began to address cross-cultural and racial appropriation of hip-hop. Sunaina Maira's ethnography of South Asian youth in New York and their identifications with blackness and hip-hop (2000), as well as Bakari Kitwana's groundbreaking observations of White American youth and their aesthetic identifications with hip-hop which inform this study (2006), are early examples of scholars of color trying to make sense of how non-Black and non-African American, Black youth around the world consume hip-hop's blackness, yet often never have to assume the social, cultural, and political consequences of living while Black. The more recent discussion of the racial and cultural appropriation of hip-hop in the United States and its export abroad to places such as England speaks directly to hip-hop's African American blackness and the aesthetic manifestation of it, absorbing all of the music and culture's polycultural contributions.[6] Many non-African American youth see performative codes of African American identity as representative of hip-hop "authenticity." However, my work contributes to these conversations by offering the language of hip-hop dance as a set of codes that can be embodied by non-African Americans to indicate blackness and hip-hop. If we think of dance as a site of knowledge production that occurs through embodied acts of exchange, then separating the original gestures from the racial, ethnic, and cultural identities of the artists who created them leaves us with no way to understand the history of the gesture. For example, in studying modern dance, one may aspire to learn the choreography of African American dancer/choreographer Katherine Dunham, who sampled many African and African diasporic dance gestures into African American dance vocabulary.[7] However, if we attempt to learn a particular move created by Dunham within the larger repertoire of modern dance, we are translating the social and historical context as well as the emotion of the gesture is part of the embodied process. If we do not know that the gesture is linked to a synthesis of African American, West African, and

Caribbean dance traditions, we can master the move technically, but the performance will lack the emotional intention that is shaped by the cultural history that produced the gesture. When non-African American dancers perform a piece from Dunham's archive, they automatically ignite the past and present of the gestures they perform, creating conversations between their bodies and those of the original dancer.

Just as any language can be learned through processes of exposure and immersion, many non-African American hip-hop dancers have been dancing blackness since hip-hop's inception. If we follow Meiling Cheng in examining the music and culture as a site of multicentricity whereby diverse racial, ethnic, and gender groups engage the music and culture, each individual interpreting it in his or her own way, then these groups can be understood to operate as independent "centers" that exist within hip-hop—always intersecting and overlapping, blurring notions of authenticity, cultural particularism, and "origins." Cheng argues that the notion of multicentricity privileges different entities' rights to "centricity," in that "it has the discursive effect of allowing each center—or unit, kind, group, the 'genus' in heterogeneity—to assert its autonomy, even when it simultaneously compels each center to acknowledge the copresence of its own margins and of other centers."[8]

Consequently, if we examine African American expressions of blackness in hip-hop as "one" of many centers within the music and culture, we can see the privileging of this particular translation of blackness in hip-hop as a locus of hip-hop "authenticity." By locating the samples of African American dance tradition that are a part of hip-hop dance, we can see how a particular set of cultural practices shapes diverse dance practices around the world. We can also see how cultures intersect, exchange, and impact one another in profound ways. Hip-hop dance can be understood as a multicentric crossroads where the performance of African American blackness by non-African American performers represents the possibility of exploring new venues of cross-racial and cross-cultural exchange and decentering the "Eurocentric" models of concert dance that exist in the United States and abroad. Understanding hip-hop dance as a facet of hip-hop theater in the United States reveals the international importance of hip-hop-inspired art and the possibilities of collecting the embodied histories of hip-hop music and culture that escape the written archive. The cross-cultural and racial exchanges created through hip-hop dance signal the overall significance of Black cultural production on the global arts community.

Situating Hip-Hop Dance within Hip-Hop Theater in the United States and England

As hip-hop began to make its way to Europe in the early 1980s, the music shaped the social, cultural, and artistic perspectives of the youth who encountered it. Outlets such as MTV linked hip-hop lovers of all races and ethnicities in the United States and abroad. In London, British youth learned the visual, sonic, and embodied texts of performance connected to African American culture in hip-hop. MCs, graffiti artists, and DJs sampled from the sounds and styles of famous African American hip-hop artists whose songs they heard on the radio or whose videos they watched on television. Hip-hop dancers imitated the moves they saw in videos or live productions that traveled to England, and they began to create their own versions of the moves. This sampling from the visual and aural texts, as well as the embodied gestures of African American hip-hop artists in hip-hop dance, were intended to create hip-hop identities that reflected these dancers' personal experiences as British subjects. British-based hip-hop artists developed their versions of hip-hop[9] that remixed African American hip-hop styles with those of the diverse African diasporic, Asian diasporic, and European youth living together in various neighborhoods in London. These specifically "British" iterations of hip-hop—often referred to as "Brit-Hop"—include, but are not limited to, Trip-hop, UK Garage, Bhangra, and Grime.

The British version of hip-hop music and culture was muffled under what Heike Raphael Hernandez calls "the African American presence." This presence suggests that African American culture has shaped, and continues to shape, traditional "European structures."[10] By the late 1980s, hip-hop in the United Kingdom began to find its own voice and cultural particularity, reflecting the diverse racial and ethnic groups that consumed U.S.-based hip-hop music and culture in Britain.[11] However, this "voice" was still largely patterned on the cultural and linguistic codes of African American rappers.[12] For example, White hip-hop communities in London and its environs often translated the blackness of hip-hop by imitating speech cadences and raps of Bronx-born African Americans to show their hip-hop "authenticity," and thus translated the blackness of hip-hop into terms used to construct their own identities. Many British hip-hoppers found superficial ways to connect themselves to hip-hop, so when White youth in the United Kingdom created these translations, they were often dismissed by "Black" Brits of Caribbean and Asian descent, who refused to accept these performances of American blackness as authentic because the performers were White. However, many White, African, Caribbean, Asian, and other ethnic groups in London identified with African American culture because they shared the social plight of being poor, as expressed in many Black American hip-hop narratives.[13]

By the late 1980s, an emerging hip-hop dance scene mirrored the emerging rap scene in England, and British hip-hop enthusiasts began to create their own polycultural mixes of hip-hop-inspired art that was still strongly influenced by African American cultural retentions. The history of hip-hop dance theater in the United States begins as early as the 1970s with the advent of popping and locking, which later became the core movements of hip-hop dance.[14] By the 1990s the influence of hip-hop music and culture in the United States began to influence other artistic forms around the world, such as theater and fine art. Hip-hop dance productions can be understood as the precursor to the "hip-hop theater" movement as we understand it today. In the United States, hip-hop theater privileges solo performances, spoken word, and plays, yet hip-hop performance more generally includes dance, performance art, and other creative practices inspired by hip-hop music and culture. As hip-hop dance groups, such as the Rock Steady Crew[15] and the backup dancers of rappers, toured Europe and Asia—coupled with MTV's circulation of their videos—many transnational hip-hop scenes emerged, creating new and innovative translations of hip-hop that spoke to diverse national and regional experiences.

The call-and-response tradition that is apparent in hip-hop dance is found in audience reactions to hip-hop dance moves. As audiences became more fluent in hip-hop dance language, dancers could communicate with audience members through their skilled execution of particular moves. Hip-hop dance originated as "street" dance and was most often performed on street corners or in impromptu party spaces. Audiences gathered around the dance "cipher," or the circular location where the dancers created their performances. When dancers were successful, the crowd would cheer, yell, and/or clap. When they were not, audience members would chide them, yet give them encouragement to bust another move. Because of the global popularity of hip-hop dance today, the cipher (an improvised stage in the round), is often still recreated on street corners as well as on theater stages in mainstream venues all over the world. As hip-hop circulated to the United Kingdom in the 1980s, the diverse racial and ethnic populations in London began to connect to the polycultural components already extant in African American culture. Dancers from all of these backgrounds remixed their own performative codes of subjectivity with those of African Americans in hip-hop with the hopes of creating their own hip-hop identity in London. Many Londoners refer to hip-hop as "American," but London is a premier city that has its own thriving hip-hop dance practice.

When Danny Hoch founded the Hip Hop Theater Festival in New York in 2000, hip-hop-inspired theater and dance productions were surfacing in the United States as well as England. At the time of Hoch's festival, many of the artists he assembled knew one another as emerging theater, spoken word, and dance artists inspired to create artistic works informed by the four elements of hip-hop music and culture (i.e., breaking, emceeing, DJing, and graffiti). hip-hop dance had been flourishing on street corners and underground venues around the United States, but it was not until artists began to teach it in classical dance studios and feature it in concert dance spaces that the official "hip-hop dance" moniker took on a new meaning that associated its practice with non-African Americans.

In 2001, Hoch introduced an international roster at his annual Hip-Hop Theater Festival in New York by featuring Black British solo performers Benji Reed (*The Holiday*) and Jonzi D (*Lyrical Fearta*). As discussed in chapter 3, their hip-hop-inspired productions marked the first international dance productions in the history of the U.S.-based festival. However, the festival still focused primarily on "written" theatrical texts. Hip-hop theater in England refers almost exclusively to hip-hop "dance" theater and is just beginning to include more intertextual performances like plays, solo performance, and other hybrid forms under its sign. Hip-

Hop inspired these new fusions of spoken word, dance, fine art, and theater, which can easily be traced to the concept of sampling and remixing made famous by hip-hop DJs. Today, artists such as Jonzi D and Danny Hoch are responsible for discovering much of the hip-hop theater talent (Jonzi D in the United Kingdom and Hoch in the United States) and giving them their big "breaks." African American choreographer Rennie Harris, for instance, participated in Hoch and Forbes' Hip-Hop Theater Festival with his dance ensemble Puremovement.

In 2002, Jonzi D created his own hip-hop dance theater festival, Breakin' Convention, which organizes hip-hop dance theater artists from around the world at a three-day festival in London. Hip-hop theater in both the United States and the United Kingdom are still considered "underground" theater movements that are just beginning to "cross over" to mainstream, subscriber-based theater production companies. One could attribute the rise of hip-hop themed plays and dance performances in those companies across the United States and Europe, specifically England and France, to the rising popularity and commercial viability of hip-hop music and culture. Both Danny Hoch and Jonzi D have been responsible for breaking ground in translating hip-hop music and culture into the art of theater.

Back to Life, Back to Reality[16]

Dance is one facet of hip-hop culture which has its own set of performative codes that connect to larger African American dance traditions in the United States. These gestures make up the specific dance language of hip-hop and reflect hip-hop's early exchanges between African American, Latinx, and other African diasporic youth. Many young African American dancers are not conscious of the links between hip-hop dance steps and other Black dance traditions in the African American dance repertoire. While their racial and cultural backgrounds do not predispose them to understanding hip-hop dance, many grew up with the moves as part of their cultural experience. They did not learn by going to dance class; they learned from one another and from television and film. However, many African American youth have not and will never realize that the gestures they perform are connected to the history of slavery in the United States and contain the residuals of African dance practices disseminated throughout the Americas, performed in recreational and spiritual dances such as the ring shout, the calenda, the chica, and the juba. African American dancers who dance hip-hop are connected to the social and historical contexts that created these moves.[17]

These aforementioned dance gestures have been incorporated into African American Dance Vernacular and practice linking hip-hop to an African past. Many African American youth have learned these dance codes through processes of what I call *corporeal transmission*, which is the process of a dancer teaching another dancer by showing him/her how to perform the move. African American dancers do not explicitly state that the hip-hop moves they perform are connected to their "African past"; they simply perform them as part of their learned cultural practices and summon this past in performance. Many African American dancers know these dances have been absorbed into many African American dance traditions, and they now perform them under different titles in their social games and popular dances. For example, the young African American dancer and singer Chris Brown, whose music represents a crossroads of hip-hop, R&B, and electronica, paid tribute to the many African American dance traditions in hip-hop dance such as the juba[18] and the cakewalk in his 2007 MTV Music Award show performance.

Because many African Americans see these gestures as always already part of hip-hop dance language, they identify the moves as hip-hop. Gestures from many Black American dances are connected to African American children's games that are all passed down orally and physically in the demonstration of the dance from one child, adult, or elder to another. Other Black American dance moves such as the strut and the shimmy can be found in hip-hop dance, yet many Black American youth have never seen these dances performed in their "original" contexts and have little knowledge of the ragtime or jazz music eras in which they were performed. Dance historian Suzanne Carbonneau contends:

> Hip-hop is an extension of traditional African dance and culture, the latest in the succession of American vernacular forms including the cakewalk, animal dances, the Charleston, the lindy hop, rhythm tap, bop, funk and disco that are derived from an African aesthetic. As such, Hip-hop must be regarded as a spiritual endeavor.[19]

Hip-hop dance, broadly defined, can be understood as a dance genre performed to hip-hop music that employs a majority of gestures, turns, movements, and attitudes associated with breaking, yet also incorporates other African, African diasporic, Asian, and Latinx dance vocabularies based on their intersections with African American culture. Despite thirty-plus years of hip-hop music history in the United States and abroad, the history of hip-hop dance is still primarily oral and corporeal. A wide range of scholars (Robin D. G. Kelley, Michael Eric Dyson, Mark Anthony Neal, Marcyliena Morgan,), dancer-choreographers (Doug Elkins, Jonzi D, Bill T. Jones, and Rennie Harris), and dance historians (most notably Katrina Hazzard-Gordon, Jacqui Malone, and Brenda Dixon Gottschild) all link hip-hop to Black American dance traditions and improvisation.[20] Additionally, all read hip-hop music, culture, and dance as part of the African American continuum of cultural production that can be linked to other African American art forms, as Carbonneau suggests.

Because there are so many hip-hop dance moves in the United States that vary by region, here I present what can be read as the "core" moves of b-boying/b-girling that began in the United States and has been translated through dance practice by youth of all races and ethnicities around the world. The term *breakdancing* is a contested term in hip-hop dance, as it was invented by the media to describe the actions of "break" boys and girls who danced in the "breaks" of hip-hop music. While regional African American dance influences such as krumping and clowning impacted hip-hop and signal its dynamic qualities, these core moves are the most familiar hip-hop gestures upon which dancers from all over the world build their hip-hop dance repertoires. These dance gestures are all linked to African American dance in the United States.[21] Breaking, or b-boying/b-girling in hip-hop, is a term used to describe many of the improvised movements that the dancers use, including the shifting of hands, feet, and legs, in a rhythmic fashion to shift their bodies on the dance floor. The term *break* refers to the dancers' responses to "breaks" in the music. While many of these start-and-stop movements are rehearsed and presented in choreographed routines, they are part of an embodied repertoire of gestures that are used in improvisational dance battles and/or freestyle sessions. Breaking usually happens on the floor and is usually a mix of choreographed dance routines and improvised moves made up by the dancers, but most of what is improvised is the remixing of existing steps and personalizing them in innovative ways. However, new moves surface constantly and are incorporated into the larger dance vocabulary once they've circulated through embodied transmission (or showing and doing) from one dancer to another. Most breaking moves on the floor begin with what is called a six-step pattern: shifting the body on the floor, moving from side to side. This body shifting allows dancers to perform footwork on the floor and to position their bodies to pop up to do standing moves. A sampling of foundational popular breaking gestures that are often translated or remixed into hip-hop dance vocabulary in the present are as follows:

Standing Moves

- **Popping**—The dancer moves the body with the appearance of popping joints. These "pops" correspond to the beats in a hip-hop song.
- **Locking (also "Campbell locking")**—The dancer makes a sudden move and "locks" it in order to link it to another in both jerking and fluid movements.
- **Toprocking**—The dancer makes a swaying motion that includes hand gestures, shoulder contortions, arm movements, and footwork, which indicates the dancer is preparing for "battle." These moves are varied and often improvised.

Floor Moves

- **Spinning**—The dancer uses body, back, and legs to push the body clockwise and counterclockwise in quick turns on the floor. Popular spin moves include back, head, and elbow spinning.
- **Freestyling**—The dancer combines any series of moves with creative samples from other dance languages and responds on the spot to another dancer's innovations.
- **Down rock**—The hand and foot work on the dance floor used by dancers to shift the body. Most of this work is done on the floor.

Power Moves (These moves are lauded by audiences and respected by other dancers because of their difficulty.)

- **Swipe**—The breaker leans back and forth, whipping the arms to one side to touch the ground in the movement of a cartwheel with the legs following fast to twist 360 degrees to land on the ground.
- **Windmill**—The dancer spins with the legs flailing in the air to indicate a windmill's blades.
- **Headspin**—The dancer spins the body on the head in a circular fashion.
- **Flare**—The dancer supports the body with his arms and swings the legs around the stationary torso in continuous circles, never allowing legs to touch the ground.
- **Suicide**—These are dramatic moves used to punctuate a dancer's routine. They include flipping forwards and backwards in various maneuvers and then dropping suddenly on the back. These moves are usually reserved for the end of a dance routine and often shock audiences because the move appears to have hurt the dancer.
- **Freeze**—This is when a dancer balances all of the body's weight on one part of the body and "freezes" it in midair for a remarkable amount of time. Many freeze moves are held on the hand, head, forearm, elbow, and/or shoulder. Freezes have various forms and names that refer to the "look" of the freeze or the body part that it isolates: e.g., armchair freeze, planche, etc.

Other Foundational Moves

- **Waving**—The dancer makes a motion that moves from one side of the body to the other to create the effect of a rippling ocean wave. This gesture often begins with the fingertips or toes and the motion ripples upward or sideways.
- **Floating**—The dancer moves the body sideways, using heel-toe shifts to travel across the floor.
- **Sliding**—The dancer moves the feet in a gliding fashion as if floating on air, and shifts body weight in different directions.
- **Snaking**—The dancer shifts the body, moving head first, then following with shoulder and hips in a snakelike, slithering motion. This move is often referenced in R&B dance vocabulary and is not always used as a "hip-hop" move, yet it is often used by dancers in various translations to transition from one gesture to another in hip-hop dance.

I offer very cursory definitions of these moves in an attempt to translate meaning in words that can really only happen in practice. You have to be there to witness it, to learn to recognize it for yourself. As surely as we can understand the European code of a *tour jeté* as specifically French and part of the larger ballet dance vocabulary, we should also be able to recognize when dancers "toprock" that they are inhabiting a gesture that links them to a specific Black dance tradition of African American hip-hop dance. This is not to say that toprocking does not sample from other dance genres as it being performed, but the act itself is coming out of African American hip-hop dance. Like verbal language and written text, dance languages reveal the social relationships between groups—their translations, mistranslations, and various remixes—which occur through processes of embodied exchange. Once a fluency in the foundations of hip-hop music and culture is achieved, the performances by non-African American people focus less on imitation and more on creating their own identifications with hip-hop that speak to their own cultural and national experiences.

Beat Street[22]

In hip-hop dance, concepts of "street" dance, a term used to associate a particular set of dance styles with urban populations, began to be categorized as "social" dance in the mainstream dance world because of their ethnic specificity. However, within Black dance traditions, hip-hop dance was already social and continues in the tradition of several African American dance forms.[23] For those who practice it as a lifestyle, hip-hop doesn't need the studio for credibility or legitimacy. You legitimize yourself as being fluent in the codes of hip-hop (based on talent, technique, and cultural fluency, not racial origins) by showing off your skills in the cipher. This process applies to every element, from MCing to turntablism.

Because of its global popularity, hip-hop dance began to intersect with concert dance; it was ushered out of the streets and into so-called legitimate theater spaces. By "legitimate" I mean theater and dance spaces that privilege concert dance styles based in European (i.e., White) culture. Here I distinguish between "social" dance, wherein the primary function is to facilitate some type of social exchange, and "concert" dance, which is choreographed and performed specifically for an audience. While most of the social dances (swing, country-western, ballroom, etc.) are partner-based, dance forms such as hip-hop are also categorized as social dances, even when they do not adhere to the form of partnering. Social dances are usually are transmitted both orally and corporeally.[24] Showing someone a dance step is an example of corporeal teaching. "Calling" a dance step by stating what it is orally to an individual or group informs the dancers of what the step is and assumes their fluency in the language of that dance genre. For example, "do the wave" or "pony" are examples of moves derived from hip-hop and 1950s Black popular dance, respectively.

In many cases these dances are created in response to a social, political, spiritual, and/or musical inspiration, even when the performer may translate these movements as spontaneous "feelings" which are translated into particular dance moves. As Joseph Schloss points out in his work on New York b-boy and b-girl culture, at times we can learn more about music by dancing to it than by listening, because the body offers us meaning that can help us understand the social and political contexts. Recounting his methods in his own hip-hop dance classes, Schloss offers this important insight that helps define my concept of corporeal transmission:

> I have started to make students in my Hip-hop classes dance at the beginning of each meeting to the music we will be discussing that day. I have found that there are things that one can learn instantly by dancing to it, which may take hours to articulate verbally. When you discover what kinds of movement can be performed to a song—and what kinds cannot—you discover a wealth of information about the social and physical environments it was meant to be heard, how those musicians viewed those environments, what their priorities were, and so forth.[25]

When non-African American dancers perform hip-hop moves that are connected only to entertainment and commercial values, they often neglect social, cultural, personal, and artistic connections to the movements. They connect to the rhythm and beat of the music, focusing solely on the execution of the gestures themselves, and they miss the meaning—what the gestures are meant to address about the social and physical surroundings in which they are performed. This is not to say that African American dancers cannot miss these nuances of the dance language of hip-hop. Most often, disconnections between a dancer's general ability and his or her ability to execute the technique of hip-hop dance gestures is not uniquely based in a failure to make visceral connections to the rhythm and beat of the music, but also a lack of knowledge about the gesture itself. These disconnections may also be complicated by the dancer's lack of understanding of what a gesture means (e.g., anger, joy, pain, etc.) that provides the motivation for the moves. Additionally, notions of "eight counts" are not a hip-hop dance practice that comes directly from the streets. When "trained" dancers (i.e., those who have studied dance, usually in classical forms) attempt to dance hip-hop, they often impose notions of "counting" to the beat, which steals focus from their own bodies' viscerally feeling when to move to the music. When hip-hop dancers who have not been formally trained teach one another, they rely on instincts and their physical connections to the beat of the music to demonstrate the moves. The student watches, repeats, and revises until the move is mastered. Often, directives on how a particular move should be performed are punctuated with sound or theatrical emphasis, not count emphasis. For example, if a move is supposed to punctuate a point for emphasis, a dancer may say "Do it like: 'Bam, bam, po' or 'Ah, Ah, tsi!'" using sounds that accentuate the repetition of a move and where the emphasis occurs to indicate the punctuation and execution needed to get a gesture right. Counting in dance is derived from European traditions, whereas most African and African diasporic dance forms rely on more physical and visceral connections to timing that are based on both individual and collective responses to the music.[26] Dancers who have danced together for long periods of time usually develop their own dance sound language to arrive more quickly at shortcuts to combinations. Counting is something that is most often reserved for studio hip-hop dance practice or used with choreographers who mix formal classical dance training and street dance practices.

Conversely, concert dance refers to those moves that are created specifically for an audience. Hip-hop dance theater is both social and concert, as it interfaces with the protocols of both dance styles. We must consider that hip-hop dance is built upon a foundation of African American dance traditions. In the past twenty years, hip-hop dance has shifted from its categorization as "ethnic" social and/or "street" dance; it now attracts invitations from many concert venues that typically privilege European dance forms. Traditional concert dance obeys the protocols of theater practice that operate under the idea of suspended disbelief, whereby the audience agrees to believe what they see on stage is "real" for the time of the performance. The fourth wall is never broken. Hip-hop dance theater, however, performed today in "traditional" venues, often disrupts this convention. Hip-hop theater performers such as Danny Hoch have refused this theatrical convention and often create interactive and improvised theater experiences that solicit responses from the audience and imitate the cipher, using their bodies to talk directly to or "call" to the audience, soliciting a response. This dynamic quality of hip-hop theater is also present in hip-hop dance theater, which invites its audience to participate in the rhythm and movement and meaning-making of a performance. Though routines are often choreographed, there is usually a space for dancers to improvise in every performance. In both, dancers, actors, and audience members participate in what Raymond Williams calls a "structure of feeling."[27] This term emphasizes the emotional connections that exist with and/or between specific groups, classes, or cultures.[28] Hip-hop dance privileges a visceral understanding of knowledge production that is learned through embodied practice, observation, cross-cultural exchange, and *feeling* in the moment. As hip-hop dance gains global popularity and is performed by people of all races and ethnicities, it decenters conceptions of "classical" dance as a superior art form and instead samples and remixes heavily from European forms as representative of the ways in which Black dance traditions around the world continue to shape global dance practices. Hip-hop dance theater in the United States and in England is a site that can be used to trace these embodied connections that occur through the crossroads of exchanges that produced hip-hop dance in the United States, and that is (re)membered (or disparate bodies and gestures reconnected) in dance. In the United States, Europe, and Asia, hip-hop dance is one of the most transnational, racially, and ethnically diverse representations of hip-hop music and culture's global presence.

Translating Hip-Hop's Blackness in Jonzi D's *TAG . . . Me vs. The City*

Jonzi D, as mentioned earlier, is a Black choreographer who is London's premier hip-hop dance theater choreographer and producer. He is responsible for developing the careers of some of the most promising hip-hop dancers in England. His relationships with both social and concert dance are strong, as he was trained at London Contemporary Dance School and is a pioneer of hip-hop dance theater in the United Kingdom. His company, Jonzi D Productions, is an associate company of Sadler's Wells Theatre, which names itself as London's premier venue for international dance. This relationship between Sadler's Wells and Jonzi D began because of his widely successful three-day, annual hip-hop dance conference, Breakin' Convention, which began in 2004 and united hip-hop dancers from around the world. The global appeal of hip-hop dance caught the attention of the Sadler's Wells producers. Today, Jonzi D's productions are regularly featured at Sadler's Wells.

There was great anticipation among London's hip-hop enthusiasts for Jonzi D's hip-hop dance theater show, *TAG . . . Me vs. The City*. The show's limited run at the Sadler's Wells Peacock Theater was sold out when I saw it in 2006. The performance I attended had a multiracial audience from a wide range of ethnic, age, and class groups. Many young theatergoers, between the ages of ten and eighteen, attended the show with their parents. There were also sixty-something ticket holders who seemed more enthused by the excitement of something new in the theater than by hip-hop itself. The energy in the lobby was palpable as many guests mingled before the show, sipping drinks, eating snacks, and chatting with anticipation and curiosity.

Featuring some of the United Kingdom's finest hip-hop dancers, *TAG* attempts to use hip-hop dance and the shared knowledge of its gestures to bridge racial, ethnic, and class divides. The show's cast consists of both classically trained and street dancers of diverse racial and ethnic backgrounds. Jonzi D is able to indicate the polycultural exchanges that exist within hip-hop's blackness, as well as its multicentricity, by showing dancers of different races engaged with hip-hop dance. This multiracial representation of hip-hop addresses the music and culture's multicentric engagements with African American dance and draws our attention to the ways in which hip-hop inspires artistic practices across racial, ethnic, and national lines. The choreographer also explores the physicality of graffiti art and its connection to rapping and breakdancing.

The narrative of *TAG* follows a White graffiti writer named Banxsy as a troubled youth. His love for hip-hop and graffiti defines his life and provides an outlet for him to claim his identity. Thus, the dancers are physical representations of the various graffiti styles that have shaped his life and helped him articulate his experiences. Through the use of a video projection screen, we are able to see the work of several of London's premier graffiti artists who have influenced the lead character's life. Many of the supporting dancers' movements sample from the styles of these famous graffiti writers, which vary from Japanese anime to Arabic script, thus indicating the intersection of African American articulations of hip-hop with global culture. Hip-hop music, mostly from the United States, is the soundtrack to the protagonist's life story performed in hip-hop dance styles.

TAG opens in blackness, only to startle the audience with a white flashlight and sirens, signaling the jeopardy that many graffiti artists experience as they risk being arrested by the police for putting up "burners" around the city.[29] The spotlight reveals large, spray-painted sculptures upon which dancers are draped. The sculptures spell the word "TAG," but their abstract designs and shapes allow them to also stand individually as art. As the music—a hip-hop score created by DJ Pogo and featuring an exciting fusion of African diasporic music from hip-hop to reggae and jazz—five dancers, representing the diversity of the graffiti writer's experiences, start to "drip" off the letters and break their way downstage. The dancers' bodies performing these fluid moves imitate the paint of graffiti writers, linking the elements of hip-hop. They are also referencing the term "physical graffiti," often used in hip-hop to refer to dance and specifically to pay homage to dancers such as Jorge "Pop Master" Fabel Pabón, an original member of the Rocksteady Crew who uses the term.[30]

Standing downstage, apparently lifeless, the dancers await the arrival of their host—the White male whose experiences they represent. Emerging from the shadows of the police strobe is the lead dancer, performed by a popular UK hip-hop dancer named Banxsy, who borrows his name from internationally acclaimed London street artist Banksy.

He is dressed in baggy pants; layered, oversized t-shirts; and a tight-fitting skullcap. His life is illustrated in many "colors" as two White, two Black, and one Asian dancer begin to dance his experiences. The dancers represent the many components of his identity as a hip-hopper. Banxsy begins to "spray" the other dancers with "paint," using popping moves and an aerosol can as a prop. The dancers come to life by also locking and popping their joints to indicate that they are dripping into place at the mercy of his aerosol paint can. We hear sounds of a paint can being shaken, with the metal ball rolling and mixing the paint in the can. Other sound effects include the swishing sounds of paint spraying or the whisper of Banxsy's breath blowing the paint represented by the dancers' bodies blending into various shapes. The character seems to be directly connected to the London-based social activist graffiti writer, Banksy, whose prolific political graffiti has been seen around the world.

In *TAG*, the character Banxsy creates a physical "blending" process that represents the technique of many graffiti writers, who must blow the paint in the direction they want it to drip to shape letters. The dancers contort their physiques; some are suspended upside down for minutes as others quickly plop to the stage, flipping onto the sculptures in acrobatic twists, turns, and suicides. The term *suicide* here names a move that involves a breaker doing a front flip and landing on his, her, or their back. The move usually results in the crowd applauding, when witnessed in a U.S. context, due to the difficulty of the move.

The music that animates the score varies from old school hip-hop beats, sampling from African American rappers such as Run-D.M.C. and Eric B. & Rakim, to African American jazz to European Brit-Hop and techno sounds, creating an aural collage. The dancers' movements correspond to Banxsy's paint strokes. The backdrop of the performance features video of subways cars and other public spaces in London that showcase the work of different aerosol artists (used as synonymous with graffiti artists) who have influenced the White protagonist's life. These videos are projected onto the stage and serve as transitions between the dance sequences. Dancers wave and pop themselves into shapes that spell "TAG," collaborating together in partner styles, which reveals the social dance element of hip-hop dance theater. Katie P, one of two White dancers (including the lead male Banxsy) is the only woman, emblematic

Fig. 7. Scene from *TAG . . . Me vs. The City*. Photo courtesy Mike Kwasniak.

of the lack of female representation in hip-hop. She defies the stereotypes of gold digger and video vixen and is presented as equal to her male colleagues. She confidently uprocks to the beat of the music, then starts her six-step, finally descending to down rock, showing off her impressive hand- and footwork. She rises to roam about the stage in aggressive moves, inserting hardcore gangsta gestures, grabbing her crotch and letting the audience know that she can hold her own among an all-male cast. Fusing old school and new school hip-hop, Katie P's gestures show that she is ready to battle and stake her claim as a b-girl who can dance. Many of Katie P's translations of hip-hop gestures seemed heavily influenced by jazz and modern dance and reveal their influence on her translation between dance languages.

B-boys Soopa J and Nathan Geering are the two Black dancers in the show. They have varying levels of fluency with hip-hop dance vocabularies (at least based on what was presented in the show). Soopa J performs only big power moves (swipe, windmill, and flare), which are at the core of breaking styles. Geering appears more comfortable with the old school hip-hop moves of popping and locking and seems less comfortable with floor work. However, his incorporation of new hip-hop moves, such as krumping, indicates his awareness of the most current hip-hop vocabulary and demonstrates direct links to new moves performed by African Americans in the United States. Tommy Frazén, a dancer of Asian descent, is technically adept at performing standing and floor moves of hip-hop dance, yet what is missing from his performance is an organic connection to the rhythm of hip-hop music. His style is more mechanical and lacks an individual flair.

As an ensemble, the dancers give the audience an amazing master class in hip-hop dance technique. However, missing from the performance is a larger connection to the narrative of the White male lead's experiences with hip-hop culture other than graffiti. We never understand how the other dancers' differences, which cannot be avoided or ignored, connect to Banxsy's life. Equally disconnected are the video projections of moving subway cars, graffiti scenes around London, and sound effects of the "street." Though they provide the audience with a general context for the moves performed, we have no idea how they connect to the life of the protagonist. However, as "physical graffiti" the dancers' bodies are easily read as part of the White male hip-hopper's identity. He is White on the outside, yet hip-hop/Black on the inside. As all of the dancers embody gestures that are historically tied to African American dance, they reactivate this African American presence on stage. The lead seems to overcompensate for his whiteness by showing how "down" he is with hip-hop, using hypermasculine gestures of crotch grabbing and thrusting, toprocking moves that reveal his anger and fight against "The City" in the title. Jonzi D's use of aggressive hip-hop gestures such as toprocking, popping, and locking showcase the White dancer's fluency in hip-hop dance, but they are upstaged by his comment that this character's life has been impacted by "blackness," "whiteness," and "Asianness" because of the histories their bodies bring to the story.

Both Asian and African diasporic communities in London have colonial histories that speak to their attraction to hip-hop as a site to address social and political inequalities, racism, and disenfranchisement. Additionally, references to "blackness" in London often refer to the experiences of and cultural production from both Asian and African diasporic groups. White working-class youth in London also have a history of connecting to African American music genres (namely jazz, soul, and R&B) to articulate their experiences and allegiances with African American struggles for civil rights.[31] All of the dancers in *TAG* create conversations with their bodies about the relationships between their ethnic identities as British subjects and how those relationships are in conversation with African Americans. Perhaps because the lead character's whiteness links him to the status quo of the British establishment, he must prove his "anti-establishment" status by flipping off the audience and showing them that he's not just White but "hip-hop" on the inside. This superficial engagement with the "rebellious" quality afforded to hip-hop seems shallow and does not add any depth to the overall development of the character or the story.

As a Black choreographer, Jonzi D's use of a White character to show how hip-hop shapes the everyday representation of White British identity is important. Yet the impact of African American culture on White British youth identity formation through hip-hop is presented mostly in superficial ways. Jonzi D's characterization of b-boy life is best used when he allows the dancers to improvise in a breaking cipher. Each dancer has a turn at portraying an assumed side of the White lead character's life. This is when we see the versatility and fluency of the dancers' knowledge of hip-hop dance vocabulary. Jonzi D's decision to restrict the dancers mainly to confrontational b-boy/b-girl battle vocabulary, with some partner work, misses opportunities for more in-depth exploration of hip-hop dance language. The show's narrative of the White b-boy in despair is weak, yet it provides important opportunities to observe how choreographers are also translating larger messages beyond the main narratives of their characters. Equally important are the relationships of power that Jonzi D's choreography seemingly shifts in the performance. The Black, Asian, and White cast are not animated at all until the White male gives them "life" by spraying them into being.

However, there are several ways that Jonzi D as the Black male choreographer is able to make a complex critique of hip-hop's association with African American expressions of blackness in hip-hop, issues of cultural appropriation, and Black authenticity. First, his diverse cast represents the ways in which racial, ethnic, and gender groups influence how White male youth in London articulate their identities. Second, Jonzi D's choice to engage diverse racial and ethnic groups with African American hip-hop dance language creates corporeal conversations with African Americanness and the social and cultural history of hip-hop.

Third, Jonzi D addresses how other racial, ethnic, and national groups are impacted by African American dance. Finally, as a Black male choreographer presenting hip-hop in a traditional "concert" dance space, Jonzi D challenges what counts as concert dance and how those assertions are shaped by race and ethnicity.

Jonzi D's attempt to create an ensemble production of African American hip-hop without African American dancers is not an anomaly, as b-boys around the world do this every day. Notable, however, is his isolation of the codes of hip-hop dance—particularly breaking moves—to reveal what is lost in translation when other racial, ethnic, and national groups translate it. The most remarkable part about this piece is that the White lead character's *lack* of fluency in hip-hop limits his capacity to articulate his experience through this dance language. Consequently, the character is bound by his own superficial understanding of hip-hop. Banxsy's identifications with hip-hop are directly connected to hip-hop stereotypes of the thug/gangsta characters used by many White males to construct a hip-hop "masculinity" that exaggerates the always already exaggerated postures of African American male stereotypes. Jonzi D's *TAG* is most successful when it reveals the effects of the circulation of African American male stereotypes in hip-hop and how they are sampled by Whites to create pseudo-rebellious identities like the one that Banxsy represents.

Many young White males (often identified by Black people as *wiggas* and *wannabes*, as discussed in chapter 1) have used African American male experiences in hip-hop as templates of anti-establishment behavior.[32] In *TAG*, it is unclear whether we are expected to sympathize with Banxsy's onstage persona and if this is even possible. As an African American artist inspired by hip-hop and fluent in its cultural codes, I translated his performance as the White kid who grew up listening to hip-hop in London and felt as if "coloring" his whiteness[33] could justify his rage against his social circumstance so he could fight the establishment, or, in this case, "The City." Jonzi D's representation of Banxsy as a White kid who is "hip-hop" before he is "White" links the character to a larger group of White youth who identify with hip-hop's blackness and its polycultural links to African, African American, Asian, Latinx, and other cultural contributions across gender lines within hip-hop. However, the theatrical presentation of such a character, though hopeful, often gives license for Whites to create a hip-hop "style" that is disconnected from the social and cultural experiences of minorities.

Banxsy does not want to be part of the White system of authority in London that has oppressed his creativity as an artist. However, his whiteness makes him always already a beneficiary of privilege. By "tagging" an autobiographical story of his life, he hopes to incite empathy for his predicament as this social outcast. Class is an important consideration when we address issues of White privilege, and it is used by Jonzi D, as class is also an important point of identification for many young, White Londoners who identify with commodified images of hip-hop's "rebellious" messages. Though tagging is radical behavior in any context because it is in fact illegal, writing on public property by Black and Latinx youth in the Bronx in the late 1970s was an act of resistance that allowed them to reclaim public spaces that often ignored the needs of their communities and dismissed their art.[34] For those White artists who leave graffiti behind after their rebellious stage in life is over and translate their skills into more socially acceptable art forms, their whiteness still affords them more opportunities and privileges than are given to their Black and Brown contemporaries. The representations of Banxsy's "soul" (both a reference to the soul of the body and "soul" music as performed by African American people), performed by dancers of various racial and ethnic backgrounds, bring diversity to Banxsy's "inner life" as a character,[35] yet he benefits from his whiteness and the novelty of being a White boy in mainstream London who loves hip-hop.[36] As the lead character in this show, he can attract and make hip-hop more palatable for the predominantly upper-middle-class White subscriber base of Sadler's Wells Theatre. Most of the dancers appeared to be studio-trained, having learned hip-hop dance in classes and/or clubs and not as part of their cultural experiences. Though this is what I perceived, it is possible that many of the dancers, Black and White, were trained through street dance and adjusted the vernacular quality of their moves to fit the audience and performance space.

Though the virtuosity of the performances allowed those of us in the audience to experience the show on a purely entertainment level, the performance lacked an emotional and visceral connection to the physicality and theatricality of hip-hop dance theater. How do we see these disconnections manifested in performance? Many of the issues of emotional and visceral connection that were missing from these translations of hip-hop dance are based in experiences that escape the written archive because they are "feelings" that are evoked when we witness a performance—one that is based in the performer's ability to translate the feeling into the gestures performed. This takes me to the next facet of the process of embodied translation, which is using the lived experiences of the artist to aid in translating the gestures.

(Re)membering Hip-Hop: Processes of Embodied Translation in *TAG*

Using the story of a White graffiti artist from London, Jonzi D is able to (re)member the impact of African American articulations of blackness in hip-hop that are often lost in translation across national spaces. *TAG* addresses the importance of embodied texts and how dance languages are shaped by race and ethnicity as well as the racial, ethnic, and cultural backgrounds of the performers who engage them. By "embodied practice," I mean the search for both successful and unsuccessful translations that seek to find the connections that other racial, ethnic, and national groups make to African American culture through hip-hop dance.

The process of corporeally translating the specificity of hip-hop moves to audience members and dancers is the responsibility of the choreographer. However, Jonzi D cannot teach an entire audience the history of hip-hop dance and its social protocols. For example, many audience members did not respond to the power moves performed by the dancers, nor the songs played by the DJ (tracks from such famous rappers such as Eric B. & Rakim) that usually move hip-hop crowds because they evoke particular "old school" hip-hop history. Brent Hayes Edwards's concept of *décalage*, the lapse in time, space, and meaning between the translations of lived experiences, speaks to the ways that the cultural memories of blackness embedded in American hip-hop dance are translated as African Americanness abroad and their impact on non-African American performers. Jonzi D's use of racially and ethnically diverse dancers to translate the similarities and differences between cultural specificities of blackness through hip-hop is suggestive of the polycultural blackness of hip-hop. Underscoring my analysis of this improvised exchange of cultural practices through the body is Joseph Roach's concept of performance genealogies:

> Performance genealogies draw on the idea of expressive movements as mnemonic reserves, including patterned movements made and remembered by bodies, residual movements retained implicitly in images or words (or in the silences between them), and imaginary movements dreamed in minds, not prior to language but constitutive of it, a psychic rehearsal for physical actions drawn from a repertoire that culture provides.[37]

Roach's reading of performance genealogies is informed by the way in which bodies in performance have the capacity to record, remember, and reactivate history and their ability to transcend national borders.[38] In this way, Jonzi D's hip-hop dance theater is able to articulate the polycultural elements of African Americanness in hip-hop. Roach's work is also on conversation with Diana Taylor's notion of repertoire and the ephemerality of gestural language. Following Roach and Taylor, I read the body as a repertoire of experiences, behaviors, gestures, and ideas that are not recorded as written text, yet can be understood and accessed as a process of "writing" histories that can be "transferred" from one body to another through dance.[39] Because the "body" of hip-hop is ultimately hybrid due to its diverse cultural deposits and the global circulation of blackness associated with it that is specifically linked to African Americans, the (re) membering process in dance can be understood as one that reconnects many of the parts that are often forgotten as elements of the whole.

These moments of decalage—or what Brent Hayes Edwards describes as a "'gap,' 'discrepancy,' 'time-lag,' or 'interval' in meaning that often loses bits and pieces of meaning"[40]—in *TAG* represent how dancers share and exchange corporeal histories which may or may not succeed in translating and reactivating the "old school" feelings archived in hip-hop movements. Though a hip-hop dancer born in the 1990s may not know the history or particular cultural origins of a backspin move, she/he/or they have improvised an understanding of its significance and the importance of including it in his or her repertoire of physical moves to evoke a communal feeling of nostalgia, technique, and street credibility.

They Reminisce Over You—Jonzi D and Rennie Harris—(Re)membering the Artistry of African Americans through Hip-Hop Dance[41]

Jonzi D and his African American contemporary Rennie Harris are Black, middle-aged men engaged with hip-hop as an African American art form. They have enough experience in living and making the culture of hip-hop that they remember when hip-hop was uniquely Black music that inspired Black dance from b-boys and b-girls in the United States and subsequently became a global music and dance form. However, by comparing their intentions in engaging hip-hop, we are able to discover spaces of décalage, or what is missing in embodied translation when non-African American artists perform hip-hop's specific African American blackness. Jonzi D is dedicated to creating outlets for dancers around the world to learn hip-hop dance and to articulate their experiences within it. Rennie Harris's engagement with hip-hop dance explores it as an African American cultural practice. These subtleties reveal how non-African American performers often miss important moments of "feeling" that escape their lived experiences and cannot be incorporated into their performance of a hip-hop gesture.

As a Black British choreographer and dancer who has toured Europe, Africa, and the United States performing hip-hop dance, Jonzi D has been instrumental in bringing hip-hop dance theater into London's more classically based dance houses. Rennie Harris is an African American choreographer and dancer who is at the forefront of the hip-hop dance theater movement in the United States and has also toured Europe performing hip-hop. Jonzi D has a long-term residency at Sadler's Wells Theater, a premier dance theater in London. Harris is the founder of the troupe Puremovement, an African American hip-hop dance company in Philadelphia. Both choreographers see hip-hop dance as a unique art with its own vocabulary and want to preserve its history. What separates these two choreographers is their views on *how* hip-hop dance is learned and experienced by dancers and *what* hip-hop dance is within the larger scope of dance practices around the world. Both professionals see the intersection of hip-hop with other dance forms.

Rennie Harris's dance company, Puremovement, is focused on the complexity of the "blackness" of hip-hop. Harris founded his dance company in 1992 with the hope of preserving the hip-hop culture through dance workshops and mentoring, similar to Jonzi D's The Surgery, a workshop for emerging hip-hop dancers that provides a space to learn and critique. Harris's Iladelph Festival, which began in 1999, is one of the longest running hip-hop dance festivals in the United States and attracts many of America's hip-hop dance pioneers. While Jonzi D uses dancers of all races to indicate the reach and complexity of hip-hop's influence, Harris instead privileges the use of African American dancers and explores other dance genres and their translation through the blackness of hip-hop. According to his website, the company is committed to providing the audiences with "a sincere view of the essence and spirit of hip-hop rather than the commercially exploited stereotypes portrayed by the media." Unlike Jonzi D, Harris is not classically trained and has been a street dancer his entire life. He was commissioned by the Smithsonian Institution's Folklife Center at the age of fourteen to teach "stepping,"[42] a Philadelphia-based dance that also has various translations in Chicago, Detroit, and Georgia. Both Jonzi D and Rennie Harris reiterate a fundamental belief that hip-hop ultimately expresses universal themes of struggle, adversity, and social discontent. Harris's dance piece *Rome and Jewels* reflects hip-hop's sampled aesthetic as the choreographer remixes several interpretations of *Romeo and Juliet* to articulate his version of the story. Sampling from *West Side Story* and Baz Luhrman's 1996 hyperreal film adaptation of the Shakespeare play (entitled *Romeo + Juliet*, which starred Leonardo DiCaprio and Claire Danes) Harris creates his own remix of the Shakespeare classic, translating previous adaptations into hip-hop dance language. The choreographer uses the *West Side Story* adaptation of *Romeo and Juliet* that focused on tensions between rival gangs, the Jets and the Sharks, to inform his translations of "family" as relationships between rival African American street gangs. Harris sampled from these translations of the original Shakespeare text to explore how non-Black theatrical forms have influenced African American cultural practices.

Using hip-hop English to rename the feuding families in *Romeo and Juliet*, Harris remixed the Montagues to become the African American gang the "Monster Qs" and the Capulets to become the "Caps." Harris samples from hip-hop styles of self-adornment associated with "old school" and "new school" hip-hop clothing and its relationship to the

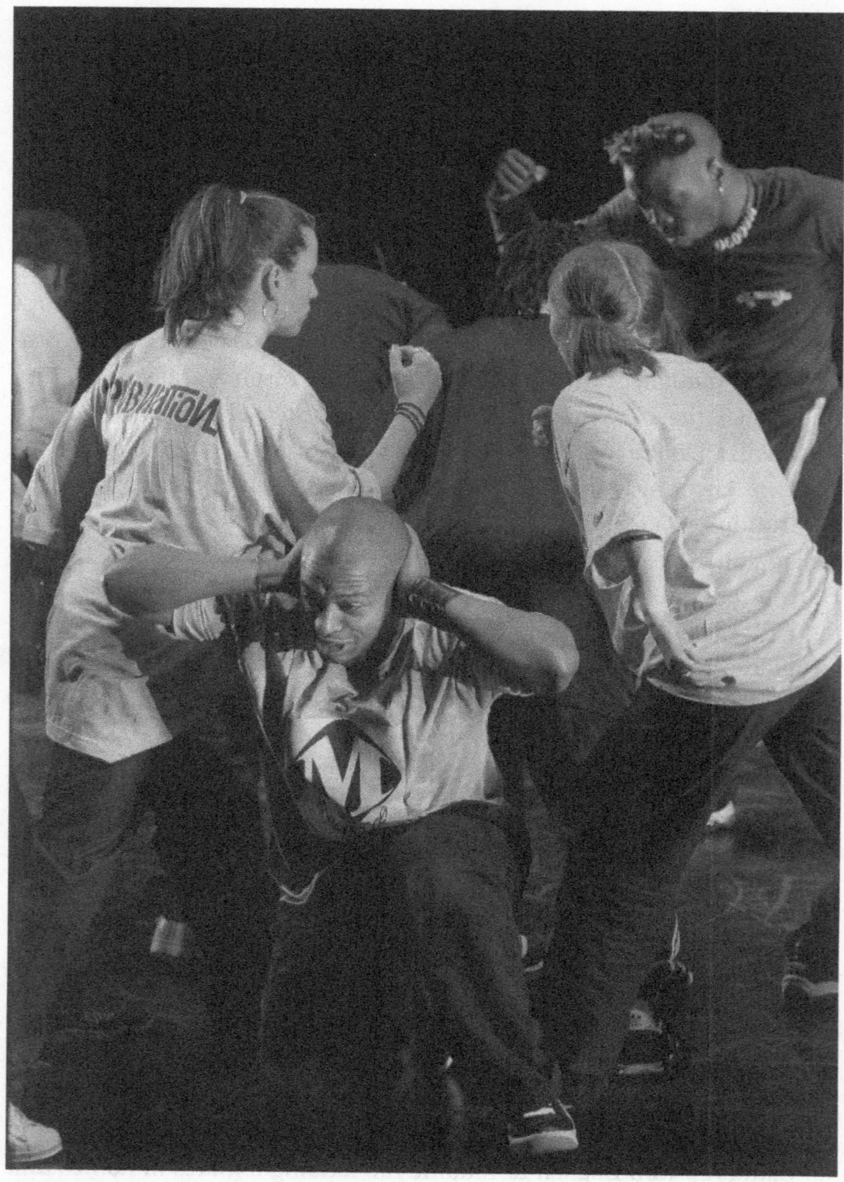

Fig. 8. Scene from *Rome and Jewels*, choreographed by Rennie Harris. Photo from a 2000 rehearsal, before the first performance in Philadelphia. Photograph by Bob Emmott ©.

gestures performed. Rome and the Monster Qs are dressed in baggy Black street clothes and dance representing more contemporary hip-hop styles. Tybalt and the Caps are dressed in red outfits that cite specific old school hip-hop fashion, such as the Adidas warm-ups[43] that have become a part of hip-hop visual and fashion iconography. The Caps break in ciphers and perform backspins and power moves in b-boy styles. The color of the clothing can also be read as representing gang color feuds in African American gangs in the United States. The two gangs clash because Rome has been seen with Tybalt's woman Jewels. This specific choice to make Juliet the center of the feud between gang members also mirrors hip-hop rivalries in the United States between "East Coast" and "West Coast" rappers Biggie Smalls and Tupac Shakur, respectively. Both rappers were murdered, and many link their deaths to this rivalry between crews.

In *Rome and Jewels,* Harris makes a connection to this history in hip-hop by focusing on the rivalry between the men, leaving the female character Jewels as an ephemeral and invisible object of their desire. The invisibility of Jewels can be read in multiple ways. In one way, her absence can be understood to reinscribe the misogyny in hip-hop and the silencing of women in any facet of hip-hop, breaking, MCing, graffiti, or turntablism. In another way, Harris's choice to focus on relationships in gang culture is always already inclusive of women. Harris's choreography suggests that cisgender relationships are complex and concern not only women as lovers, family members, friends, competitors, etc., but also have central hip-hop narratives and iconography that represent more than popular culture's representation of hip-hop as a site of female objectification. Harris does not gender the choreography in this production. If you can dance it, you can perform it. Harris makes skill-based instead of gender-based choreography decisions. Performance studies scholar Imani Kai Johnson argues that b-girls have to be "badasses" who are not afraid to challenge the heteronormativity of b-boy culture:

> As much as confrontation, aggression, and an outlaw persona are intrinsic parts of breaking's aesthetic, being a b-girl means being an outlaw—a badass in "normal day life." This is due in no small part because b-girls incur a much greater social cost for participating in a dance culture that is seen as being by and for young men. As a result, breaking's inherent qualities are often interpreted differently on the bodies of women.[44]

By not separating Jewels from the pack and incorporating her within the body of dancers, Harris renders her a badass. Though women are both metaphorically and literally invisible in the history of hip-hop dance, Harris makes Jewels forgotten in this dance piece and as hyper visible and necessary to the narrative of hip-hop dance. Perhaps Harris is showing us the impossibility of Black men loving Black women in any relationship (familial, romantic, or platonic) until they reconcile the self-loathing and erasure of women within hip-hop's history. It is impossible, Harris seems to say, to engage in any love relationship—the love of hip-hop, breaking, or another human—without loving one's self. At one point in the production, Rome says to Jewels, "Shall I compare thee to a summer's day?" quoting the original Shakespeare text, yet Jewels is never seen. Harris uses down rock moves (fast hand- and footwork that shifts the body) on the floor to simulate sex between Rome and Jewels, which further centers the female presence as one that is desired and needed by Black cisgender men, yet not necessarily appreciated, respected, or revered. However, this creative choice to make the female character invisible can be read to represent her illegibility as an equal player in hip-hop representation. Women and nonbinary players engaged with hip-hop culture deal with gender bias daily. *Rome and Jewels* reflects conversations between African American men about their lives in their inner circles as well as the ways they articulate their struggles as men, irrespective of women.

However, despite these sexist undercurrents and brief moments of subversion where Harris attempts to challenge the misogyny in hip-hop, his sampling of Shakespeare's story and remixing it with coming-of-age narratives of African American men attempts to represent life on the "streets" where many African American men come of age and define their place in the world. Rome's journey to becoming a man is plagued by violence, poverty, and uncertainty about his life chances. By claiming either territory as a gang member or the right to love, he finds agency, even if he is surrounded by factors that speak to his demise. As in *TAG*, Harris uses video projection to create vivid backdrops of the streets. But Harris, unlike Jonzi D, mixes in more verbal narrative to complement the dance narrative; thus, we are able to connect Rome's journey to the images on the screen and the dance moves, rather than the images operating separately from the whole of the production. The Caps and the

Fig. 9. From *Rome and Jewels,* choreographed by Rennie Harris. Photo from a 2000 rehearsal, before the first performance in Philadelphia. Photograph by Bob Emmott ©.

Monster Qs creep through the streets. Their bodies appear as disjointed images that slither about, seeking out the enemy hiding in the shadows and second-guessing every step as they look over their shoulders to locate their target. Rome delivers a monologue that speaks to his life chances as a product of the street. Citing preachers, war heroes, and pimps, Rome chooses his gang as his family and the core of his identity. His worldview is shaped by his experiences in the streets, and gang life represents protection, comfort, and brotherhood, perhaps even a surrogate family.

The final dance sequence visually samples directly from scenes in the film *West Side Story.* Each gang dances, the gangs clash, and then each dancer enters the breaking cipher to show off individual skills. The two women in the production dance with no reference to their gender or sex in acts that unsettle the hypermasculine production. Mercutio dies in Rome's arms, and Rome's crew dances to show their anger over his death. Rome instructs his gang, "Break him off," which translates from hip-hop English to standard American English as "Get them." The dancers in red begin a forceful sequence of dance moves that include strong footwork, ensemble moves, and even suicides. "O, I am fortune's fool," declares Rome, faithful to the original text, as he, too, falls to the ground. Harris samples from hip-hop verbal language and dance language and remixes those fragments with samples from Shakespeare's original texts. Harris's fluency in hip-hop dance language allows him to find the similarities and differences between the language of hip-hop and Shakespeare's vernacular.

Finding African American experiences "within" Shakespeare's *Romeo and Juliet* means Harris is able to see the intersections of European and American theatrical forms, specifically the ways that Shakespeare addresses class issues and his perspective of rights for the "common man." Harris states, "Shakespeare was and is the essence of hip-hop. The lyricists of today—the rappers—probably come closest to his dynamic of writing."[45] Harris's perspective that the rhythm of Shakespeare's writing is the "essence" of hip-hop may be an attempt to canonize hip-hop by showing the connections between African American working poor and working-class British identities. However, this is a dangerous gesture that could undermine Harris's larger goal of preserving hip-hop culture and its various expressions as expressions that must be validated against so-called classical art forms. Harris also samples superficial translations of Shakespeare and reduces some of the complexity of the original plot and characterization in *Romeo and Juliet* by sampling not from the original text, but from copies made of copies. Focusing simply on the rivalry between the Capulets and the Montagues can be read as reductive; however, Harris's choice to focus on issues of masculinity and men's struggles with socially prescribed roles of gender and class positions in society is innovative. As far as the role of gender and the performative codes of femininity in the play are concerned, many read Shakespeare's Juliet as a "damsel in distress," yet she is a powerful female character who is assertive and demanding. She knows exactly what she wants and what she is willing to sacrifice for it. Her voice is muted in Harris's version, however. Harris argues his exploration of these various samples of Shakespeare's work was more to indulge his own process as an artist and his interest in healing male relationships and sexist perceptions embedded in African American masculinity. Sampling from predominantly White texts and remixing them as blackness has always been a part of hip-hop. Locating blackness inside historically White texts can be subversive. We must be careful that such identifications of blackness do not seek to erase the importance of Black experiences of racism, trauma, and invisibility or to make predominantly White theater audiences feel less fragile as they witness expressions that address histories of inequality and anti-blackness. More contemporary instances of Black and Latinx performers occupying White texts to create a narrative between White oppression and Black and Brown subjection that is lost in translation are in Lin-Manuel Miranda's *Hamilton*, which I discuss in chapter 5.

Nonetheless, Harris's ability to translate the connections between hip-hop street life and Shakespeare achieves exactly what *TAG* aimed to accomplish in identifying with African American culture in hip-hop: that we are all connected through our differences and can learn through the exchange of cultural practices. As an audience member, I never separated the execution of these hip-hop moves from the bodies of the dancers that performed them. In addition, the connections between the narratives being danced with the bodies of the performers were synthesized, so I could read the performance as a narrative and not a start-and-stop performance of individual hip-hop dance moves connected by music and light transitions, as occurred often in *TAG*. I was immersed in the dancers' abilities to use their bodies to translate the gestures they performed to advance the story. Many of these nonverbal codes embedded in hip-hop dance gestures were never fully explored in *TAG*. For example, instead of "battle" moves being used to demonstrate ability as they were in *TAG*, in *Rome and Jewels* they are used as narrative tools that successfully portray the rage of rival gang members. The performers also use the moves within their original context in hip-hop dance history, as many popping, locking, toprocking, down locking, and freeze moves continue to be used in dance battles. Harris argues that "rappers and lyricists, hip-hop poets of this generation, probably owe something to Shakespeare's writings and complexity as much as any poet today."[46] In *Rome and Jewels* dancers use verbal texts that sample Shakespeare and remix them using hip-hop English to break the fourth wall and to present asides to the audience about the story, much in the way that a chorus operates in classical drama. This call-and-response component of hip-hop is reiterated here in hip-hop dance theater, making a specific point to dismiss concert dance styles that may object to this call-and-response between the dancers and the audience. The dancers in *Rome and Jewels* were predominantly African American and fluent in hip-hop dance language. This level of corporeal fluency and connection to the embodied text of the choreography afforded the dancers the opportunity to concentrate on embodying the nuances and subtext of the narratives and not simply the perfection of movements. Comparatively, Jonzi D's dancers were proving their fluency in various hip-hop moves and did not always connect to the dance practice as a whole but as separate parts. Harris's use of Shakespeare reflects hip-hop's ability to borrow from and be inspired by other cultures, yet use these cultural samples to further explore experiences that reflect African American subjectivity. Jonzi D was able to use his dancers' diversity to represent the cultural sample within hip-hop and its impact on different racial and ethnic groups in London.

As hip-hop continues to influence artistic practices, we will see more nuanced translations that personalize non-African Americans' connections to hip-hop dance and their personal relationships to blackness that are more visceral and emotional. We will see more and more fluent translations of African Americanness in hip-hop by non-African American artists reflecting the cross-racial and ethnic collaborations that hip-hop enables through dance in the United States and in the United Kingdom. In discussing the recent phenomenon of dancers around the world learning hip-hop dance moves, Rennie Harris observes:

> You may know the movement, but not the culture. I would never approach modern dance without trying to understand it. But black culture always gets kicked into this thing of entertaining. It's approached as a commodity, without understanding the history. People forget that the true foundations of Hip-hop are an extension of traditional culture in the States. The understanding of it is different between the US and Europe.[47]

We can also read Rennie Harris's sampling of Shakespeare and its adaptations as his attempt to understand European cultural traditions and history. By making connections between African American life and Shakespeare, Harris addresses the recycling of knowledge and its translation in various mediums. He does not sample Shakespeare as a commodity, but explores the story and his dancers' relationships to it. *Rome and Jewels* won a "Bessie Award," or New York Dance and Performance Award given for an exceptional achievement by an independent dance artist in 2001, perhaps because Harris's work suggests the impact of Shakespeare on many racial and ethnic groups who may not typically see themselves as having a relationship to classical texts. Hip-hop's multicentricity allows for these types of social improvisations to occur. For Harris, what cannot be translated in performance is lost, and what can be translated is incorporated into African Americanness through hip-hop. Since *Rome and Jewels* Premiered at Jacob's Pillow, Harris has become one of the most prolific hip-hop choreographers in American history. Other notable works include *Lazarus* (2018) and *Lifted* (2017). In 2020, Harris was a scholar in residence at University of Colorado-Boulder's Dance Department when he was awarded the Doris Duke Artists Award in 2020, which awards extraordinary contributions to the arts. His 2018 production *Funkdified*, exemplifies hip-hop's impact on Black and non-Black audiences by centering street dance, funk music, and integral components of American identity. Likewise, Jonzi D's capacity to translate hip-hop dance language across national, cultural, and ethnic borders had placed him at the center of the hip-hop dance theater movement in the United Kingdom. He has received numerous awards and distinctions for his choreography and community work including a Member of the Order of the British Empire (MBE) award in 2011. Jonzi D's company was associated at Sadler's Wells from 2004–2010. He has been the executive director of the Breakin' Convention since 2004 and has several notable production that build on *TAG . . . Me vs. The City*, including *Ivan* (2006) and *Markus the Sadist* (2009) a hip-hop-inspired musical.

Jonzi D's philosophy is to teach and perform hip-hop as a vehicle of cross-cultural exchange. Rennie Harris is committed to teaching and performing hip-hop as an act of archiving and teaching African American culture. Jonzi D identifies hip-hop as a "Black American" dance, as does Harris. However, Harris believes that one's lived experiences as an African American subject greatly inform the translation and performance of the dance. Harris's philosophy underlies the spiritual component of hip-hop dance that is often dismissed in dance theory and suggests a visceral quality that speaks to the "feelings" that cannot be translated in hip-hop dance practices and that are often overlooked in dance studies. Here, I have explored how these different philosophies of choreography intersect and disconnect in order to understand how specific translations of blackness are articulated as African Americanness in hip-hop.

Conclusion

When I spoke with Jonzi D about the concept for *TAG*, he stated that he wanted to reflect the diversity within hip-hop; he argued that London has a particular hip-hop voice, despite the dominant American representation in hip-hop music and culture. For him, hip-hop is a place where and a tool with which one can experiment creatively, using styles and images in order to construct a persona that communicates an identity the performer wants to portray at a particular moment. When I asked about his positions on hip-hop and blackness, Jonzi D argued:

> We have to be careful about what we are saying is "black" because of the many black people throughout the African diaspora and Africa. But if we are talking about Hip-hop, there is a very specific "black American" thing that we all imitate a bit. Like "you know what I'm sayin'" and the moves and everything you know . . . we all talk it . . . but Jamaicans, Indians, whites—we all relate to it.[48]

In my discussion with Jonzi about how he defined hip-hop, he mostly referenced African American history in hip-hop, mentioning old school Black American icons, hip-hop aesthetic references such as clothing styles and language, and archival "beefs" or disagreements that have existed between various hip-hop artists over time. Yet, he was more interested in how hip-hop is being used as a site of cross-racial and cross-ethnic connection for groups that find social connections through ideas of "American" blackness. Jonzi D's ability to translate the blackness of hip-hop as a site of cross-cultural exchange specifically recognizes blackness as a multicentric construct and acknowledges specific African American cultural expressions that dominate in hip-hop. For example, in *TAG* he uses the dancers to create a cipher on stage wherein the dancers stage a freestyle battle. Each dancer enters the cipher to perform an improvised routine. Nathan Geering, the twenty-something, Black British dancer mentioned earlier in this chapter, is well versed in old school toprocking and krumping. He exudes a confidence and comfort with the gestures that suggests he has danced them hundreds of times before. Yet, when he enters the cipher and begins to break, he engages in some power moves in which many of his back spins end with his feet positioned in the air in a "freeze" position. This move is usually applauded in American breaking circles as a power move because of its difficulty and for the length of time the dancer is able to keep his feet in the air. I was shocked that not only was I the only audience member to translate this move and initiate a clap, but that the dancer did not pause in the break and wait for this acknowledgement by the audience. Certain gestures, such as the aforementioned power move, are a call to the audience to clap and for the dancer to wait in the break for the acknowledgment. This is one example of translating an "old school" hip-hop move where the dancer's lack of knowledge about the culture of the gesture caused him to miss an important moment in the performance and in the choreography. When I spoke to Jonzi D about the cipher and his choreography, he informed me that he created the context for the moves by giving the dancers the story and the emotions that he wants conveyed to the audience. He then allows the dancers to improvise, changing their moves from show to show. Jonzi D acknowledged, however, that the audiences rarely clap and the dancers cannot recreate any experiences from more realistic ciphers that occur on the street because, for the most part, they have not experienced them. Much of the emotion in hip-hop dance must be obtained through connections to the dance language and how it is used. Jonzi D's word-for-word translation of hip-hop reflects the needs of the audience. Perhaps this is a limitation inherent to translating social dances for concert venues. What cannot be translated through embodied gestures between cultural, ethnic, and national experiences is not based on racial authenticity. In the case of Geering, he is racially Black and British, thus non-African American, yet the context of the gesture is coming out of a largely African American dance practice that many across racial lines can learn over time and practice.

What Jonzi D and the dancers in *TAG* cannot account for in their performance are the ways in which their bodies communicate as texts with the audience. Hip-hop dance as an "American" art form often attempts to distance itself from any association with African American culture because to some who equate authenticity with racial origins, this dialectic between hip-hop and blackness appears to limit its possibility to be read as international or "universal." If hip-hop is always already produced through a hybrid blackness emanating from African American cultural experiences, then the way hip-hop is sampled in the United States in all facets of popular culture suggests that it always maintains its blackness, even when non-Black consumers borrow, consume, and embody it. However, African Americans respond in kind to cultural commodification by continuing to sample and remix cultural contributions of other groups under the sign of hip-hop and African Americanness, thus disrupting ontological notions of authenticity conflated with hip-hop.

In his discussion of the ethics of sampling in DJ culture, Joseph Schloss identifies a series of sampling rules that many DJs adhere to in order to establish themselves as legitimate artists, archivists, and engaged hip-hop cultural producers. One of the rules that many DJs adhere to is "no biting," a rule that operates as an inferred policy of ethics between turntablists and producers. To bite (or take without crediting) another DJ's sample is considered a type of sonic plagiarism.[49] However, as Schloss alerts us, sampling is the foundation of hip-hop, so then the defense of a sample has less to do with proof of origins and authenticity and more to do with creative integrity and "ethical obligation."[50] Similarly, to bite African American dance moves, and to perform them as "universal" dance moves that have no links to history, place, social conditions, etc., is to a great degree an unethical citation practice and a theft of intellectual and creative property. The recognition of the sound or gesture is part of the archival work that is intrinsic to hip-hop aesthetics. The more references you can recognize, the more meaning is produced. If we can envision blackness as a multicentric set of cultural practices that can have multiple idiomatic translations across national and ethnic lines, then African Americanness as articulated in hip-hop is but one of many "blacknesses" that describes not only racial identity, but cultural identity as well. Angela Ards argues that blackness can be defined in multiple ways and must be understood within specific social, historical, and cultural contexts to effectively access the meaning of how cultural practices can ultimately be understood:

Of course, words in one language don't always have exact equivalents in another. Take "Blackness," for example. There are as many varied and contested ways to describe Black racial identity in English (Black, Negro, nigger, colored) as there are in French (*noir, negre, homme de couleur, bon neg*), with no term capturing all the shades of meaning of another. In other words, an ineffable "something" is always lost in the translation.[51]

Ards's comments find synergy with Brent Hayes Edwards's concept of décalage, or what is lost in translation within blackness across national lines. Few b-boys and b-girls enter into hip-hop dance without understanding the fundamentals of hip-hop dance language, such as popping and locking. However, this knowledge is not learned from reading histories of hip-hop dance. The translation of African American hip-hop gestures by non-African American dancers is mediated by the racial, ethnic, and national identities of the performers. Corporeal transmission in dance is much like an oral history, except the body is used to record and disseminate histories, instead of the voice. Jonzi D's improvisational process as a choreographer and director allowed the dancers to use their bodies to translate and remix hip-hop's blackness on stage, yet many of the dancers mistranslated the important social meanings contained by the gestures, even when imported into British social contexts. Like watching new actors learning Shakespeare, it becomes very difficult to sit through a performance of a text when it is clear as an audience member that the actor does not truly understand the intention and meaning of a line, even when he delivers it in a very convincing manner. Jonzi D, as translator, was able to use dancers to translate between American hip-hop and British hip-hop, yet the lack of fluency of many of the dancers' movements revealed sampling of experiences from other cultures without always understanding the context. The uniqueness of British hip-hop lies in the capacity of the artist to use the performative codes of African Americanness to articulate personal and collective stories under the sign of hip-hop. What is emerging is a new dance language that, while rooted in African Americanness, creates a hybrid relationship that stresses the multicentric possibilities of hip-hop's blackness. What I witnessed in *TAG* was a representation of hip-hop dance language in translation. This in and of itself allows us to see the magnitude and multicentricity of blackness in hip-hop.

Jonzi D's and Rennie Harris's different approaches to translating the racial, ethnic, and national specificities of hip-hop's dance language are important contributions to the evolving aesthetic of hip-hop theater and performance. Both artists (re)member the multiple racial, ethnic, and national contributions that are dynamic within hip-hop, that have shaped and are continually being shaped by African American articulations of blackness. The impact of African American cultural production on American and international dance culture is undeniable. Just as the Harlem Renaissance inspired Blacks in France and the Caribbean to create art movements inspired by jazz and African American culture, hip-hop is inspiring artists around the world and influencing their social and concert dance styles worldwide. Rennie Harris noted this influence in an interview in *Dance* magazine in 2011:

> Concert dance basically has appropriated everything under the sun, which has affected it in every way. So I think you have to ask, "How has Hip-hop *not* affected concert dance?" Hip-hop has affected all of mainstream culture, aka white culture. It has affected the language of an entire nation when you have white kids speaking the slang.[52]

Documenting hip-hop's influence on mainstream dance culture influence is essential to further our understanding of how cultural practices are exchanged, translated, and reconfigured through acts of performance. Moving beyond appropriation to ask how the sampling and remixing of Black dance forms such as hip-hop has changed mainstream practices in positive ways is what this chapter has worked to answer. By (re)membering hip-hop's cultural history, its connection to African American life, and the specificity of social conditions in the United States that produced it, new opportunities arise to explore hip-hop as a site that facilitates cross-racial and cross-ethnic exchanges that can subvert the dominant discourse of excellence and legitimacy that marginalizes Black and other forms of dance created by people of color. The choreographers and dancers in these productions are cultural translators who can rewrite and remix the wrongs of past appropriations and thefts by acknowledging the multiple samples within African American blackness and hip-hop that incite non-African American artists to push the art form beyond its national cultural and historical context.

This chapter seeks to magnify the broad-ranging impact that African American expressions in hip-hop dance have on the artistic practices of non-African Americans around the world. Perhaps we can rewrite the narrative of hip-hop dance to include its liberating impact on how people across racial, ethnic, gender, class, and/or sexual identifications live their lives. Hip-Hop dance continues to inspire new ways to empower people to find points of empathy with the resilience of African Americans to dance our way out of our constrictions.

FOUR

MUSICAL MASH-UPS OF AMERICANNESS / Lin-Manuel Miranda's *In the Heights* and Matt Sax's *Venice*

The first musical that I knew the words to was *Grease.* I also knew for a fact that I could play Rizzo or Sandy in my high school's production. I would have been happy with either role. I prepared my audition song (a terrible choice—Sheena Easton's B-side "Calm Before the Storm") and rehearsed my lines in the bathroom mirror. On that nerve-wracked day in the late 1980s, my dreams of being Sandy or Rizzo were deferred. I distinctly remember my drama teacher telling me that I was not a "fit" for either role. At that time in my life, the only musical I had ever seen with African American leads was *The Wiz* (and that was the film version with Diana Ross and Michael Jackson). I knew that my suburban high school would never think of putting on *The Wiz.* But after high school I went on to college, where I discovered more musicals by artists of color and fell in love with Black and Latinx theater.

In the early 2000s, I found a musical to replace my love for *Grease*: *In the Heights*, created by Pulitzer prize-winning playwrights Lin-Manuel Miranda (concept and music) and Quiara Alegría Hudes (book). It features a majority Latinx cast with one African American character. *In the Heights* was the first musical I saw live that had been created by people of color, for people of color. It placed our narratives front and center in the American theater. Emerging on stage is a mash-up of Latinx diasporic immigrant stories and first-generation Latinx dreams, creating a sonic and visual worldview that is deeply rooted in the urban landscape fused with hip-hop and Latinidad.[1] Miranda, a Puerto Rican actor, writer, and composer from New York, began crafting the show as a student at

Wesleyan University in 2003.[2] In the music he composed for the show, Miranda used hip-hop as a vehicle to remix the foundations of Broadway musical forms. Borrowing from African American and Latinx hip-hop and remixing them with salsa, merengue, bolero, reggaetón, ragtime, and jazz, Miranda made the connections between African American and Latinx culture already embedded in hip-hop visible before a live audience. The production premiered in 2005 at the Eugene O'Neill Theater Center in Connecticut, later moving off Broadway to the 37 Arts Theatre, in 2007.[3] I loved *In the Heights* because I felt that even though it was about Latinx people, that I could see myself in it. As an African American woman, I saw myself in the hip-hop narratives and the stories the characters told about their quests for the American dream. Their desire for success, education, and a pathway to wealth resonated with me as the child of a first-generation, Algerian African American woman and an African American man of mixed heritage.

I had very different feelings when I saw the hip-hop and rock inspired musical *Venice*, created by Matt Sax and Eric Rosen. On the one hand, I was excited about the spectacle of the musical. On the other hand, I felt ambivalent about the dystopian scenes and darkness of the show which used abstractions of hip-hop aesthetics to create a *Venice* that also samples from diverse music (from hip-hop, rock, and opera) and literature (Shakespeare's *Othello* and DC Comics). Sax and Rosen use this multicentric soundscape to provide the backdrop for a narrative about a multiracial man struggling to identify between the Black and White social worlds in a fictional U.S. city named Venice. The musical was produced in 2010, during the first tenure of the Obama administration, and attempts to mirror the racist discourse that ensued after the election of the first African American president. I saw the premiere in Kansas City in 2010, and again when the show moved to the Public Theater in New York in 2013 with a different cast. I was poised to love everything about the musical. It features a racially ambiguous (assumed to be biracial Black and White) lead, a multiracial cast, and music that reflects the diversity of American cultural identities. However, the musical numbers, book, acting, and dancing all felt forced. The actors' bodies and the music represented entertainment industry prescripted "diversity" as far as physical representation, but there was something substantive missing. Both of these hip-hop-inspired musicals had casts composed of people of color and used hip-hop music, yet one story—*In the Heights*—was told from lived and witnessed experiences that were remixed to create a fictional story. *Venice* seemed to have many sampled parts from many different cultural influences that all came together under the sign of hip-hop, yet there was no origin story, no lived experiences translated into fiction, that I could connect to in the narrative. Two Jewish American musical theater collaborators made a musical about what the world may feel like after we abandon race; in contrast, a Puerto Rican American artist and a Puerto Rican American/Jewish American artist created a musical that still had remnants of the heartbreak of becoming American within a social and historical climate in the United States that constantly reminds Latinx Americans that their worth and experiences are not as valuable as those of their White fellow citizens. This chapter explores contrasting perspectives of musical theater teams creating theatrical mash-ups (works containing elements from more than one source) that challenge how we understand American identity and its representation in Broadway theater. These musical theater mash-ups attempt to reorient audiences to hip-hop culture by sampling from familiar Broadway aesthetic representations in sound, dance, and structure and remixing these fragments with hip-hop to present a reflection of an American mosaic. Dick Hebdige describes the remixing of cultural experiences as a mosaic effect in hip-hop:

> Just as in a mosaic the overall pattern is made by placing bits of differently coloured stone together, so Hip-hop is made by splicing together fragments of sound from quite different sources and traditions. And just as you can see the joins between the stones in a mosaic if you stand close enough, so you can hear the breaks and joins between different sounds in a Hip-hop record if you listen carefully.[4]

These theater works offer alternative cultural perceptions of hip-hop that specifically reference American blackness, yet make the "breaks and joins" between blackness and other racial, ethnic, and cultural experiences visible and audible in utopic and dystopic mash-ups that challenge how we understand stories of American identity.

Triple Threat[5]

Lin-Manuel Miranda triples as playwright, actor, and composer. He writes and sings stories forged at the hyphen of his Latino and American identities. Miranda allows his characters to form themselves in the breaks of the music, drawing from a variety of musical and embodied dance languages, thereby leading the characters to connect to, and to overcome, the limitations imposed on Latinx people in pursuit of the American Dream. By identifying points of cross-racial connections between histories of oppression, Miranda makes a social commentary on the citizenship of Americans who live at the hyphen. He makes visible the shared sights and sounds of the interracial and ethnic coalitions that can be formed in acknowledging these shared struggles for legibility.

Venice, conceived by Matt Sax (lyrics, performance, book) and Eric Rosen (book, direction) moves beyond the specific indexes of racial identity to translate W. E. B. Du Bois's 1903 term "double consciousness" into a cipher through which the normative whiteness of the signifier "American," and the importance of hip-hop to its popular configuration in the twenty-first century, battle for ground in theatrical acts that challenge the authenticity of normative whiteness in off-Broadway and Broadway theater. *Venice* premiered at the Copaken Stage of the Kansas City Repertory Theatre in April 2010 and then moved to New York's Public Theater Lab in May 2013. The American musical theater formula, once painfully marked as White for artists of color, is remixed live on stage as racial boundaries are pushed to the limit when a fictional city located in the American South comes under attack by corporate greed and power.

In the Heights and *Venice* are different from the other performances and plays that I have explored in this book. These musical theater works reference hip-hop's African American expressions of self-adornment, and embodied and discursive language as a mashed-up worldview at the core of hip-hop. In *Venice*, hip-hop becomes an alternative to racial, cultural, and national identities that works to highlight the multicentricity of citizenship based on shared experiences of belonging or exclusion. Hip-hop becomes an identification that supplants race and unsettles the structures and reference points that are used to register racial expression as indicative of identity. By abstracting from blackness in hip-hop,

Fig. 10. Lin-Manuel Miranda in *In the Heights*. Photo courtesy Joan Marcus.

Fig. 11. Matt Sax and the ensemble of *Venice*. Photo courtesy Don Ipock.

Sax and Rosen are able to present race as a distraction that limits understanding of the sociopolitical ideologies that challenge the quality of life of all people. The play works to unsettle our assumptions about blackness and whiteness by forcing the audience to render them insignificant constructs in the face of a national crisis. Both plays reveal the artists' intentions to understand the relevance of both the interiority and the exteriority of race and hip-hop.

While the audiences of these musicals may take their hip-hop beats and African American cultural samples for granted, these playwrights are scripting remixes of change that allow artists and audiences to have a dialogue about race and nation through performance in unlikely spaces and contexts. Hip-hop's non-African American artists are flipping hip-hop inside out to reveal the cross-cultural samples within it that validate their participation as important contributors to the culture. The result is a visceral mash-up of performance genres and music that challenges how we understand race and its improvisation in contemporary performance in national and international contexts. Hip-hop becomes an epistemological point of departure for Sax, Rosen, and Miranda, though their perspectives diverge based on story and intention. In Miranda's story, the personal trials of a multicentric Latinx community play out before the audience. *Heights* is deeply connected to Miranda's personal intention to share stories of Latinx people by placing it in the United States and illustrating the historic relationship between hip-hop and Latinx culture. *Venice* creates a dystopian future where existing constructions of race are no longer legible as a site to express identity. While the dystopic story portends to be about life and war, the musical attempts to resignify race as an irrelevant tool of human categorization. The playwrights move beyond the personal to suggest that the only way to uplift humanity is through a dystopic deconstruction of race, class, and nation. In both works, theater provides a space for Miranda, Sax, and Rosen to test out possibilities for revisionist and future imaginings of identity that are facilitated by hip-hop's particular blackness.

Lin-Manuel Miranda's *In the Heights* and Matt Sax and Eric Rosen's *Venice* remix notions of Americanness and hip-hop that challenge the Black–White binary to define what race is to us in the twenty-first century. A mash-up is a creative combination that fuses content from different sources in order to tell a story that has multiple (and often conflicting) stories playing at once. In most instances, the origins of the sample content are left in their original form, just repurposed in new relational contexts within new material. A theatrical mash-up, then, is one that samples and remixes indexes from diverse sonic, visual, and embodied sources, and plays disparate and shared theatrical elements in new contexts. These two musicals mash up traditional Broadway formulas, hip-hop musical lyrics, and other Black and Latinx musical forms (such as R&B, rock, and reggaetón) to reflect the struggles of marginalized Americans who must negotiate the hyphens of their human experiences as they try to attain full citizenship. These artists reveal the double consciousness of Black American identity that is imbedded in hip-hop music and often lived through its cultural samples that reside within expressions of hip-hop. The characters in these plays sample a doubling of Black identity, at once marginalized and American, as described in W. E. B. Du Bois's definition of double consciousness:

> It is a peculiar sensation, this double-consciousness, this sense of always looking at one's self through the eyes of others, of measuring one's soul by the tape of a world that looks on in amused contempt and pity. One ever feels his twoness—an American, a Negro; two souls, two thoughts, two unreconciled strivings; two warring ideals in one dark body, whose dogged strength alone keeps it from being torn asunder.[6]

Du Bois's prose attempts to capture the embodied process of living as Black and American; it is a process which produces the vexed feelings at the core of double consciousness. Non-African American artists symbolically identifying with the twoness of blackness through hip-hop provide blueprints for diverse groups to see themselves "through the eyes of others." Oftentimes, these non-Black artists engage hip-hop in ways that reproduce the very hierarchies that hip-hop works to dismantle. For Miranda and Sax, hip-hop is a worldview, a way of knowing and experiencing life, not simply an aesthetic. The Puerto Rican American and Jewish American histories of these creators are also embedded in hip-hop as hidden transcripts of hip-hop's blackness. In their musicals, Miranda and Sax flip those non-legible transcripts from the inside of hip-hop to the outside, making visible intersections with African American culture. These two musicals critique the centricity of generic transcripts of White American life as the default point of departure for American musical theater. They mark and complicate whiteness as a racial experience that is reliant upon blackness to be legible. Every time hip-hop shows up on the Great White Way, with or without Black people, it signals the undeniable influence of a predominantly Black art form.

Is it Live or is it Memorex?

As a kid in the 1970s, I remember a commercial for Memorex, a popular brand of audio cassette tape, with the great jazz vocalist Ella Fitzgerald. Fitzgerald sang a jingle that asked the question, "Is it live or is it Memorex?"[7] As a note she sang shattered a wine glass, viewers discovered that her voice had been recorded on a Memorex tape, its sound purportedly so authentic, it could not be distinguished from a live performance. What TV viewers heard was Ella Fitzgerald. We were entertained by her voice and presence in the commercial. Our experience did not change when we discovered that her performance was recorded and that she was not singing live.

This is similar to my experience watching hip-hop when it is engaged and performed out of a Black context. I saw *In the Heights* when it came to the Richard Rodgers Theatre on Broadway in 2008 after playing off Broadway to rave reviews. The show ran for two years and gained an international fan base that I had not witnessed since Jonathan Larson's *Rent* in 1993.

Much of the Harlem Renaissance was dedicated to debunking myths about blackness projected by Whites in the mainstream. Black artists and scholars worked to define Black aesthetics and to identify what types of Black cultural production and artistic practices could facilitate a self-determined representation of Black life. The desired outcomes for many African American artists creating Black art, literature, music, and theater were tenuous. Many Blacks wanted to prove to White Americans that Black art was of equal value to the Western canon. Others wanted to prove that Black cultural production was fine as it was created and did not need authentication from outside the Black community. W. E. B Du Bois's "problem of the color line" attempted to articulate "the strange meaning of being black here in the dawning of the Twentieth Century."[8]

African American artists and writers worked to make American art that spoke to their unique experiences walking the tightrope of the color line. Black artistic petitions for equal visibility and acceptance were courageous and inspired, yet the works remained underground for most of the 1920s and 1930s. During the Black Arts Movement, Amiri Baraka and other leaders criticized the artists of the Harlem Renaissance for what they perceived as a failure to improve the everyday social and economic conditions of Black Americans. The aesthetic of Black art during the 1960s was changing its shape. Drawing from the past, yet revising it, the Black Arts Movement shifted the intention of *showing* from the Harlem Renaissance to *proving* by focusing on the pursuit of freedom of expression as captured in jazz music. For Black Arts Movement theater artists such as Amiri Baraka, Adrienne Kennedy, and Sonia Sanchez, Black music, specifically jazz, greatly impacted their writing for the stage. These artists used theater as a tool for fashioning strategies of resistance that could challenge White hegemony, revise traditional play formats, and challenge aesthetic preoccupations with Western ideals of theater and performance. William J. Harris writes of Baraka's use of jazz as a tool of translation to mobilize Black voices for social change:

> Baraka believes that black music captures the ever changing voice of the black masses in its forms. It is there in the music that one finds the current vernacular of the African American people. In the 1960s Baraka's project became the translation of the black free jazz voice into one for his poetry, a project similar to that of Langston Hughes. Throughout his career, Hughes kept changing verse styles—first blues, then bebop, and then free jazz—to catch the transmuting voice of the African American masses.[9]

For Harris, Baraka's view of Black music as an archive of social, cultural, and political struggles explains the improvisatory power of Black artists to remix the content and sound of the music to fit particular social and political needs. Harris connects the shifts in vernacular, tone, content, and style to history and memory. If the Hip-Hop Arts Movement continues in the tradition of the Black Arts Movement, it makes sense that its dominant samples of blackness are incorporated through hip-hop. In 2004, Danny Hoch's "Towards a Hip-Hop Aesthetic: A Manifesto for the Hip-Hop Arts Movement" spoke of hip-hop arts as a mash-up of transnational influences that combines socioeconomics, diverse cultural practices and retentions, and contributions from diverse racial groups.[10] Riffing on Du Bois's 1926 statement about Negro theater in *The Crisis*, Hoch's manifesto offered his improvised definition of hip-hop theater:[11]

> Hip-hop theatre must fit into the realm of theatrical performance, and it must be *by, about and for* the Hip-hop generation, participants in Hip-hop culture, or both. The clamor for more Hip-hop theatre on the legitimate stage is not unlike the cry of theatre artists of color during and after the Civil Rights Movement. But few Hip-hop theatre pieces fit into a solely African-American slot, or an Asian American or Latinx one. This is because the face of the Hip-hop generation is considerably more diverse. And this is a good thing, because Hip-hop shouldn't fit into a tokenized "slot," and certainly not one that narrows its scope. It's a bad thing because theatres don't seem to have a category for this work, and therefore don't know what to do with it. That's okay, they'll catch on soon enough.[12]

Sampling from early meditations on Black theater by W. E. B. Du Bois in the early twentieth century, and later by Larry Neal and Amiri Baraka during the Black Arts Movement, Hoch argues that hip-hop theater is "by, about, and for the Hip-hop Generation."[13] Hoch's citation of Black, Asian, and Latinx struggles of self-definition to define hip-hop theater speaks directly to the ways that many White and non-African American artists source blackness to validate their struggles for self-determination. Hoch's definition of hip-hop theater also suggests that White, Black, and Latinx struggles have been absorbed by blackness and mashed up in conversation for years. For many years, I could not reconcile his definition. It troubled me because it seemed like an easy way to obfuscate the importance of African American cultural production that dominates the visual, embodied, and sonic realities of hip-hop and its perception in the American and global racial imaginary. Years later, my sentiments about Hoch's manifesto have shifted, but my mind has not changed. Hip-hop is still a Black American art form, but its particularity is indeed multilayered and complex. Such is the complexity that built the foundation upon which the Hip-Hop Arts Movement is built and the remixed American Dream narratives that are mashed up by Miranda, Sax, and Rosen.

Flipping American Dreams

In the Heights helped to shift the center of Broadway's focus on White American life to spotlight the interwoven lives of Latinx people in Washington Heights, an ethnic enclave in Manhattan in the throes of gentrification. It is one of Manhattan's most diversely populated neighborhoods, particularly with Latinx people of different ethnicities. Usnavi, the main character, is a first-generation business owner. He was born in the Dominican Republic and immigrated with his family to the United States as a child. He inherited a small bodega from his parents and is working hard to get his piece of the American Dream. Selling coffee, sundries, and corner store fare at the bodega, Usnavi has big dreams for his life. Grappling with his debt to uphold the legacy of his family in America and his desire to return to the Dominican Republic to find his roots, Usnavi is the personification of the dreams of many Latinx in the United States. When I saw the production on Broadway in 2008, I was sitting in the third row, surrounded by a reasonably diverse audience. The opening number, "In the Heights," was unlike anything I have ever seen on Broadway. The show's main character, Usnavi, played by Lin-Manuel Miranda, began to rap the opening rituals of his day as owner of a city bodega in Act 1, Scene 1 of the musical:

> LIGHTS UP ON WASHINGTON HEIGHTS, UP AT THE BREAK OF DAY.
> I WAKE UP AND I GO THIS LITTLE PUNK I GOTTA CHASE AWAY.
> POP THE GRATE AT THE CRACK OF DAWN, SING
> WHILE I WIPE DOWN THE AWNING . . . HEY, Y'ALL. GOOD MORNING.[14]

Miranda sets the scene, bringing his own storytelling style and speaking directly to the audience. Referencing African American rapper Doug E. Fresh and The Get Fresh Crew's "The Show" in his opening rap, Usnavi tells the mainstream that the American Dream is in technicolor and that he is in charge of his destiny. The questions of rightful belonging, Americanness, and Latinx identity spring from experiences that Miranda dealt with growing up in Inwood, a Manhattan neighborhood. Washington Heights, like Inwood, has fought the threats of gentrification as young

Fig. 12. Lin-Manuel Miranda and the *In the Heights* cast. Photo courtesy Joan Marcus.

middle- and upper-class twenty-something Whites moved in to take over the distressed business fronts, only to build hip bakeries and flower shops that pay no reverence to the rich Latinx roots of the space. Usnavi and his friends are holding on to their businesses and their histories as they question the value of the American Dream. With the slow-moving threat of gentrification on the horizon, they question their lives, harbor nostalgia for the various homelands they never really knew, and work to make a place for themselves in the United States that feels like home even as their citizenship and belonging are questioned daily. Living at the hyphen of his identity as a Dominican American, Usnavi sees parts of his life and his possibilities through the eyes of his adopted grandmother, Abuela Claudia, a Cuban woman who immigrated to the United States after World War II and raised Usnavi after his parents died. The "New World" lens that Usnavi learns from his abuela operates as a mash-up of Du Bois's double consciousness. Usnavi negotiates a tripartite, not just a double view, of being a Dominican American. By narrating his American Dream in English, Spanish, and hip-hop, he challenges Americanness as he centers marginalized worldviews from diverse Latinx perspectives.

Usanvi's cousin Sonny is visiting for the summer; he helps Usnavi in the bodega and provides moral support. The love of Sonny's life, Vanessa, is a hairstylist with big dreams, but is trying to find the courage to take the first step to leave the neighborhood and the dysfunction of her home. The Rosarios, a forty-something couple, run a car service company across from the bodega. They immigrated to the United States from Puerto Rico and are in the midst of realizing their own version of the American Dream. They are business owners; they have a strong nuclear family and a beautiful daughter, Nina, who returns home for the summer after her first year at Stanford University. Puerto Ricans, represented by the Rosarios, are not the first immigrant community to occupy the space. Miranda acknowledges this in the show by referencing the Irish immigrants who lived in the neighborhood years before, represented on an old sign that reads "O'Hanrahan's," visible just underneath the Rosarios' car service awning. Usnavi's close friend Benny works at the car company as a dispatcher. He's a former "street kid" turned future entrepreneur, and is the only African American character in the show.

The positioning of Benny and Usnavi as best friends metaphorically connects the shared histories of Blacks and Latinxs finding common ground in their exclusion from mainstream American Dream narratives and through their engagement with hip-hop. The neighborhood is a palimpsest of first- and second-generation Latinxs mapped over intersecting histories of other immigrant and forced migrant populations who have lived in Washington Heights. This new generation has set their sights on making it big as they claim their contributions to American history. The brick walls and grates of the set are tagged with graffiti; tiered fire escapes and corner shops with painted-over signs and billboards look as if they were moved directly from the streets of New York. The bodega, beauty shop, and car company are symbols of entrepreneurship and sustainability that many Latinx Americans have forged in ethnic enclaves across the United States. Miranda boldly asks, "Whose America is it?" Miranda creates an intergenerational dialogue about the complexity of identity, notions of belonging, and the power of music to help theorize how we remix the diverse influences that fuse our identities. He unsettles the idea that there is some monolithic Latinx identity by offering what Brian Herrera calls a "parahistory." Parahistories, Herrera argues, are "those histories that [are] at once analogous and parallel to, but also distinct and separate from, a performance's central, official history."[15]

Mi Gente—Multicentric Latinx Identities[16]

In *In the Heights*, Miranda plays the hidden transcript of Latinx influences and innovations that helped to shape the foundation of hip-hop culture. Black and Puerto Rican studies scholar Juan Flores speaks of the erasure of Latinx contributions in hip-hop and the erasure of the history of important Puerto Rican MCs in the national and global memory of hip-hop's foundation:

> This omission, of course, is anything but fortuitous and has as much to do with the selective vagaries of the music industry as with the social placement of the Puerto Rican community in the prevailing racial-cultural hierarchy. As the commercialization process involves the extraction of popular cultural expression from its original social context and function, it seems that the "Latinazation" of Hip-hop has meant its distancing from the specific national and ethnic traditions to which it had most directly pertained.[17]

Flores reveals that not only do Latinxs sample from blackness, but also that hip-hop samples from Latinxness to forge its multicentric construction. Miranda also samples language, musical styles, and gestures associated with White Broadway musical shows by George Gershwin and Steven Sondheim, and also with salsa, merengue, bolero, and R&B to reveal the multiple innerworkings of hip-hop that go unacknowledged. By privileging a Latinx perspective of hip-hop, he offers a prescriptive lens to show why Latinx people make claims to hip-hop in acts of self-definition that underscore how Latin histories have been subsumed under the dominant expressions of hip-hop's African American particularity. In a keynote speech to the Latino Journalists Association in 2009, Miranda spoke of his intention in creating *In the Heights*:

> I remember the first time I went to Puerto Rico for summer vacation. Prior to that, the way I saw Hispanics on TV were as janitors, criminals, and

> talking Chihuahuas.[18] And I remember being struck, even at that age, being in Puerto Rico and realizing "oh the doctors are Puerto Rican, the lawyers here are Puerto Rican, oh the journalists here are Puerto Rican. . . . And here is where we belong we can do anything we want." But back in New York, we are janitors, criminals and talking Chihuahuas.[19]

Visiting Puerto Rico was an awakening moment for Miranda. The child of a psychologist and a social activist, Miranda grew up going to the best schools, had a transnational worldview, and understood Cole Porter just as much as he did Jay-Z. Yet, visiting Puerto Rico opened him up to the personal legacy of his American Dream narrative and the difference between a fictionalized idea of home and one that could be forged by remixing his experiences in Puerto Rico with those he had in the United States. This was the first time that Miranda could see the value of being Latino was enough and needed no authentication from White structures of legitimization in the United States. This twoness—this double consciousness of Latinx identity—is to be at once Latinx and American, and being proud of both. Miranda showcases a new school understanding of hip-hop as a worldview rooted not in negative projections of Latinxs, but in the redemptive capacity of hip-hop's oral narrative poetry to enable truth telling. Echoing Danny Hoch's analysis of hip-hop not being possible without all of its parts, Miranda plays with a new understanding of racial sincerity. For Miranda, there are no generic Latinx immigrant experiences, but very specific ethnic and national cultural experiences that matter to the Cuban, Dominican, Columbian, Puerto Rican, and other representations of Latinx life that come together under the multicentric sign of Latinxness within *In the Heights*.

Usnavi from the Block

The story of Usnavi and his friends and family on the block unfolds over an extremely hot Fourth of July weekend when their stories come into conflict during the first act. Nina has dropped out of college because she didn't make the grades. Benny dreams of starting his own business and sees himself with Nina. Sonny tries to stay out of trouble, but is always tempted by Usnavi's nemesis, Graffiti Pete, who tags the local stores.

Graffiti Pete, with his illegal tagging, embodies Usnavi's fears: he is what mainstream society says that young Latinos will become. Usnavi works hard every day, taking care of the store and his abuela, all while wondering what his next move in life would be if he won $96,000 in the Lotto. If he can get up the nerve, one day he will tell Vanessa that she's the love of his life. Abuela offers Usnavi melancholy reminders that his true home is the Dominican Republic, and Daniela, the beauty shop owner, provides the telenovela gossip of the block.

The big number of the first act, is Scene 7, "96,000," which is a mash-up of all of the main characters' stories and the musical soundtracks that follow them on their journey to truth, a truth written on their own terms using a hybrid of Spanish, English, and hip-hop. The number is sung in a remixed format that I had never before witnessed on stage. Three main hooks are sung in a round, as if a DJ is scratching each part live before the audience. The hooks are taken from the individual testimonies that each character gives about what he or she would do with the longed-for Lotto winnings. The ensemble scratches in with a constant refrain of "Ninety-six thousand—No me diga!" Though impossible to capture the enveloping sound on the page, capitalization used here mirrors the traditional use of capitalization that marks that a performer is singing. The song is spliced between three principal performers and plays something like this:

VANESSA	BENNY	USNAVI
I'LL BE DOWNTOWN	FOR REAL, THOUGH I'LL	IT'S CRAZY WHEN WE
SEE YOU AROUND	TAKE A BREAK AND WE'LL	GET INTO THESE CRAZY
IF I WIN THE LOTTERY PARTY EVERYBODY HERE	THROW THE BIGGEST BLOCK	HYPOTHETICALS[20]

The story is served by the aesthetics of hip-hop, allowing multiple narratives to intersect as in a traditional Broadway ballad. R&B and rap stylings are vocally mashed up right before the audience. Lin-Manuel Miranda's sophisticated use of hip-hop allows the audience to step inside the music to see the characters as they see themselves, making the lenses of double consciousness the perspective of the audience. Sampling and remixing become devices used to translate experiences and feelings in the real, fragmented fashion in which they are lived. Miranda does not mine hip-hop for flashy devices, but uses it as a way of seeing the world differently than the mainstream formulas of Broadway will allow. Miranda explores new territory on the stage as he uses sampling and remixing as theatrical devices that challenge how theater is made, how we view it, and how we experience it in live performance. Watching the actors sing the song, one can envision a DJ hand mixing and scratching their individual voices together to weave a sonic and visual scene of intersection that allows the different experiences of Latinxness to remain ethnically and nationally specific, while stressing the urgency of a pan-Latinx solidarity.

In the second act, the musical continues in the same fashion as the characters' stories weave in and out of one another. These neighborhood characters are relatable; they mirror the multitude of Latinx representations floating on billboards, on television shows, and in the very neighborhood in which they work so hard every day. In true Broadway formula, Usnavi wins the Lotto, but not without great sacrifice. His abuela passes away and Usnavi has to decide where his home is. Usnavi has another awakening moment in the riveting number "Carneval del Barrio," sung in English and Spanish with ensemble:

USNAVI
YES!
MAYBE YOU'RE RIGHT, SONNY CALLIN' THE CORONERS!
MAYBE WE'RE POWERLESS, A CORONER FULL OF FOREIGNERS.
MAYBE THIS NEIGHBORHOOD'S CHANGING FOREVER
MAYBE TONIGHT IS OUR LAST NIGHT TOGETHER, HOWEVER!
HOW DO YOU WANNA FACE IT?
DO YOU WANNA WASTE IT, WHEN THE END IS SO CLOSE YOU CAN TASTE IT?
YOU COULD CRY WITH YOUR HEAD IN THE SAND,
I'M A FLY THIS FLAG THAT I GOT IN MY HAND![21]

Miranda underscores the twoness of living at the hyphen of being simultaneously Latino and American. As his predominantly Latino neighborhood is threatened by gentrification, Usnavi asks, "Who has the right to occupy the space?" Playing on the double entendre he occupies as a Puerto Rican American actor infiltrating Broadway and as a character challenging the Whites in power infiltrating his neighborhood, Miranda, like many other historically underrepresented artists, makes an important effort to decolonize the structures of Broadway that prevent fair representations of diversity. From Will Marion Cook's *In Dahomey* (1903) to Lorraine Hansberry's *A Raisin in the Sun* (1959) and Russell Simmons's *Def Poetry* on Broadway (2001), artists from historically underrepresented racial backgrounds in the United States have made critical disruptions in American theater history. Miranda joins this legacy of artists, yet also offers a plot twist. He challenges the normative whiteness of American Dream narratives and Broadway by sampling from these exclusive narratives and remixing them into new structures, language, and forms that are definitively hip-hop.[22] His efforts saw a resounding success. *In the Heights* ran on Broadway for a total of twenty-nine previews and 1,184 performances, and was nominated for thirteen Tony Awards, ultimately winning Best Musical, Best Choreography, and Best Orchestrations in 2008. It was also nominated for the 2009 Pulitzer Prize for Drama.[23] *In the Heights* will find a new international audience in June 2021 when, according to David Morgan of TheatreMania.com, the film version of *In the Heights*, directed by Jon M. Chu, will be release on HBO Max and movie theater in June 2021. The movie was scheduled for a June 26, 2020, release, however, the coronavirus pandemic shifted the premiere dates. Lin-Manuel Miranda and the musical's original book writer, Quiara Alegría Hudes, created the film adaptation.

It's the End of the World as We Know It[24]

Matt Sax and Eric Rosen's *Venice* also challenges how we understand racial, ethnic, and national identity.[25] The musical takes place in a post-apocalyptic future in a fictional city called Venice, which has been embroiled in a civil war for twenty years. Most of the characteristics of a dystopia are in place: We have a futuristic city controlled by corporate and military standoff; exaggerated worst-case scenarios of people in a state of emergency, living in safe zones; challenging party politics; and surveillance of citizens by corporations and the government. This is textbook dystopia, remixed hip-hop style. Sitting in the audience at the Copaken Stage in Kansas City, where I saw *Venice* in its first iteration, I felt as if I was being projected into a distorted future. The opening number of the musical involves a character called Clown MC (played by Sax) breaking the fourth wall and introducing how the story will unfold. He is in front of a laptop, typing the story as words begin to fall down the walls in real-time projections. An infectious remix of sounds scratches together parts of bass beats and remnants of Broadway ballads into a dissonant soundtrack that floods the playing space. The audience is immersed in the world of the play, yet finds itself without language to talk back to the multiple indexical references that are simultaneously thrown at them. Opera, rap, R&B, gospel, and militaristic hip-hop dances all fuse before us in a chaotic opening that asks us to check our preconceived notions about hip-hop and race at the door. The demand on the audience to read the prologue in the opening scene as it is typed and projected onto the stage shifts the visceral response to the musical dissonance to one that is logocentric. Such a move assumes, first, that the audience can read, and second, that they will understand and comprehend English. This is already a test for the audience to gain access to the fictional Venice. However, Rosen's and Sax's use of multiple languages—sonic, linguistic, and embodied—allows the audience to enter into the play from any number of perspectives. The Clown MC begins to narrate the story:

CLOWN MC

(Typing) Willow was the daughter of the president. Venice was the son of a beloved leader of a movement for peace.

CLOWN MC

(Typing) Until one day a massive terrorist attack killed 20,000 people, plunging the nation into chaos. Both of their parents were killed. The government was destroyed.

(Typing) Now orphaned, the two children were torn apart.

CLOWN MC

(Typing) She was taken to the Safe Zone, a haven for the elite in the distant countryside.

(Typing) He was left behind in the destroyed city.

(Typing and/or spoken.) Since then, the two have written letters to each other every day, dreaming of the time they'd reunite.[26]

As the words are typed onto the set of the musical (see figure 11), the music is distorted and engulfing, the lights are dim, and the letters bounce back into the audience, shining a light on us as a character involved in bringing meaning to the play. We are inside the words and thus enliven the space. One could argue that Sax and Rosen are attempting to mash up Du Bois's color line, blurring lines of pretext and context of racial transcripts to trouble how we make sense of bodies in space. All racial references that produce meaning in relationship to the other are twisted and distorted. The narration scrolls down. Venice is destroyed by a massive terrorist attack that kills tens of thousands of people. A military occupation divides the nation into a Safe Zone for the elites, and leaves the rest trapped in the ruins of the fallen city. The Clown MC, our narrator and guide, describes life under military occupation and introduces Venice Monroe, a charismatic leader with a plan to restore the nation's democracy.

The city is divided into two camps of believers—those for revolution and those who want to keep the current regime of oppression. Venice, the man who is the namesake of the city, is the son of a peace movement revolutionary named Anna. Venice was conceived after Anna was raped by the military; she chose to keep her child as a reminder that peace can be birthed out of chaos and violence.

Living with the story of his violent conception and his mother's violent death, Venice battles to reform society. He is depicted as a racially ambiguous man, though this is never spoken—light-skinned males of Latino and Lebanese descent were cast in the Kansas City and New York productions, respectively. Venice's revolutionary stance is reminiscent of Tupac Shakur's, and the character's racial ambiguity suggests the hopes for peace projected on seemingly multiracial bodies in the twenty-first century, particularly that of then-President Barack Obama. Willow (who is cast as White) and Venice, once childhood friends ripped apart by the war, are now to be reunited as husband and wife when the borders between the cities are lifted to reunite revolutionary causes. The Clown MC represents the plight of the underclass of Venice. The people of the city have been abandoned by the state because of their revolutionary spirits and desire to dismantle corporate greed. The Clown MC raps this exposition (thus capital usage):

CLOWN MC
LET ME TELL YOU A STORY
LET ME PAINT YOU A PICTURE
LET ME—LET YOU IN ON THE WORLD I ENVISION
IT MIGHT BE STRANGE TO YOU
OR MAYBE SIMILAR TO YOUR OWN WORLD—
MIGHT FEEL THE SAME TO YOU
I AM YOUR LIFELINE
YOUR FORWARD AND HINDSIGHT
REPORTER OF ORDER OF STORY
YOUR TIMELINE
TO TELL THIS STORY IS A MEANS OF RESISTANCE
SO MY EARS FOR THE NIGHT—YEAH I NEED YOUR
ASSISTANCE.[27]

The Clown MC talks directly to the audience, mimicking the African griot traditions embedded in hip-hop MC strategies, much like a clown/jester character in Shakespeare. He is an information giver, a clever character aware of his position as a keeper of tales. Leading the ensemble, the Clown MC and the people shout/sing to the audience:

ALL *(sans WILLOW)*
WE'VE BEEN LEFT FOR DEAD
STUCK HERE WHILE THE WEALTHY FLED
DRAINED OUR LIFE AND FUCKING BLED
BOMBS EXPLODED ROUND OUR HEADS—GET SOME REST
WE'RE TIRED—WIRED—UNINSPIRED—.[28]

Venice returns to the city to usher in a new era of peace. He shares the name of the city and becomes a racially ambiguous Obama-type figure who is poised to bring the warring sides of the city together. He is depicted as a man of mixed racial heritage, with one Black parent and one White, similar to Barack Obama, "the son of a black man from Kenya and a white woman from Kansas."[29] The description of the state through this number depicts city sounds and images that project a scene from the 2007 Richard Lawrence dystopic film *I Am Legend*. Sax and Rosen play on trauma and euphoria as intersecting emotional landscapes. The traumatic events of 9/11 and Hurricanes Katrina and Sandy that circulate in the American imaginary remind us of our humanity and connectedness in times of crisis. By suspending racial and class differences as foci, Sax and Rosen are able to provide an emotional anchor to the musical that suggests sincerity as a whole. As Daphne Brooks reminds us, sites of trauma have the capacity to recall histories of miscegenation and violence through sonic and visual racial performatives, even when the intention of the artist may be to focus on unity in the wake of national trauma.[30] Because Sax and Rosen never mention race, they count on current and past histories of race embedded in parts of the sampled narratives (Iago and Othello, histories of slavery in trauma sites, Black women's bodies as sites of sexual pleasure in the role of Daisy) to ground the audience in the miscegenation of history. They suggest that the musical's context cannot be understood within told structures of race and power and that the characters are transgressing the boundaries of those indexical sonic and visual markers. Everything is everything. To find the truth of the characters, Sax and Rosen tell the audience not to be fooled by the fictions of race that we bring to the world of theater by default, but to trust what is in front of us—to live in the unstable sonic and visual chaos of race's deconstruction through their musical mash-up.

Through the distorted projection of samples of race, class, and power; class is not the determining factor; humanity is. The authors suggest that we as the audience do not have a referential for humanity, thus the dystopic backdrop of corporate greed and the military industrial complex as the nexus of power in the musical. Likewise, the racial malleability of the lead character Venice allows the audience to project their idea of what Venice is racially. His power-hungry half-brother, Markos (Markos is Iago to Venice's Othello), is cast as a Brown-skinned man of African descent who constructs an evil plot to undermine his brother's marriage to Willow. Willow is the child of the slain former president of Venice. Markos's thirst for power and bitter jealousy toward his brother prompt him to ruin his brother's plan to bring peace back to the city. Markos works for Theodore Westbrook, the new CEO of Westbrook Enterprises, a company that controls the Safe Zone and military occupation of the city.

Daisy, a Black military sex worker, services the desires of all the men in the play. The character Willow, cast as White, represents virtue and victory. Though this observation is based on my historical references to racial hierarchies that persist in American culture post-slavery, the performer's bodies bring to the stage the socio-historic stereotypical projections of a White female's expectations of protection and a Black female's hypersexuality. It is difficult to disconnect from the fact that Willow sings and Daisy raps/sings and that Daisy's sexual labor is violently depicted, while Willow's virtue inspires affection from all of the men in the play. Such representations reinforce the devalued representations of Black female sexuality and the inflated projections of fragile White femininity. Sax and Rosen attempt to alienate us from these types of thoughts, almost in Brechtian form, with the intention of directing the audience to focus on a justice–injustice binary that stands in for couplings of race and gender. The musical attempts to immerse the audience in the future world of the play, yet ignores the fact that the sampled storylines from *Othello* ask the audience to make connections to existing racial meanings from the past that persist in the present racial state of America in the twenty-first century. Markos, the play's villain, is cast as a dark-skinned Black male, countering Venice's light-skinned, racially ambiguous appearance. Willow, as a White female, is ultimately sacrificed in the show as the object of desire that sparks a heated fight between Markos and Venice. Though Sax and Rosen make efforts to tell us that race does not matter, in the everyday lives of people of color who suffer through anti-Black racism, as well as anti-immigrant and White supremacist rhetoric, the American racial imaginary is far from being erased. The traces of hope that these artists leave in *Venice* require us to immerse ourselves in the suspended disbelief of the theater to imagine what our lives might be like if we allowed ourselves to believe that systemic inequality will eventually fall.

As the audience struggle to make sense of the characters' relationships, Sax, as the Clown MC, brings comic relief to the audience. Riffing on the fool and clown characters in Shakespeare's works, Sax plays on

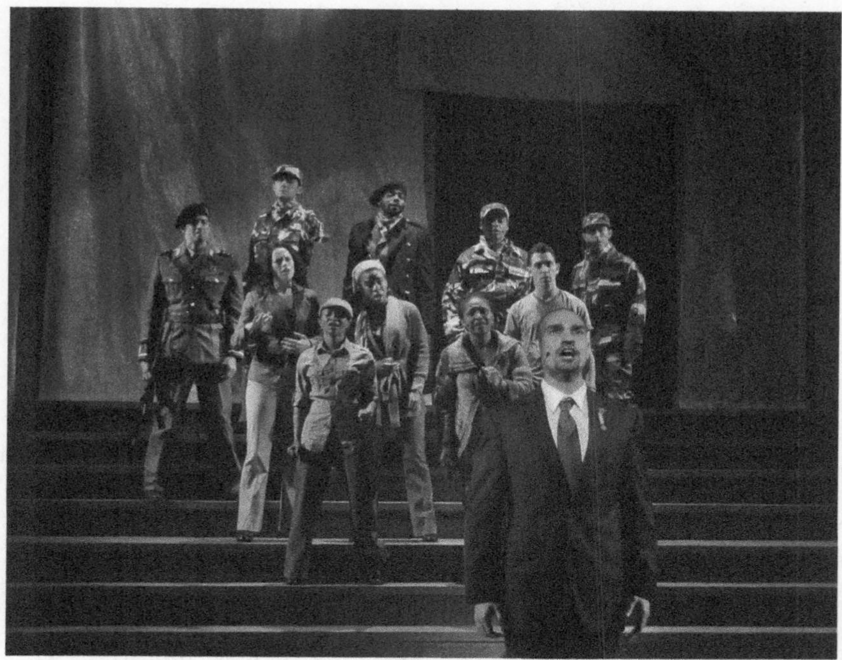

Fig. 13. Scene from *Venice* with Matt Sax. Photo courtesy Don Ipock.

the often-working-class status of Shakespeare's commoners, who see the world from below or are hired to entertain the king as comedian/social critic. A proficient rapper, Sax raps the narration and works as a physical bridge between scenes, using his body to deliver comfort to the audience as he cuts them into the story beat by beat. The hip-hop dance numbers are chaotic and seemingly abstracted from hip-hop dance, improvisation, and modern dance. The comfort of Sax's rapping style projects images of Black masculinity onto the scene as the performer makes it clear that though he did not learn how to rap uniquely for this play, he is borrowing this device to destabilize how we understand whiteness. The Clown MC has consumed the language, embodied gesture, and styles of self-adornment of hip-hop as his worldview. The line between what we think is his whiteness and the blackness of hip-hop is attached to argue that culture is selective and race is a fictitious construct. Our old knowledge of how race and class are lived cannot fit within the life of the musical. As soon as we try to use what we think we know to understand the story, the Clown MC mixes the intention again, mashing up our way of knowing. The blackness, Latinxness, and whiteness of the lead characters—Venice, Markos, Anna, Willow, Clown MC, Theo, and Emilia—do not connect to anything historical or racial in the play besides the state of war and unrest. The only way that we know they are Black, Latinx, or White is through the racial scripts that are mapped on their bodies, based on racial transcripts that audience members bring to the performance. The audience is asked to suspend their own projection of what a leader and American citizenship look like.

In an interview with playwright and musical theater producer Shoshanna Greenberg in *The Huffington Post*, Eric Rosen contends that the futuristic framing of *Venice* is one that mirrors social unrest today: "It's not a warning of a possible future; it's happening. It's more of an allegorical world than a futuristic one. The conflicts that inspire the play are happening all over the world now."[31] Sax and Rosen use hip-hop to bait the audience, yet the structure of their musical is sampled from *Othello*, which assumes that the mainstream audience knows Shakespeare's play and can import meaning from those iconic relationships to the musical. If the audience does not recognize their sample from this classic play, Sax and Rosen throw in a bit of sibling rivalry, corrupt government politics, and a tragic love story to appeal to a millennial generation that grew up on reality shows. Sax's Clown MC, like the other characters, becomes alienated and forces us to focus on the story between the bodies that want peace. The audience's confusion in response to the narrative and sonic dissonance in the musical is reflected in extreme theater reviews that either laud the piece as one of the most amazing musicals of the early twenty-first century or demand some type of qualification to make sense of it. The *New York Post* describes *Venice* as "one of the worst theaters shows of 2013":

> Dystopia's a hot subject right now, so this musical took it and . . . crashed. It was actually surprising to see this debacle at The Public Theater, which can usually be relied on for a minimum of professionalism.[32]

The idea of "crashing" the subject of dystopia might be just what the playwrights intended. Perhaps *Venice* had to blow up musical formats and racial projects as we know them in order to challenge race as a device that reproduces hierarchies of power and privilege on and off the stage. Though there is no racial or cultural particularity for the characters, their embrace of hip-hop consumes all of the musical forms that are remixed in the performance. Many of the critic's reviews seem to find the show's layers tedious and the style turgid. Ben Brantley, then theater critic of the *New York Times,* says of Sax:

> Mr. Sax . . . is an original voice and presence, a rapper from the suburbs who regularly morphs from self-conscious square to wriggling, blissed-out Slinky. You can feel the joy he takes in summoning the characters into being as *Venice* begins, assessing the actors with sly and shy glances as they appear onstage. Unfortunately, the creatures that spring from this teeming imagination are, to outsiders, about as lifelike as toy soldiers. Though the cast includes a bevy of attractive and seasoned young performers . . . their skills don't always mesh with Mr. Sax's sensibility. They are also burdened with an unwieldy tale to tell, unassisted by the special effects that Hollywood can be relied on to provide as plot-hole-concealing camouflage.[33]

In an interview with Sax, I asked about the inspiration for the show. He said that any number of events that have shaped American life inspired him and Rosen. Hip-hop allowed the playwrights to sample from traumatic events that have dramatically altered American identity and its projection around the world—foreign terrorism, the Obama election, Arab Spring, Occupy Wall Street—and remix them as part of the language of the show. Interrogating what and who inspires revolutionary action from everyday people, Sax pushes the boundaries to ask: How useful is race in helping to inspire social change? What happens if we completely mash it up and resignify its meaning intentionally? For some critics, this move to unsettle the audience's relationship to race was inspiring and daring. Richard Zoglin of *Time* magazine was willing to be uncomfortable in the chaotic mash-up that forces the audience to participate in the spectacle. He argues that much of the cohesion in the otherwise challenging narrative structure in *Venice* is owed to hip-hop:

> Indeed, I've never before seen rap music used so well as a narrative device in a stage musical. While Sax's rhymes may have less street authenticity than Lin-Manuel Miranda's similar Hip-hop narration for *In the Heights,*

> they are also less sentimental and carry more operatic grandeur. The other musical numbers, too, propel the story, deepen the characters and heighten the emotional temperature. All along the way, the goal of the show's creators seems to be something rare in musicals, particularly rock musicals: to communicate with the audience rather than provide a string of virtuosic big moments for the singers onstage. This is a musical that gets no ovations until the end.[34]

The fact that Zoglin begins his review talking about Sax's rap prowess by using Lin-Manuel Miranda's skill sets in *In the Heights* as a validating frame, and then names *Venice* as a "rock musical," is indicative of American theater's incapacity to understand hip-hop without a body of color. White men in theater spaces "doing" hip-hop make White critics nervous because understanding performances of blackness, even without Black bodies, requires a literacy of Black life that many theater critics do not possess nor desire to obtain. Whiteness as the dominant legitimizing center of the art world is shifting. Hip-hop-inspired theater and performance challenges the de facto practice of measuring Black cultural production against rubrics of whiteness and Eurocentricity. Hip-hop becomes a space to resist racial projections and hierarchies. As a nation, we have not figured out how to qualify one another outside of racial identification and cultural production, so we try to fit what we see and experience into comfortable categories that limit full possibilities of humanity and opportunity. Hip-hop's influence on the theater world has begun to produce a new wave of theater arts that claim hip-hop as a way of knowing, being, and becoming in the world.[35]

Conclusion

In *In the Heights*, I saw Latinx artists challenge stereotypes of representation on Broadway by offering a multicentric representation of Latinx identity and its intersection with blackness. Lin-Manuel Miranda's use of hip-hop to showcase a diversity of Latinx shared experiences of oppression and their connection to African American culture and the American Dream showcases minoritized quests for full American citizenship. On an even playing field, hip-hop would not need validation by White critics or legitimizing on or off Broadway. The fact that Black and Brown people narrating their oppression, hopes, and dreams in hip-hop has become the hottest commodity in theater is ironic. Mainstream theater needs hip-hop as a vehicle to relate to the non-White world, yet Broadway can't relate to hip-hop (or the Black and Brown people who created it) unless it scrubs hip-hop's blackness into a non-threatening presentation that fits within recognizable Broadway formulas.

Though *Venice* presents itself as a dystopic equalizer that tries to destabilize our sensorial relationship to race, the idea of destabilization is sampled from hip-hop itself. White artists writing about oppressions ventriloquized through blackness can do so with a safety net of privilege that is never afforded to people of color. Hip-hop content conveyed through language, embodied gestures, and styles of self-adornment are cultural practices extracted from the people that have material consequences. The resulting performances have a myriad of possible results, yet missing are the bodies and the lived experiences of jeopardy that people of color live every day, regardless of gender, sexuality, ability, class, nationality, or ethnicity. Hip-hop is born out of artistic resistance to systemic inequality and racism that fuels the continuum of African American music genres that petition for equality. No matter how much the mainstream wants to claim hip-hop as its own, borrow it as a creative vehicle for artistic mash-up, or be inspired by its constant reinvention, hip-hop without people of color is an artistic genre, not a cultural experience that is connected to experiences of oppression, survival, and triumph, but rather a series of technical applications, no matter how well intended, that feel like hip-hop-lite.

Case in point: In 2016, Porchlight Musical Theatre in Chicago produced *In The Heights* with the role of Usnavi played by a White actor. The theater company cast Latinx actors in other roles, but justified its lead casting even after protests surrounded the production. To add fuel to the fire, the *Chicago Sun-Times* lauded the production's "authentic" cast. *NBC Latino* interviewed local Chicago actors about the casting choices:

> With [*In The Heights*], people felt excited, we felt like we had to show up and audition. It was important to be in a show that is from us, by us, with our own voice . . .
>
> We were excited about it and then seeing that lead role go to someone who was not Latino, we realized that it was not an equal playing field. How can a white person act Latino better than a Latino?[36]

Porchlight Theatre's production renders *In the Heights* a different play. Without a Latino lead in conversation with the music and the book, the role is whitewashed. Usnavi is rendered as insignificant as a White male in blackface. In *Venice*, Sax and Rosen specifically avoid the possibility of such physical whitewashing moves by using hip-hop as a vehicle to understand Americanness when our understanding of race is destabilized. However, historicizing hip-hop by pushing it into a "raceless" dystopic future suggests an America without race is only available in the aftermath of tragedy or war. In a twenty-first-century racial climate that continues to marginalize Black and Brown people as inferior contributors whose presence challenges America becoming "great again," people of color still rely on racial particularity, no matter how problematic it is that people of color are cast in roles written for Whites when the director want to appear to be "edgy" or colorblind. But can't people of color have musicals that tell their stories from their perspectives? Why is it that a musical that departs from a non-White perspective must be read as "universal" or prescribe to its conventions and legitimizing frames (being produced at majority White venues and/or directed by White directors who have been vetted as acceptable) in order to be worthy of mainstream production? The musical mash-ups of hip-hop in *In the Heights* and *Venice* follow jazz music's cross-racial influence on mainstream American theater and culture. As mainstream White audiences consumed jazz music, it moved away from being marked as African American music, or "race music," to America's music. Since the early twentieth century, jazz music, similar to hip-hop, has been a way for African American people to express their post-slavery experiences in America. To reject jazz, and similarly hip-hop, as a cultural expression rooted in the African American experience, paves a path that erases the social, cultural, and economic sanctions of slavery and its aftermath that have produced the social conditions of inequality that make it necessary to describe and evaluate the contributions to the American theater by the racial and ethnic identities of its citizens.

Though whitewashed versions of *In the Heights* and young African American girls being cast as Sandy or Rizzo in *Grease* supposedly represent progressive politics, these are the last things people of color need to produce diversity, equity, and inclusion in the theater. As Daniel Banks asserts, hip-hop is always already inclusive:

> Hip-hop was and is something—and to grapple with it seriously reveals the overlapping ethnic, cultural, and geographic influences in today's world, as well as the ways in which racism, classism, and sexism continue to serve as systemic tools of oppression by the media. Hip-hop culture struggles against the basic tenets of the marketplace as embodied by much of popular music and, specifically, the rap music industry with which many people associate the name Hip-hop.[37]

Banks reminds us that the mythical hip-hop community of practitioners and consumers who see themselves as connected through the music and culture of hip-hop, even when that culture is not one that they were born into, must be acknowledged as part of the culture. Like the hip-hop artists of the early 1970s who wanted to create and perform new imaginings of blackness that rejected racial and social discrimination, so too do non-Black and Latinx artists use hip-hop to challenge the status quo. The sampled stories within hip-hop's matrix cannot be separated from the African American and Latinx people who struggle for freedom and equality. People of color live under an expectation of violence, exclusion, and invisibility daily. Making art that expresses how we live and feel as Black people living in the United States and other parts of the African diaspora is how hip-hop and other Black art forms survive mass consumption. Black art forms are not revered in the mainstream unless they are vetted through White legitimizing frames and desired for consumption. Hip-hop is constantly being rediscovered by the White mainstream as a thrilling novelty, yet as hip-hop shows up on Broadway, it is rare that Black and Brown people are telling their stories from their perspectives. This is why Lin-Manuel Miranda's and Matt Sax's works are important. Neither artist attempts to speak for, or like, Black people. They use the art form to express their specific relationship to the music and culture. Hip-hop's capacity to constantly reinvent suggests a survival instinct within the creative space of hip-hop that anticipates that parts of culture will be sampled and remixed anew. The struggles for equality have not been won for Black and Brown people, so sampling the parts of the music and culture that express our oppression and resilience cannot be done without traces of sorrow and the desire to live freely, without the expectation of violence or erasure.

FIVE

HAMILTON: AN AMERICAN MUSICAL'S GHOSTS / Digging up American History

> Now things have been turned upside down. Now the masters, the producers of this profit hungry production, which has already made 30 million dollars, are using the slave's language: Rock and Roll, Rap and Hip-hop to romanticize the careers of kidnappers, and murderers.
>
> —Ishmael Reed on *Hamilton: An American Musical, CounterPunch*, 2015

The first time I heard about *Hamilton* was in 2009. Then President Barack Obama invited the musical's creator, Lin-Manuel Miranda, to the White House with a group of other nationally recognized artists for an event entitled "An Evening of Poetry, Music and The Spoken Word." I imagine that upon receiving an invitation from the first African American president in the history of the United States, every invitee brought his or her "A" game to the performance. Miranda used his audience with the president and his guests to reveal an excerpt from what he then thought was a "concept" album on the life of Alexander Hamilton. He introduced the sample from his work with this prelude:

> Uhm I'm thrilled uh . . . the White House called me uh . . . tonight . . . uhm . . . because . . . uh . . . I am actually, working on a Hip-hop album . . . uh . . . it's a concept album about the life of someone I think embodies Hip-hop: Treasury Secretary Alexander Hamilton. You laugh! But it's true! Uhm . . . he was born . . . uh . . . a penniless orphan in San Croix, uh . . . of illegitimate

birth uh. Became George Washington's right hand man . . . uh . . . Became treasury secretary. Caught beef with every other founding father. Uh . . . and all on the strength of his writing . . . I think he embodies the word's ability to a make a difference. So, I am going to be doing the first song from that tonight. I'm accompanied by—Tony- and Grammy-winning music director Alex Lacamoire. I will be playing Vice President Aaron Burr. And snap along if you like.[1]

Miranda proceeded to launch into the song "Alexander Hamilton." This would later become the opening number of his phenomenally successful show *Hamilton: An American Musical*:

How does a bastard, orphan, son of a whore and a Scotsman, dropped in the middle of a forgotten
spot in the Caribbean by Providence impoverished in squalor
grow up to be a hero and a scholar?
The ten-dollar founding father without a father
got a lot farther by working a lot harder
by being a lot smarter by being a self-starter
by fourteen, they placed him in charge of a trading charter
And every day while slaves were being slaughtered and carted away
across the waves on him he kept his guard up
Inside he was longing for something to be a part of
the brother was ready to beg steal borrow or barter
Then a hurricane came and devastation reigned
our man saw his future drip-dripping down the drain
put a pencil to his temple connected it to his brain
and he wrote his first refrain a testament to his pain
Well the word got around they said this kid is insane man
took up a collection just to send him to the mainland
Get your education don't forget from whence you came. And the world is gonna know your name.
What's ya name, man?
Alexander Hamilton.
My name is Alexander Hamilton.
And there's a million things he hasn't done.
But just you wait, just you, wait [. . .].[2]

The audience members who witnessed this performance rose to their feet for a standing ovation, led by Barack Obama himself. It was a moment of triumph for Miranda. Yet the fact that the first U.S. president of African descent invited a Puerto Rican American rapper, composer, actor, and musician to perform a musical number that dramatizes the life and times of U.S. Founding Father Alexander Hamilton is not without irony. Hip-hop and Alexander Hamilton would seem an unlikely coupling. Yet as Miranda demonstrated, the two have much in common. Hip-hop is the bastard language of many African American and Latinx sons and daughters who feel they have lived in the shadows of Hamilton's legacy. As an African American President and a Puerto Rican rapper-composer made history at the White House, the ghosts of White men who would never have imagined them there haunted Lin-Manuel's captivating performance and his subsequent international recognition as a lost Latino son of the American theater returned home.

In the PBS special on YouTube that shows Miranda's performance, the camera pans over the audience, revealing some who seem both uncomfortable and amazed by Miranda playing Alexander Hamilton. You can almost see thought bubbles, which I imagine saying things like, "What is this?" "What is he saying?" "American history told through rap?" A non-African American musical theater artist rapping a mash-up of hip-hop, the history of a Founding Father, classical Broadway musical theater, and R&B completely counters the preexisting high art narratives usually portrayed in PBS specials and American theater. Remixing the legacies of Alexander Hamilton and hip-hop through a Latino male's body places audiences in the vortex of lost American history sung in raps that chronicle avoided truths of "slaves [who] were being slaughtered and carted away" and immigration narratives that criminalize and exploit Latinx people in the United States, all of which are lost in the infectious raps.

Cut to the present: *Hamilton* went from being a "concept album" in 2009; to off-Broadway, must-see theater in 2015; to a Broadway juggernaut that won the Pulitzer Prize in 2016. At the time of this publication, it will have grossed over one billion dollars. Miranda attempts, through *Hamilton*, to challenge the American racial imaginary and its impending hierarchies. Teaching early American history using the bodies of Black, mixed race, Asian, and Latinx actors to play White Founding Fathers is a revisionist history that challenges the normative whiteness of Broadway. Hip-hop music and culture, born out of poor Black and Brown New York boroughs in the late 1970s, inspired poor communities to identify with its rags-to-riches redemption narrative that inspired the global pop phenomenon. Before Lin-Manuel Miranda, Alexander Hamilton's narrative was inextricably tied to the privilege, power, and anti-Black violence of America's Founding Fathers. What happens, then, when hip-hop music and culture are used to tell Alexander Hamilton's story? How is hip-hop used as a device to reveal the ghost narratives of Black and Brown people lost in the annals of American history, yet present in the daily experiences of anti-Black violence?

This chapter explores the concept of ghosting in hip-hop as a device of selective absence and presence in the musical *Hamilton*. Lin-Manuel Miranda's knowledge of hip-hop and Broadway musical forms allows him to sample hip-hop's music and narratives and remix them with Hamilton's biographic information, such as his orphan status and Caribbean origins, to connect the ghosts of Black and Brown people whose humanity was, and continues to be, devalued in America's present. These ghosts, their descendants, and their trauma, helped to build the foundation of American ideals of freedom with which Alexander Hamilton and his colleagues are credited in the musical.

The tripart concept of *ghosting* that I am tracing in *Hamilton* operates as a residuum of sampling. Sampling is defined here as the act of borrowing a racially and ethnically specific aspect of identity, and using it to amplify or embellish another identity without acknowledging the body or history from which the piece was borrowed or copied. The result of such linguistic, visual, embodied, or gestural borrowing can result in corporal and historic erasure. I use the concept of ghosting in three ways. First, I argue that sampling is a form of ghosting in that it allows an artist to reference a singer, musician, and/or any piece of sonic or visual artwork or lived experience as a *ghost image*, a sonic or embodied gesture that can be used to develop original content that may or may not have anything to do with the original usage or intention of the person who is associated with the sample. Second, I use ghosting as a noun in its traditional definition, here cited from Oxford English Dictionary, to signal the act of being spiritually present after dying. Third, I use Black vernacular uses of ghosting in hip-hop as "a state of being gone, done, not be[ing] legible."[3] I contend that the musical *Hamilton* offers a ghosting of blackness in all of these iterations. The act of sampling is in itself an act of haunting by the past in the present where the original piece of work that is sampled (music narrative, visual art, embodied gesture, etc.) to perform an aspect of someone's identity derives from a life lived. Ghosting, in popular culture today, has less to do with ghosts and their haunting in the present, and more to do with cutting off communications with someone. The Urban Dictionary defines ghosting, when used as a verb, as "end[ing] a personal relationship with (someone) by suddenly and without explanation withdrawing from all communication."[4] In this chapter, the ways in which the Black, Latinx, and Indigenous presence of the past is presently referenced in the bodies of the performers of color, yet, painfully, the "ghost"—"gone, done, not being legible" in the narrative of the musical—is of principal concern.[5] Miranda samples from the ultimate source of whiteness, the biographical narrative of one of the Founding Fathers of democracy, to signal the ways in which Black and Latinx stories, cultural expression, language, styles of dress, and embodied gestures are sampled under the rubric of Americanness. Black and Brown people, and their experiences, are the ghosts of American history. Our bodies are discarded as our stories, clothing styles, music, dance, and expression are used to make America's story. Miranda shows audiences that the soul of America is built on Black and Brown narratives, including many untold stories of trauma. By sampling America's history from the White perspective of Alexander Hamilton, a telling that excludes the violence perpetrated against Black and Brown people, Miranda remixes history through hip-hop, using Black and Brown bodies to recover those narratives.

Playwright Suzan-Lori Parks argues in her 1992 introduction of *The America Play*, entitled "Elements of Style," that ghosts in theater are real to her. She states, "They are *not characters*. To call them so could be an injustice. They are *figures*, *figments*, *ghosts*, *roles*, *lovers* maybe, *speakers* maybe, *shadows*, *slips*, *players* maybe, maybe someone else's pulse."[6] The experiences of Black, Latinx, mixed race, and Asian actors who perform the musical *Hamilton* are the *pulse of the musical*. The unspoken traumatic experiences expressed in the bodies of the actors and the unsaid text of the past remixes with the narrative content of the Founding Fathers and daughters to suggest that their ancestors have spiritually and generationally survived the trauma and premature death brought about by slavery, indentured servitude, sexual assault, and attempted genocide. Their stories have yet to be acknowledged by the White mainstream audiences or theater critics who subscribe to Broadway's mainstream narrative formulas. Miranda's use of hip-hop and actors of color to tell Alexander Hamilton's story seemingly challenges Broadway and America's whitewashing of American history. But does it? The majority of critical responses to the musical have almost uniquely qualified it as an American masterpiece that depicts post-racial America. Content creator and critic Kylie Umehira finds that "Theater critics, journalists, and civilians alike held a practically unanimous opinion about *Hamilton*: that it is one of the best pieces of musical theater in this generation. It was praised not only for its well-crafted songs, relevant political rhymes, and unprecedented artistry, but also for its intentional non-White casting."[7] However, Umehira finds that such assessments of the musical adhere to a White worldview that does not consider the ways in which the musical reifies White representations on Broadway as legitimizing frames of reference, even when actors of color are "playing" White:

> Though *Hamilton's* insistence in casting non-white actors is admirable, the show itself does have some problematic elements. I have found that in *Hamilton*'s retelling of American history, the musical adheres to the typical whitewashed history many Americans are familiar with. Though most of the actors in *Hamilton* are people of color, all of the characters portrayed in the musical are white; there are no people of color featured as characters. I believe this deficit is only underscored by Hamilton's privileges as a white man.[8]

Umehira's insistence that Lin-Manuel Miranda's use of African American and Latinx actors is perhaps the only agency that Black and Brown people get in *Hamilton* underscores my assertion about ghosting in the musical. Miranda's use of hip-hop and its narratives to rewrite an incomplete history that White mainstream audiences refuse to see or hear is not necessarily his fault. The stories play out right there on the stage, but we have to *want* to see and hear them. What is *Hamilton* really about? Does the story have the capacity to change based on who is watching? Make no mistake, historian Ron Chernow's popular biography of

Hamilton is the foundational source material for Lin-Manuel Miranda's narrative. However, the show's core narrative is not uniquely Miranda's musical interpretation of Chernow's book. The use of hip-hop's sampled music and culture, coupled with untold histories that play America's history back to us, creates conversations between the past and the present that ask some Americans to imagine a post-racial present, and others to relive the unreconciled traumas of the past.

In this chapter I work to disentangle those meanings while holding onto all that is good about the musical. How we can use what hurts in *Hamilton* to move forward the national conversation about race? How might the musical help us acknowledge the foundational traumas that facilitated American democracy in acts of national reconciliation and healing? I engage key songs in Acts One and Two that map the trauma of Black, self-identified mixed race, Asian, and Latinx actors playing White characters. These actors play against the ghost narratives of their ancestors whose physical and emotional labor and sacrifice built the nation's infrastructure.

First Time Ever I Saw Your Face[9]

I have been a fan of Lin-Manuel Miranda for a long time; *In the Heights* is one of the best musical contributions to the American theater that I have seen in my lifetime, and I truly believe that Miranda is a genius. Thus, I was excited to see the next iteration of his musical creativity. I attended my first viewing of *Hamilton* at the CIBC Theatre in Chicago in 2017, hopeful that I would experience something fantastic. My wish came true; *Hamilton* is both fantastic and fantastical. When I reached the theater, outside was a school bus carrying about forty African American high school students from the Chicago area. I could not help but wonder what it would mean to these teenagers to see people like themselves—Black and Brown actors—on stage, dressed in the distinguished clothing of the Founding Fathers, depicted not as property—slaves and indentured servants, as many people of African descent in America were at that time—but as men and women fighting for change as they imagine America as a place for freedom?

The audience comprised these students and a host of others: a multiracial group of folks from all walks of life. In all my years going to Broadway shows, and Broadways tours such as this one, I never saw another audience that looked like that of *Hamilton*. There were people from diverse racial and ethnic backgrounds. I saw same-sex couples of all races. I saw grandparents with their grandchildren. I saw mothers and fathers with their children. I saw America as I lived it—an always already diverse group of people, all descendants of immigrants, both forced and selective. The theater in Chicago was a beautiful art deco structure with intimate seating. The winding staircase and bar areas were filled with anticipatory audience members. The atmosphere was full of energy and excitement. Some folks were seeing the show for the first time, while others were there for the fourth or even fifth time. I heard young people singing songs from the musical in the lobby. I heard conversations in the restroom about how great the show was and what the audience members were hoping to see and feel. I saw the show in Chicago and New York and the audiences in both venues were similar, so clearly there is something about the aesthetic of the show that attracts and represents hope to many Americans. For the most part, I will focus my exploration of ghosting in *Hamilton* on my experiences at the Chicago show in the fall of 2017. I divide the chapter into acts/tracks that performatively mime the theatrical and hip-hop structures of the musical. I mark the ways in which Alexander Hamilton's narrative, as riffed upon by Miranda, plays two simultaneous tracks of performance for the audience. One is for the people of color and Whites who can decode it, and the other models the standard musical structure of two acts with book, songs, and musical dance numbers.

Ghosts of America and Hip-Hop's Past

At the Chicago show, the announcement came for the audience to turn off their cell phones. The audience clapped. I could feel the heaviness in the air, as if the audience was holding its breath collectively as we all waited for the show to start.

The first number is a narrative that maps Alexander Hamilton's arrival in New York City in the summer of 1776, seeking a meeting with his American idol, Aaron Burr. Each principal male character (John Laurens, Marquis de Lafayette, tailor's apprentice Hercules Mulligan, and Burr) introduces himself by rapping a line of Alexander Hamilton's bio. As they take turns setting up his biography, the actors form a diagonal across the stage, spinning in and out of the light. The movement of this sequence is a nod to R&B choreography, reminiscent of groups like the Temptations and New Edition. The first character to appear in the spotlight is Aaron Burr (played by Leslie Odom, Jr. on Broadway and Akkron Johnson in Chicago). He starts the first number with the same line that opened Lin-Manuel Miranda's performance at the White House. This time, however, the words are sung by a Black man: "How does a bastard, orphan, son of a whore and a Scotsman, dropped in the middle of a forgotten / spot in the Caribbean by Providence impoverished in squalor / grow up to be a hero and a scholar?" Then the second actor, playing the roles of John Laurens and Philip Hamilton (Jamaal Fields Green in Chicago and Anthony Ramos on Broadway), is illuminated on stage as he takes up the second line of the opening number: "The ten-dollar Founding Father without a father / got a lot farther by working a lot harder / by being a lot smarter, by being a self-starter / by fourteen, they placed him in charge of a trading charter."

The third spliced line is rapped by Thomas Jefferson/Marquis de Lafayette (played by Daveed Diggs on Broadway and Paris Nix in Chicago). This line, one of the most powerful in the entire musical, allows us to connect the absent Black and Brown bodies of the past to those of the actors on stage: "And every day while slaves were being slaughtered and carted away across the waves/he struggled and kept his guard up. /Inside he was longing for something to be a part of / the brother was ready to beg steal borrow or barter."[10] As the actors perform, Alexander Hamilton's ghosted body begins to haunt the space through their singing and rapping. The fourth line is given to us by James Madison (played by Okieriete Onadowan on Broadway version and Jamal Fields Green in Chicago): "Then a hurricane came and devastation reigned / our man saw his future drip, dripping down the drain / put a pencil to his temple, connected it to his brain / And he wrote his first refrain, a testament to his pain." Aaron Burr returns to center stage to deliver the last line of the song before the chorus that finally brings Alexander Hamilton from the darkness into the light:

> Well the word got around they said "this kid is insane, man" Took up a collection just to send him to the mainland. "Get your education don't forget from whence you came, and the world is gonna know your name. What's your name, man?"

Then Alexander Hamilton (played by Miguel Cervantes in Chicago and Lin-Manuel Miranda on Broadway) says the now-famous line at the exact moment that a spotlight hits his face: "My name is Alexander Hamilton / And there's a million things I haven't done / But just you wait, just you, wait."[11] At the performances I attended the crowd erupted into applause at the sight of Hamilton dressed in off-white and standing in a stately position.

The light shifts and Hamilton's wife Eliza (played by Phillipa Soo on Broadway and Jamila Sabares-Klemm in Chicago) enters, wearing a beautiful colonial dress, and positions herself behind Hamilton as ensemble members move in modern dance fused with hip-hop choreography to position a chair in which Hamilton sits. Eliza narrates the status of Hamilton's family. He was abandoned by his father, leaving his mother a single parent. She and Alexander became gravely ill when he was ten years old: "When he was ten his father split, full of it, debt-ridden Two years later see Alex and mother bed-ridden, half dead sittin' in their own sick, the scent thick." As the whole company circles around Hamilton and Eliza we hear, "And Alex got better but his mother went quick," and we see an ensemble member gesture to indicate her death. A fast-paced exchange follows between George Washington (played by Christopher Jackson in New York and Tamar Greene in Chicago) and Aaron Burr, tracking Hamilton's transformation from a destitute child into a hardworking student with an ambition to make money and become someone great. Aaron Burr remarks: "Plannin' for the future see him now as he stands on the bow of a ship headed for the new land in New York you can be a new man."

The number ends with the whole company singing in round: "Alexander Hamilton. We are waiting in the wings for you. You could never back down. You never learned to take your time! Oh! Alexander Hamilton When America sings for you will they know what you overcame? Will they know you rewrote the game? They world will never be the

Fig. 14. Lin-Manuel Miranda as Alexander Hamilton in *Hamilton*. Photo courtesy Joan Marcus.

same." Each principal, Mulligan and Lafayette, Laurens, Washington, Eliza (with Angelica and Maria Reynolds), and Burr all take turns highlighting their relationship to Hamilton. The final call comes from Burr: "And me? I'm the damn fool that shot him." The company reprises Hamilton's line "There's a million things I haven't done. But just you wait!" as we close on Burr asking Hamilton one more time, "What's your name man?" To this question, there is only one answer: "Alexander Hamilton!"

Again the audience erupted in applause, and this was just the first song. The first song. *What have I witnessed?* I wondered. *An American masterpiece or a horror story?* I so wanted it to be the former, but my feelings while watching the musical had my emotions and my intellect in a duel.

One wonders if the audience applauds at the moment of Alexander Hamilton's reveal on stage in Act 1 because of Miranda's celebrity or if the applause is for the audacity of a Latino playing Alexander Hamilton? The performance of Black and Brown actors telling the story of Hamilton highlights the ghosting of their stories in American history.

Their collective trauma is mentioned in the opening as the narrative speaks to "slaves [who] were being slaughtered and carted away across the waves . . ." Yet, what it felt like for me, when I saw it on Broadway and in Chicago, was more like a haunted house. I was watching Alexander Hamilton (of course through the bodies of Lin-Manuel Miranda and Miguel Cervantes) tell me, a Black woman who is a descendant of African American, Algerian, European, and Native people, that Hamilton's story is *just like* my ancestors' story. But *Hamilton: An American Musical's* story isn't at all like my story. Or is it? *Hamilton* is a bait-and-switch musical that uses sampling as an act of ghosting which haunts us with our past. It plays unreconciled traumas and experiences back to us so that we can truly see what is missing from American history. The trauma that my family continues to feel as African Americans who journeyed to American by forced and selective migration is nothing like Hamilton's migration journey as a White male emigré of European descent via the Caribbean. The residual systemic inequality produced by and through the constitutional freedoms that Black and Brown people have never been fully afforded. Waiting to be seen and heard as themselves, not by ventriloquizing Hamilton's stories and history, the performers of color in *Hamilton* play the important ghost messages of hip-hop and history's past that ask us to think about what revolution really looks like.

In the next major number of the musical, "Aaron Burr, Sir," we see Miranda use the act of remixing to summon the ghosts of late rappers Tupac Shakur and The Notorious B.I.G., as well as samples from his own musical *In the Heights,* and Rodgers and Hammerstein's musical *South Pacific.*[12] As Hamilton introduces himself to Burr, Burr carries himself like an established rapper, with street smarts and swagger. He is dismissive of Hamilton, finding his pursuit quite amusing. The scene is reminiscent of moments in early 2000s hip-hop films such as *Brown Sugar* (2002), where a young MC approaches an established radio DJ with his mixtape, hoping the DJ will play his record on the radio. Similarly, Miranda writes Alexander Hamilton as a prodigy and stages the meeting outside a saloon-style location. Hamilton shares with Burr how much he has admired him and his capacity to graduate from college early. He works to prove his intellectual prowess by depositing as much information about himself as possible in a few short minutes in a truncated rap styles that volleys between Hamilton and Burr:

BURR: Talk less.
HAMILTON: What?
BURR: Smile more.
HAMILTON: Ha!
BURR: Don't let them know what you against or what you're for.
HAMILTON: You can't be serious.
BURR: You wanna get ahead?
HAMILTON: Yes.
BURR: Fools who run their mouths off wind up dead.[13]

This important exchange between Burr and Hamilton, if read as a Black man speaking to a Latino male colleague, can easily be understood as code for how to play the politics game. Burr, as a Black man, uses the rhetorical strategy of coding the power game in politics, letting Hamilton, ghosted through the body of a Latino male, know that he must be careful of what he says if he wants to advance in the politics game. The game here is vitality. The double meaning produced through this exchange is that living while being a person of color in a White world affords no expectation of protection or privilege. As Burr signals to Hamilton, "Fools who run their mouths wind up dead." This is amplified in the historical climate of the musical, which is contextualized in the anti-Black violence of the present. Living in the "twoness" of Du Bois's double consciousness requires that Black people see themselves through both Black and White perspectives in order to access opportunity or a semblance of protection. This piece of advice could easily be translated in hip-hop turns as "slow your roll" (i.e., "don't tell White people your next move").

Miranda takes creative license here to craft a fictional meeting between Hamilton and Burr. It demonstrates Miranda's desire to establish a hierarchy between Burr's and Hamilton's status as White men, one coming from privilege and the other from a working-class experience. However, it would be much easier to watch White actors play White historical figures. Watching two men of color play White men engaging one another as they speak about the possibilities of revolution and the stakes that may have to be waged challenges the viewers to ask, "What is missing from the history that we think we know?" At this historical moment, 1776, there is no such discussion possible between men of color that does not involve slave revolt in the colonies, yet Miranda conveniently, or purposely, forgets this important fact throughout the entire musical. It contains the ghosts of a Black rebellious past where slaves worked to escape for freedom in the colonies, both a distant past (the Sono Rebellion of 1739, New York City Conspiracy of 1741, and Gabriel's Rebellion of 1800) and a recent past of African American men and women fighting against systemic inequality, racism, and oppression through the creation of hip-hop.

Miranda samples from the work of Tupac Shakur and Biggie Smalls in the third musical number, "My Shot," to narrate the ideals of many African American rappers, who wish that America would open its mind to allow them to live their best life through a "shot" at the American Dream, not a gunshot stemming from police brutality and anti-Black violence. The opaque spot for Miranda here is that his citation intends to pay homage to the lyrical fortitude of Tupac and Biggie, but he only does so by sampling their lyrical flow and form. He does not take up any of the significant content that Biggie Smalls and Tupac present in their discographies. He uses one-line samples to stand in for their larger revolutionary content. Ultimately, his remix of parts from Tupac's "Holler if Ya Hear Me" and Biggie Smalls's "Juicy" is mostly aesthetic references that are filled with White content. As Mulligan, Lafayette, and Laurens form a cipher around a picnic-style table, beatboxing, they begin table rapping to give Hamilton a beat to which to rap. The men call him into the cipher, challenging his abilities:

> **MULLIGAN, LAFAYETTE, LAURENS:** Ooh, who is this kid? What's he gonna do?
>
> **HAMILTON:** I am not throwing away my shot! I am not throwing away my shot! Hey yo' I'm just like my country I'm young, scrappy and hungry, And I am not throwing away my shot! I'm a get a scholarship to King's College I prob'ly shouldn't brag, but dag, I amaze and I astonish. The problem is I got a lot of brains but no polish. I gotta holler to be heard. With every word I drop knowledge.[14]

Here, Miranda not only employs samples of the embodied gestures (table rapping to indicate a drum and beatboxing) and language of hiphop (the use of African American Vernacular English), he also calls on the ghost narrative of Tupac Shakur by remixing the line "I gotta holler to be heard," with the 1993 album of the same title, which was a revolutionary anthem. There is an extra, grim layer added to "My Shot" with the knowledge that both Tupac and Biggie died due to gun violence, as have a disproportionate number of Black and Latino men in the United States.[15] Miranda samples the blackness of the actor playing Burr and his own brownness as a Latino male to render Hamilton and Burr people of color "*like*." Miranda borrows the narratives of Black people seeking freedom during the eighteenth century and grafts those hopes onto both Hamilton and Burr as if they wanted the liberation of Black people. Hamilton asks Burr how he graduated from college so fast. Here Miranda cleverly gives a nod to Hamilton's White privilege, which he also addresses in his book that annotates the songs in *Hamilton*. What Miranda does not mention is that Aaron Burr, Sr. was one of the founders of the university that Burr Jr., later attended—Princeton, one of the most elite Ivy League institutions in the United States.[16]

Alexander Hamilton, as conceived by Miranda and adapted from Chernow's biography, is willing to do what it takes to be a revolutionary, but he finds Aaron Burr's advice confusing. In hip-hop, if you want to be the best, you boldly step forward and make your intentions known. You self-present as if fully prepared to back up your bravado with skills. The remix of hip-hop samples in *Hamilton* occurs as Miranda asks us to believe that Hamilton is just as hungry as a young Latinx or African American aspiring hip-hop artist who wants to present revolutionary music about his hopes and dreams to the world. The exchange between Hamilton and Burr inside the saloon is where we begin to understand why Burr would rather exercise caution in making his beliefs public and why Hamilton is so certain that he has something special. Hamilton and Burr enter the saloon (the entire story takes place in one set that is transformed into different locations by use of moving pieces), where they meet up with abolitionist John Laurens, the Marquis de Lafayette from France, and Hercules Mulligan. Here, audiences who know hip-hop will recognize a cypher form in the saloon, complete with beatboxing, banging beats on tables, and rapping lines. They also will recognize the style of the raps from Laurens, who yells, "Show time! Show time! Yo! I'm John Laurens in the place to be! Two pints of Sam Adams and I'm working on three!" Miranda uses the hip-hop vernacular "show time" and "yo yo" as a shout-out to the b-boys in New York subways who begin their shows with "Show time!" and "I'm in the place to be," which is one of the most famous party-starting rap lines of old school hip-hop. Mulligan vocalizes machine-gun sounds of the type utilized by famous rappers like DMX in this quip: "Brrah Baraaah! I'm Hercules Mulligan up in it, lovin it, yes I heard your mother said 'come again!' Lock up ya' daughters and horses of course. It's hard to have intercourse over four sets of courses."[17] Through these samples from famous cultural references in hip-hop, we hear positive and negative references that link us to early 1980s DJs and MCs. The misogynistic lyrics and the hypermasculine wordplay captured in late 1990s and 2000s hip-hop is also referenced in the lyrical double entendre of "your mother said 'come again!'" and "Lock up ya' daughters and horses."

As Miranda asks the audience to follow the double narrative of American history, the whitewashed history of America and hip-hop, the experiences of self-determination and striving "to be somebody" represented in the narratives of *Hamilton* and African American hip-hop MC styles, he samples African Americans' desire for freedom by using Black bodies and language as the scaffolding for his narrative of Hamilton's journey to "make it" in America. The signature "My Shot," establishes *Hamilton*'s ghosting of blackness through Miranda's use of recognizable rags-to-riches narratives of Black and Latinx hip-hop MCs, which he uses to lend street credibility to Alexander Hamilton's otherwise very White narrative of becoming American. By focusing on Hamilton's immigrant status, stressing his original nationality as generically "Caribbean," Miranda plays on the limited cultural literacy about the racial demographic of the Caribbean and its dominant association in the American racial imaginary with immigrants of African descent. Miranda manipulates hip-hop vernacular language and hip-hop history by sampling from several iconic songs performed by iconic African American rappers who died by gun violence, namely Tupac Shakur and Biggie Smalls, and remixing their narratives with Alexander Hamilton's story, searching for places of overlap. Hamilton confronts his newfound colleagues (or rappers) in the saloon, dropping this verse to establish himself as worthy of Burr's time and his colleagues' support:

I am not throwing away my shot
I am not throwing away my shot
Hey yo, I'm just like my country
I'm young, scrappy and hungry
And I'm not throwing away my shot.
I'm a diamond in the rough, a shiny piece of coal
Tryin' to reach my goal, my power of speech: unimpeachable
Only nineteen, but my mind is older
These New York City streets getting colder, I shoulder
Ev'ry burden, ev'ry disadvantage
I have learned to manage; I don't have a gun to brandish
I walk these streets famished
The plan is to fan this spark into a flame
But damn, it's getting dark so let me spell out my name
I am the
HAMILTON, LAFAYETTE, MULLIGAN, LAURENS:
A-L-E-X-AN-D, ER we are meant to be.[18]

"My Shot" segues into "The Story of Tonight," which unites the rappers/revolutionaries in song as they "raise a glass to freedom," declaring themselves committed to building a republic that guarantees freedom for all. This melancholy number features all men of color singing about their futures. Chillingly, these Black and Latino actors playing White men announce to the audience that their futures are uncertain and that they may never live to see their dreams realized:

HAMILTON:
I may not live to see our glory

LAURENS, MULLIGAN, & LAFAYETTE:
I may not live to see our glory

HAMILTON:
But I will gladly join the fight

LAURENS, MULLIGAN, & LAFAYETTE:
But I will gladly join the fight

HAMILTON:
And when our children tell our story

LAURENS, MULLIGAN, & LAFAYETTE:
And when our children tell our story

HAMILTON:
They'll tell the story of tonight

MULLIGAN:
Let's have another round tonight

LAFAYETTE:
Let's have another round tonight

HAMILTON:
Let's have another round tonight

LAURENS:
Raise a glass to freedom
Something they can never take away
No matter what they tell you
Raise a glass to the four of us

LAURENS AND MULLIGAN:
Tomorrow there'll be more of us

LAURENS, MULLIGAN, & LAFAYETTE:
Telling the story of tonight

A discussion about the pursuit of social and political freedom in American, using actors of color who remain in a perpetual state of unfreedom as a result of systemic inequality and violence, is an ironic frame for *Hamilton.* To contextualize the social climate that surrounded Hamilton's premier, when the musical made its debut on Broadway in 2015, Black men, women, and nonbinary people in America still had no expectation of protection or longevity. The #BlackLivesMatter movement began in 2013 in response to anti-Black violence and the #MeToo movement gained traction in 2015 when White women started using the hashtag created by African American activist Tarana Burke back in 2006. The musical's phenomenon status reflects the state of American race relations in that White audience members are the primary audience who consume the musical's all-inclusive American narrative, yet people of color still fight to stay alive physically, psychologically, and emotionally on a daily basis. Broadway's capacity to continuously produce musicals that situate Black and Brown people in the past or that utilize their cultural products (i.e., their songs, styles of self-adornment, vernacular, gestures, etc.) to color the normative whiteness of Broadway culture is a problematic formula. The actors featured in the Broadway, Chicago, and other touring versions of *Hamilton* play White Americans on the verge of forging a new republic at a time when the ancestors of these performers were fighting for freedom and self-determination. The actors who perform in *Hamilton* are not only haunted by their ancestors who never got to see freedom; they themselves are still susceptible to anti-Black and anti-Brown violence. They only get to realize freedom as perceived through a "lived" experience of whiteness. By ghosting the White body with their Black- and Brown-identified American experiences, the actors symbolize a ghosting of themselves. Singing about their ancestors' haunting pasts in the present, they foreshadow their future social and physical deaths as they highlight that Black and Brown people had no expectation of protection in the past and simultaneously affirm that the only hope they have to receive protection in the present is to play White.

Sisters are Doing it For Themselves—The Schuyler Sisters

In the middle of the first act of the musical we meet the Schuyler sisters, Angelica, Eliza, and Peggy. Using an R&B girl group motif à la Destiny's Child circa 1990s, three beautiful women of color saunter into the saloon to make their presence known, right in time for a group of very drunk men to perhaps be seeking comfort in the arms of beautiful women for extracurricular post-drinking action. Burr begins the introduction of the sisters by setting up more so-called "street credibility" for himself. He

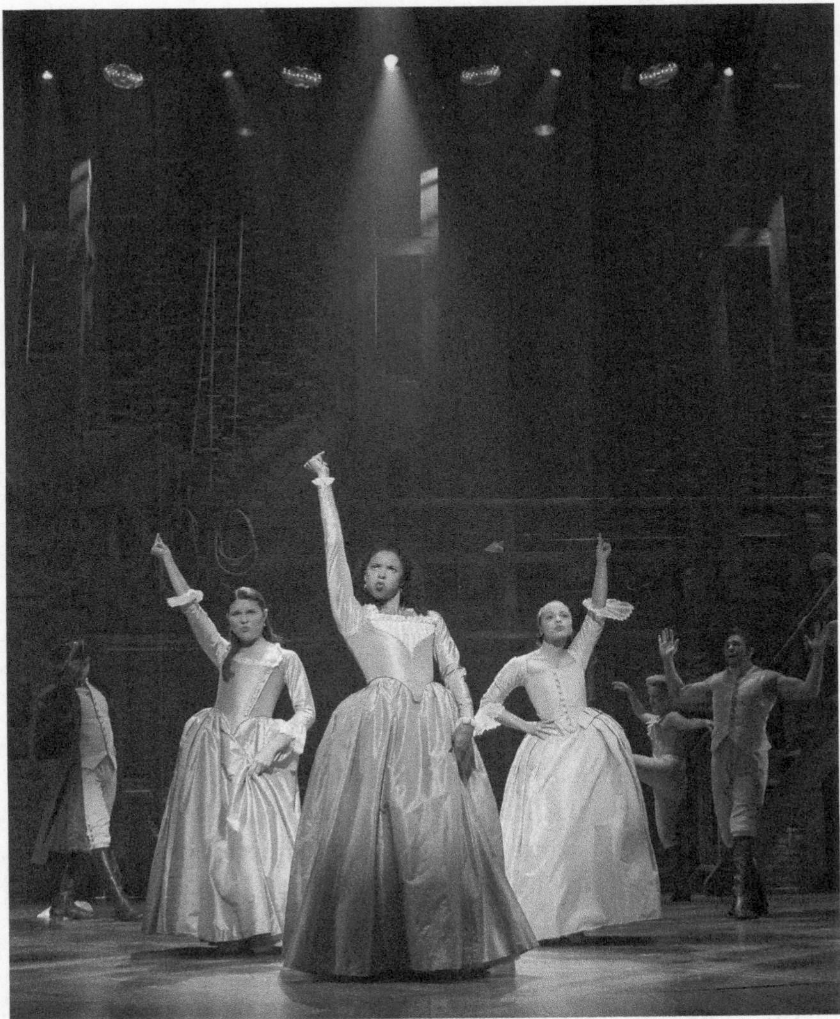

Fig. 15. The Schuyler sisters from *Hamilton*. Photo courtesy Joan Marcus.

disavows his privilege in his performance of a "White" male as he speaks to the wealth of the sisters, whom he views as "slumming it" by hanging out in the saloon with men of lesser status:

BURR:
There's nothing rich folks love more
Than going downtown and slumming it with the poor

> They pull up in their carriages and gawk at the students in the common
> Just to watch 'em talk
> Take Philip Schuyler, the man is loaded
> Uh oh, but little does he know that
> His daughters, Peggy, Angelica, Eliza

In full stereotypical sassy fashion, the women check Burr by lifting their hands in unison to "read" him with their first sung quip, "Work," used in the multiples contexts of Black queer vernacular meaning to "work it" (show what skills you have), or to "work it out" (perform excellently under high expectations), or simply "you better work," a Black queer vernacular directive which means to give something your very best effort:

> COMPANY: Work, work
> ANGELICA: Angelica!
> COMPANY: Work, work
> ELIZA: Eliza!
> PEGGY: And Peggy!
> COMPANY: Work, work

The finger-snapping body cross that the sisters employ with each iteration of "work" marks the Schulyer sisters' bodies as "Black," not White. Each sister is introduced to the audience in her performed and ghostly form. The actresses playing the sisters are Black, Latina, and Asian in the Broadway version and Black and Afro-Latina in the Chicago version. This type of physical and auditory ghosting of Whiteness changes the historical narratives of the White women whom the actresses are there to deliver. Women of color are playing White women. No matter how much mainstream audiences want to pretend they do not see color, it is the color of the women's bodies and the excluded histories that those bodies bring to *Hamilton*'s narrative, that are most intriguing and problematic about the musical. The Schulyer sisters were the wealthy White children of General Philip Schuyler and Catherine "Kitty" Van Rensselear, who were members of prosperous Dutch families in New York. According to Arnold Rogow's biography, *A Fatal Friendship: Alexander Hamilton and Aaron Burr*, Catherine was "a great beauty" who passed down her striking looks to her daughters.[19] The sisters depicted in *Hamilton* are indeed beautiful, hip, savvy women who assert themselves with agency and strong opinions, giving a wink, to paraphrase Suzan-Lori Parks, to the lack of agency held by White women in the eighteenth century and the oppression and subjugation of the Black women who served them. Black performance studies scholar E. Patrick Johnson argues the snap gesture is directly connected to African American queer cultural references and can be read as a Black vernacular form that is often borrowed and dislocated from Black bodies in American popular culture.[20]

Miranda's musical depicts the sisters as abolitionists. Angelica (played by Renée Elise Goldsberry in New York and Nikki Renée Daniels in Chicago), Eliza (played by Phillipa Soo in New York and Jamila Sabares-Klemm in Chicago) and Peggy (played by Jasmine Cephas Jones in New York and Candace Quarrels in Chicago) let the audience know immediately that their characters are confident, full of sass, and appreciative of men who work. History is remixed as the original White, rich, and fragile White women are transformed before our eyes into women of African American, Latina, and Asian descent who have no expectation of protection in American society due to their historically marginalized social positions. This creative license taken by Miranda creates a synthetic historical experience for the audience that suggests the Schuyler sisters crafted an empowered, feminist counter-narrative to the exclusion of women in the forming of the Republic. *Rolling Stone* reporter Mark Binelli argues:

> Songs about Hamilton's complicated love life get more of a Destiny's Child treatment, and the rest of the score is expansive enough to include torchy show tunes, high-camp Brit pop and nods to Hip-hop classics (from "The Message" to "Empire State of Mind" to "Lose Yourself").[21]

Conservative cultural critic and linguist John McWhorter takes great pains to counter critiques of Miranda's sleight of hand when it comes to addressing slavery, race, and ethnicity in the musical. McWhorter contends that slavery is not the foundation upon which all American narratives should be written and that important theatrical elements of the play are dismissed when framed from such a perspective of critical race studies. He offers this meditation on the critiques of *Hamilton*'s treatment of slavery: "To tar any portrait of a historical figure as incomplete without blaring announcement of their failure to pass today's antiracism test is a kind of witch-hunting in the guise of civic discussion."[22] McWhorter's tragic coupling of "tar" and "portrait" deliver a rhetorical case in point as to the ways in which Broadway musicals use blackness to "color" the normative whiteness of most of its shows and narratives. Broadway samples from blackness in choreography, song arrangement, and creative casting choices that present "diversity" sonically and gesturally without the othered body. In the instance below, excerpted from an essay about *Hamilton*'s omission of slavery as a principal storyline, McWhorter argues that conflating all racial and ethnic issues that plague American race relations, including a denial of the attempted genocide of slavery, prevents audiences from recognizing what, in his view, is really great about *Hamilton*. McWhorter takes on critics who critique Miranda's whitewashing of slavery in the musical:

> It is certainly a rather blinkered take on art. The *Hamilton* sequence introducing the Schuyler sisters is one of the most thrilling I have ever seen in the theatre, convincing me immediately that the buzz was apt for a show I was afraid wouldn't live up to its reputation. "Look around, look around," the beautiful actresses sing, trumping the whiteness of the characters they are playing in their multiple hues. Angelica Schuyler, of all people, will now likely forever be spontaneously imagined as an imperiously lovely black woman like Renee Elise Goldsberry, just as a new generation of kids spontaneously imagine America's president as a pensive black man. Dazzling stagecraft and wordplay fill the senses—this is what the theatre is for, something that would have seemed utterly inconceivable when lily-white old chestnuts like *Good News* and *Guys and Dolls* were playing on the same stage at the Richard Rodgers theatre in days of yore. To come away from such an epic happening, this gift from an awesome talent, asking "Where were the slaves?" is less constructive thought than recreational Puritanism.[23]

McWhorter is purposely missing the point. Moreover, his focus on the women in the play as objects of beauty, his fantastical reading of Angelica as an "imperiously lovely black woman," and the way he summarizes Barack Obama's presidency with a reference to "a pensive black man" are dangerous specifically because America's children, across racial and class lines, are not afforded the same educations and already receive a skewed view of history that conveniently leaves out important contributions from non-White Americans. Should the children now imagine that the Founding Fathers were all Black, Latinx, or mixed race? It is irresponsible to present the utopic dream of an America that does not see color without showing them how such a concept is necessary at all. If all Americans were treated equally, we would never have to take note of the racial identities of any American.

McWhorter is not the only scholar who believes that *Hamilton*'s interpretation of female characters and creative casting choices are empowering. Musical theater scholar Jerneja Žlof writes about early feminism in *Hamilton*: "Miranda's female characters seem to be expressing a strong desire to be heard respected and viewed as equal to and by their male counterparts. The beauty of multicultural diversity, the ethnic and racial diversity of the *Hamilton* cast and the celebration of equality, are some of the outstanding attractions of the musical."[24] Žlof reads the Schuyler sisters as imagined by Miranda as pre-feminists of sorts. The sisters are there, back in history, to haunt the past in the present by challenging the gender norms of the colonial period. As Angelica and her sisters talk back to a fictional past in the present, they sample from Black feminist rhetoric and African American vernacular in hip-hop in the same ways that third wave feminists often borrow from Black feminists to address gender inequality without citation of the Black feminist scholars who have created the narratives of intersectionality. In the following excerpt from the Schuyler sisters' number, Aaron Burr tells Angelica and her sisters that women should be treated equally. Neither McWhorter nor Žlof attends to the fact that the Schulyer sisters were not Black nor feminists in real life:

ANGELICA: Burr, you disgust me

BURR:
Ahh, so you've discussed me
I'm a trust fund, baby, you can trust me

ANGELICA:
I've been reading Common Sense by Thomas Paine

So men say that I'm intense or I'm insane
You want a revolution? I want a revelation
So listen to my declaration:

ALL SISTERS:
"We hold these truths to be self-evident
That all men are created equal"

ANGELICA (AND COMPANY):
And when I meet Thomas Jefferson (unh!)
I'mma compel him to include women in the sequel

WOMEN: Work!

Singing and partially rhyming back to Burr ("You want a revolution? I want a revelation / So listen to my declaration"), employing the African American vernacular used in hip-hop ("I'mma" rather than "I am"), Angelica takes on the cadences and content of African American female MCs such as Lauryn Hill or Nicki Minaj to convey that she and her sisters are strong and independent. The goal here is to paint the Schulyer sisters as passionate feminists with the desire to be included in the male-constructed narrative about freedom. However, having women of color sing these lyrics absolutely invokes the ghosts of history's past, as Black women such as Harriet Tubman, Sojourner Truth, Ida B. Wells, and many others fought and died for Black women to be legible as women in emerging feminist narratives. As Black female slaves took care of the homes, children, and sexual desires of slave owners, the pre-feminist narrative of Black women was swallowed by trauma.

The Schulyer sisters' ghosts are embodied by the African American, Latina, and Asian American actresses playing the sisters. Their actresses' bodies, in turn, are occupied by all of the Black women who served the pre-feminist antebellum narrative, whose stories were never told. As the number ends, Hamilton meets Samuel Seabury, a vocal Loyalist, who presents him with a counter-narrative about American revolution that Hamilton rejects in the number "Farmer Refuted Lyrics." Hamilton's sonic delivery specifically works to counter King George's pronounced "King's English" vis-á-vis Hamilton's rapped response, which creates a "Brown"/"White" sonic binary that separates England and America, with Miranda's Latino Hamilton representing the United States of the past.

A message then arrives from King George III (performed by Jonathan Groff in New York and Andrew Call in Chicago), reminding the colonists that their desire to become revolutionaries is ill-advised. In the song "You'll Be Back," we are introduced to the colonial mindset without any Black or Brown vernacular buttressing for the first time in the music outside of "Farmer." King George reminds the aspiring revolutionaries, as they are presented by Miranda, to mind their place, and that their desire for freedom cannot even be imagined outside of their relationship to England, colonialism, and whiteness:

> You'll be back
> Soon you'll see
> You'll remember you belong to me
> You'll be back
> Time will tell
> You'll remember that I served you well
> Oceans rise, empires fall
> We have seen each other through it all
> And when push comes to shove,
> I will send a fully armed battalion to remind you of my love

According to King George, Hamilton and his friends are vulnerable because their idea of freedom is an illusion, in the sense that the very idea of it is indebted to colonialism. As the act moves to its end Hamilton, Burr, and their friends join the Continental Army. As the army retreats from New York City, George Washington—not yet president but on the path from general of the army—is introduced though the number "Right Hand Man." Washington (played by Christopher Jackson in New York and Jonathan Kirkland in Chicago) realizes that Hamilton's ambition and naiveté about war and revolution might be the perfect combination to help him win the war. Although Washington wonders why no other group has employed Hamilton, he offers him the role of aide-de-camp and gives his friends positions in the army. Then he chronicles his expectations in "Right Hand Man," arguing that he needs brave soldiers to fight for the country.

"Right Hand Man" is significant because Miranda employs hip-hop DJ techniques to remix parts of the numbers from Act 1 with samples from *In the Heights*. With George Washington's reference to "thirty-two thousand troops in New York Harbor," Miranda samples from his own work. In an interview for Genius, an online database that annotates rap lyrics and other musical lyrics, Miranda notes that he repeats "thirty-two thousand" three times in "Right Hand Man." Thirty-two thousand times three adds up to 96,000, which is the exact number and name of one of the songs in *In the Heights*.[25]

The remaining numbers of Act 1 follow this pattern, offering sonic refrains from previous numbers in Act 1 that are reworked live on stage, using the actors' voices to serve as sampling and scratching devices. The act wraps up with the men attending a ball given by Philip Schuyler. It is at this ball that Hamilton falls in love at first sight with Eliza. Here, Burr tells us that Hamilton's privilege and personality have allowed him to forge ahead in social stature and opportunities with women. As a Brown-skinned man, Miranda is commenting on skin privilege and the colorism that exists both interracially and intraracially in Black and Latinx communities. Burr asserts in "A Winter's Ball":

> How does the bastard, orphan, son of a whore
> Go on and on
> Grow into more of a phenomenon?
> Watch this obnoxious, arrogant, loudmouth bother
> Be seated at the right hand of the father

Remixing the content from his opening lyrics in "My Shot," Burr warns the audience that Hamilton is obnoxious, and guides his listeners to track his envy of Hamilton's rise to the top. He talks of all the beautiful women at the ball ("so many to deflower") and compares himself to Hamilton in looks, stature, and ability. He foreshadows Hamilton's potential fortune should he be lucky enough to marry one of the Schuyler sisters.

Hamilton sets his eyes on Eliza, who falls for him after being introduced by Angelica. Angelica is also attracted to Hamilton but suppresses her feelings after she sees her sister's interest. Eliza and Hamilton are quickly married, chronicled in the number "Helpless." Still, Angelica admits her feelings for Hamilton in the number "Satisfied," which sets up dramatic tension and a love triangle involving the two sisters and Hamilton. Angelica, singing in a 1990s R&B style vocal complete with autotune-style female vocals underscored by sassy raps, sees Hamilton as "a bit of a flirt" with whom she had several "moments" before Eliza fell for him. Angelica tells the audience that she has to keep her eyes on the prize and marry someone who can help raise the Schuyler family's status, breaking down two main points. Point one is important; Angelica realizes her affection for Hamilton will remain unrequited and that if he marries her sister at least he will remain in her life:

> He's after me cuz I'm a Schuyler sister. That elevates his status, I'd have to be naïve to set that aside, maybe that is why I introduce him to Eliza, now that's his bride.
>
> Nice going, Angelica, he was right, you will never be satisfied.[26]

Point two is the romantic tension between Hamilton and Angelica, which works as an unreconciled B-side to the Hamilton mixtape. Angelica's fate is her fate. The act fast-forwards to cover Hamilton and Eliza's marriage, which is celebrated drunkenly by Laurens, Lafayette, and Mulligan. When Burr arrives to offer congratulations, Laurens teases him, and Burr admits in "The Story of Tonight (Reprise)" that he is having an affair with Theodosia Bartow Prevost. The opening of the song describes his love for Theodosia. This narrative shifts away from Burr's individual needs and he talks about why waiting is worth it when you have something to fight for. Sung in a pop ballad style remixed with a gospel tinge, Burr's lyrics speak to the ghosted experiences of Black slaves whose hopes and dreams were dashed by violence and dehumanization. The gospel refrains of the song, sung by a Black and Brown chorus, haunts the space as Burr asks the audience to "wait for it":

BURR/ENSEMBLE
Death doesn't discriminate
        Between the sinners and the saints,
        it takes and it takes and it takes

and we keep living anyway.
We rise and we fall
and we break
and we make our mistakes.
And if there's a reason I'm still alive
when everyone who loves me has died
I'm willing to wait for it.
I'm willing to wait for it.
Wait for it.

"It," for Burr, is the love and freedom promised by the revolution. Watching Leslie Odom, Jr. and Akkron Johnson sing the hopes of Aaron Burr presented traumatic feelings for me as an audience member. I wanted Burr's song to be about a Black man's quest for Black love and freedom, for which many slaves risked their lives during the Revolutionary and Civil Wars. However, the song's meaning is much more trivial; it chronicles a budding romance with Theodosia Hamilton.

The romance between Burr and Theodosia results in their marriage and first child, aptly named after her mother and sung to adoringly in the number "Dear Theodosia," in which Hamilton urges Burr to make the relationship public. Burr, however, prefers to wait and see what life has in store for him rather than take any drastic measures, as narrated in the number "Wait for It" as the company and Burr sing the double entendre embedded in every song of *Hamilton*:

COMPANY (at the same time)
I'm willing to wait for it.
Wait for it
Wait for . . .
I'm willing to-
Life doesn't discriminate
between the sinners and the saints
it takes and it takes and it takes
and we keep living anyway,
we rise and we fall and we break
and we make our mistakes
and if there's a reason

I'm still alive
when so many have died,
then I'm willing' to-

BURR
Wait for it . . . (Hamilton, "Wait for it Lyrics," 2019)

Act 1 ends with more revelations about Hamilton's character. He is pushy, "scrappy" by his own admission. His forthright approach is Miranda's attempt to capture some of the White privilege of a character such as Hamilton. However, Hamilton's narrative is altered when played by a Latino male and thus draws attention to the revolution's connection to Latinx and Hispanic roles in the struggle for freedom. The audience can't help but wonder what results such canvassing and self-advocacy would have produced for a person of Spanish descent at the time. The conflation of Spanish Europeans and Latinxs is still fraught territory in U.S. articulations of Latinxness. Many argue that Spanish people are uniquely from Spain and not Latinx. Other critics argue that Spanish-speaking people, across racial lines, are united under the term Latinx. According to journalist Tony Castroof in *La Opinion*, Latino Hispanic noblemen were integral players in helping the colonial army win independence from Britain in the American Revolution[27]

The Latino males playing Hamilton—their voices, mannerisms, and physical bodies—speak for the many Latinx men and women who have died serving America as patriots, built the country as civil and physical servants, and continue to be threatened by anti-Latinx and anti-Hispanic violence (particularly anti-Hispanic violence that occurs due to the conflation of Latinx and Hispanic peoples) that seeks to keep their bodies away from American borders inside and outside of the United States. The ghosts of Latin- and Hispanic-identified men who contributed to Hamilton's success provide important disruptions in the sanitized narratives of American history presented in the musical. One important military figure during this time was General Bernardo De Galvez. De Galvez, who was born in Spain, was the Latino governor of the Louisiana territory during the American Revolution. His story haunts this production, as he played a major role in assisting General George Washington in fighting British soldiers who were advancing into the southwestern

part of the United States, including providing weapons and food to the Continental Army between 1775 and 1777. Equally present as ghosts in this production are the militia of Native Americans, freed African Americans, and Spanish soldiers de Galvez[28] organized after Spain officially declared war on Great Britain in 1779.[29]

Washington refuses Hamilton's petition to promote him instead of Charles Lee, whom Washington ultimately chooses as his representative for the Continental Congress. Lee orders a retreat against Washington's orders, which prompts the commander to remove him from command in favor of Lafayette. Disgruntled, Lee spreads slanderous and vindictive rumors about Washington as chronicled in the number "Stay Alive." Hamilton is offended on Washington's behalf, but Washington orders him to ignore the comments. Hamilton does not wish to do so, but cannot disobey a direct order; instead, Laurens duels Lee, with Hamilton as his second and Burr as Lee's second. Laurens is satisfied after he injures Lee. Lee breaks down his position to Hamilton in a Biggie Smalls inspired song, "Ten Duel Commandments." Hamilton returns home to Eliza in "Meet Me Inside," and learns that she is pregnant. She tells Hamilton that his family has everything they need to live a happy life in "That Would be Enough."

The remaining numbers of the play follow Hamilton's journey, including the British surrender at the battle of Yorktown, the births of his son Philip and Burr's daughter Theodosia, and Laurens's death in the Battle of the Combahee River, which segues to the song "Tomorrow There'll Be More of Us." Hamilton and Burr both return to New York to finish their law studies, and in 1787, Hamilton becomes a delegate to the Constitutional Convention. President-elect Washington selects Hamilton as Treasury Secretary, despite Eliza's dismay. In "Non-Stop," Angelica announces that she is going to marry and move to London.

It's a Different World[30]

Miranda tells Hamilton's American story differently than we've ever heard it. Tracking through the first act of the musical allows me to show the reader where the ghosts in the musical are standing, how the samples operate, and the ways in which Miranda remixes American history before our eyes to challenge our visual and sonic consciousness. The varying acts of ghosting history and the haunting of untold traumas that are present on the bodies of the Black and Brown actors allow the audience to hear and see those lost stories and haunting presences in the sonic and visual gaps of the musical. Miranda codes his musical for multiple audiences. For White and non-White audiences who adhere to a mainstream telling of American history that underplays racial subjugation, institutional inequity, and slavery, Chernow's biography serves an appropriate foundation of whiteness upon which American history narratives should be constructed. Miranda, who is appealing to his mainstream Broadway audience while trying to maintain some semblance of street credibility with hip-hop communities, works to subvert these so-called foundational narratives by using a remixed version of history that places Black and Brown bodies in conversation with a whitewashed history that continues to deny slavery, violence, anti-immigrant narratives, sexual assault, and other atrocities that are part of the U.S. history of nation building. For U.S.-born African, Latinx, Asian, Native, and other Indigenous people who grew up with hip-hop, *Hamilton* acknowledges the use of oppressed labor in the making of American history in its silence of story, but presence of bodies. The irony of audiences clamoring to see African American, Latinx, and other historically underrepresented "minorities" playing Alexander Hamilton, the Founding Fathers, and the Schulyer sisters in various tours around the United States speaks to America's racial blindness when it comes to the consumption of hip-hop as an African American and Latinx cultural product that is packaged through whiteness, as well as the tone deafness when it comes to reconciling the trauma of slavery in America's present.

Miranda's use of the "people's music," i.e., hip-hop, and its physical and spoken codes, performatively subverts Alexander Hamilton's whiteness. This aspect of Miranda's sampling of hip-hop and use of its mechanics to speak a subtext within the musical is important and links the production to African American cultural practices that are embedded in hip-hop. Throughout the time of the Underground Railroad, African Americans communicated in code while speaking English in order to relay valuable information about freedom to other oppressed Black people and to abolitionist allies. The use of hip-hop language and gestures operates in *Hamilton* in many ways that are similar to the underground freedom currencies of African American slaves. As Edward Delman of the *Atlantic* points out, theater has long served as a tool to teach the masses about history:

> Perhaps the most significant lesson the show might teach audiences, and one that has particular relevance today, is the outsized role immigrants have played in the nation's history. Alexander Hamilton was an immigrant—a fact that Miranda repeatedly emphasizes throughout the show—and the musical also prominently features the Marquis de Lafayette, a French nobleman who played a crucial role during the revolutionary war.[31]

What Delman does not discuss here is the tone of racial neutrality that is used to market the musical and the ways in which such rhetoric renders immigrants as race neutral. Miranda plays on the "we are all immigrants" narrative in an attempt to undermine the metanarrative immigration debate in the United States that criminalizes Latinx and other immigrants from the so-called "shit hole" and "terrorist" nations (terms used by the forty-fifth American president, Donald Trump) listed in Executive Order 13769, whose plights and stories are invisible and inaudible in American politics.[32] What Miranda does show us, perhaps unintentionally, is that the dominant culture is constantly sampling and remixing the racial and cultural samples it finds most attractive and entertaining. The biggest racial immigration scandals that have ever threatened the democracy and freedom narratives in the United States are slavery and Native removal. They have resulted in the pain and suffering of diverse undocumented people in the United States, as well as the descendants of slaves and Native people who live in a perpetual state of anti-blackness and anti-Nativeness. Miranda suppresses such ghost narratives in *Hamilton*'s musical content, yet the bodies of the actors tell their story over the beat of Hamilton's generic life. Miranda makes Hamilton's life seem more exciting and aspirational by conflating it with the "cool" of hip-hop. But is it . . . cool? By using ghost stories of hip-hop MCs, by borrowing rap styles to play a revisionist American history that uses the bodies of minorities as reminders of what has not been said about American history, what does *Hamilton* really say about freedom and those who live in America still wishing they were free? Is there hope, or simply a series of ghosts whose stories never get told? The Black and Brown actors who have gained fame and some small part of the billion-dollar fortune that *Hamilton* has generated can't tell their ancestors' stories in full voice because society has convinced all of us that the stories of the oppressed don't sell on Broadway.

The Shadow and the Act

The December 6, 1949 issue of *The Reporter* carried a piece by Ralph Ellison entitled "The Shadow and the Act," a prolific critique of several mainstream Hollywood films circulating negative Black mythologies for mainstream audience consumption. Ellison reviewed four films: *Intruder in the Dust* (based on the novel of the same name by William Faulkner), *Pinky*, *Los Boundaries*, and *Home of the Brave*. Ellison discusses the ways in which these films work to disrupt D. W. Griffith's 1915 film *Birth of Nation,* which he argues was responsible for creating and circulating dehumanizing mythologies of the Negro:

> Usually, the *Birth of a Nation* is discussed in terms of its contributions to cinema technique, but, as with every other technical advance since the oceanic sailing ship, it became a further instrument in the dehumanization of the Negro. And while few films have gone so far in projecting Negroes in a malignant light, few before the 1940's showed any concern with depicting their humanity. Just the opposite. In the struggle against Negro freedom, motion pictures have been one of the strongest instruments for justifying some white Americans' anti-Negro attitudes and practices. Thus the South, through D. W. Griffith's genius, captured the enormous myth-making potential of the film form almost from the beginning. While the Negro stereotypes by no means made all white men Klansmen, the cinema did, to the extent that audiences accepted its image of Negroes, make them participants in the South's racial ritual of keeping the Negro "in his place."[33]

Ellison addresses the ways in which Black actors in White films of the period found agency in subverting the stereotypical roles perpetuated by *Birth of a Nation* in their interpretations of Black life as written by

White artists. In Griffith's film, Black actors and White actors in blackface perpetuated negative Black mythologies that persist in the racial imaginary of the United States today.

As the crux of Ellison's essay, he uses Faulkner's narrative in *Intruder in the Dust* to mark what Ellison perceived as a turn in the national recognition of Black men as a threat to White male virility and White female fragility. The main character in *Intruder in the Dust* is Lucas Beauchamp, a Black southern farmer who is self-determined within a racist society that views him as less than human. A White male named Chick falls into an icy stream and almost drowns. Lucas rescues him and lets him warm in his cabin. Chick cannot take having a "debt" to a "nigger" and continues to try to pay him for his efforts, much to Lucas's chagrin. Lucas stands his ground and makes his own choice as to whether to accept or reject payment from the White man, asserting a new authority that allows him to subvert the normative perception of Blacks as service-givers without dignity. Ellison observes:

> In the end we see Chick recognizing Lucas as the representative of those virtues of courage, pride, independence, and patience that are usually attributed only to white men—and, in his uncle's words, accepting the Negro as "the keeper of our [the whites'] consciences."[34]

Ellison draws our attention to what he calls "the shadow and the act," addressing the ways that Hollywood masks its desire to teach Black people and other minorities their "place" while still self-presenting as supporting racial equality:

> In the beginning was not the shadow, but the act, and the province of Hollywood is not action, but illusion. Actually, the anti-Negro images of the films were (and are) acceptable because of the existence throughout the United States of an audience obsessed with an inner psychological need to view Negroes as less than men.[35]

Ellison's observations about Hollywood's manipulation of Black stereotypes in film propaganda is important to understanding some of the ways that Miranda uses hip-hop and the casting of actors of color as a way to disrupt the same type of myth-making that happens on Broadway. Act 2 of Hamilton has twenty-three songs (there are forty-six total in the musical), which span the return of Thomas Jefferson to the United States from France to Alexander Hamilton's untimely death. Particular songs in Act 2 reveal the ghosts in Hamilton's biographical narrative that perpetuate a power dynamic that reinscribes racial hierarchies. Miranda uses the entertaining novelties of hip-hop's fundamental elements, such as DJing and remixing, to make the work theatrically "fresh" for a predominantly White audience that probably has surface-level knowledge of hip-hop.

For those audience members who do not speak hip-hop, rapping, as a form of self-articulation, allows Miranda to explore a complexity and density of references that give him the license to make direct links between the past and present of the unreconciled Black histories that are mapped onto Hamilton's narrative. The first scene begins in darkness as the words "Seventeen . . ." "seventeen . . ." "s-s-s-seventeen seventy-nine" cut through blackness as if a DJ were scratching human voices like records before the audience. We hear a remixed refrain from the first number of Act I, "Alexander Hamilton," sung/rapped by Aaron Burr. Enter Thomas Jefferson, who has returned from France. Jefferson saunters down a long staircase on casters situated stage right, singing in a jazzy scat vocal style and wearing a deep purple silk and velvet jacket and White ruffled blouse reminiscent of the late R&B and soul artist Prince. He makes his way to center stage, where he meets a cast of sultry backup dancers, all performers of color dressed in eighteenth-century silhouettes. Using older American music forms that derive from Black popular music such as jazz and the blues to support Jefferson's musical numbers, Miranda remixes samples of genres that were often subsumed under the label of "race" music in the early twentieth century to make a distinction between old and new in the present.

In portraying Thomas Jefferson, Miranda had an opportunity to address the violence of Jefferson's relationship with his slave Sally Hemmings, which has been written about extensively by both historians and fiction writers.[36] Some romanticize the relationship between Jefferson and Hemmings as a reciprocal love affair. Others discuss it as representative of the perpetual sexual violence experienced by many slaves at the hands of their masters. Miranda's writing in Jefferson's number, "What'd I Miss," highlights the ghosting of racism that Miranda refuses to acknowledge in his overall treatment of the Founding Fathers, and is tone deaf in his treatment of Jefferson's relationship with Hemmings (played by a member of the ensemble in a quick run-on):

JEFFERSON

There's a letter on my desk from the President
Haven't even put my bags down yet
Sally be a lamb, darlin', won'tcha open it?
It says the President's assembling a cabinet
And that I am to be the Secretary of State, great!
And that I'm already Senate-approved . . .
I just got home and now I'm headed up to New York

Jefferson's and Hemmings's relationship and the way that it represents the violence experienced between Black women and slave masters is reduced to a one-line quip. Miranda writes Jefferson as an arrogant Founding Father who underscores Hemmings's purportedly subservient role in Monticello. Hemmings is one of a few roles in the entire musical played by a Black female actress who is playing a Black historical female character. Miranda could have used this opportunity to allow Hemmings some agency, but the opportunity is lost and her story is absorbed by the ghost of Jefferson that is represented to the audience by a Black actor. No matter how much the Black version of Jefferson attempts to absorb the historical trauma of the man's relationship to Hemmings, the history is in the silence of what is not being said.

Several other numbers in Act 2 demonstrate the verbal dexterity that Hamilton gleans from hip-hop. Since hip-hop's inception in the 1970s, MCs who can freestyle are regarded more highly than those who cannot do this difficult task. Miranda is an accomplished lyricist and rapper, so he is able to endow Hamilton with skills that the historical figure never had, as well as the braggadocio that is important for hip-hop MCs to convey to audiences to let them know they are master wordsmiths. In a hip-hop battle sequence number entitled "Cabinet Battle #1," Secretary Hamilton and Secretary Jefferson are in a rap battle/debate, moderated by George Washington, about the merits of establishing a national bank. Washington introduces each man to the audience, breaking the fourth wall and inviting them to witness a cabinet meeting with this familiar crowd chat phrase borrowed from R&B and hip-hop artists: "Ladies and gentlemen, you coulda been anywhere in the world tonight. But you're here with us in New York City. Are you ready for a cabinet meeting?" In the cipher, ensemble members pivot from Washington on each side, sitting in chairs that surround the two MCs. Madison, on the side of Jefferson, stands as hype man for Jefferson. In Jefferson's first blow to Hamilton, he raps:

> Life, liberty and the pursuit of happiness
> We fought for these ideals we shouldn't settle for less
> These are wise words, enterprising men quote 'em
> Don't act surprised, you guys, 'cause I wrote 'em (ow)
> But Hamilton forgets
> His plan would have the government assume state's debts
> Now, place your bets as to who that benefits
> The very seat of government where Hamilton sits
> Oh, if the shoe fits, wear it
> If New York's in debt why should Virginia bear it?
> Uh, our debts are paid, I'm afraid
> Don't tax the South 'cause we got it made in the shade
> In Virginia, we plant seeds in the ground
> We create, you just wanna move our money around
> This financial plan is an outrageous demand
> And it's too many damn pages for any man to understand
> Stand with me in the land of the free and pray to God we never see
> Hamilton's candidacy.[37]

Jefferson's words ignore the trauma and magnitude of slavery completely. With lines such as "In Virginia, we plant seeds in the ground / We create, you just wanna move our money around" there is little consideration for a Black actor playing a White male slave owner who not only sold slaves but also forced them, as working property, to "plant seeds in the ground." For me, this was a breaking point in the musical. I felt traumatized by watching a wonderfully talented Black man speak words which completely trivialized the history of his—and my—ancestors' oppression.

Hamilton's response to Jefferson is telling. Miranda doesn't claim ignorance about slavery; rather, there is a lack of sensitivity in his construction of these two numbers. Hamilton's response is a rhetorical move that absolves him from any complicit behavior in slavery:

Thomas, that was a real nice declaration
Welcome to the present, we're running a real nation
Would you like to join us, or stay mellow
Doin' whatever the hell it is you do in Monticello?
If we assume the debts, the union gets new line of credit, a financial
diuretic
How do you not get it, if we're aggressive and competitive
The union gets a boost, you'd rather give it a sedative?
A civics lesson from a slaver, hey neighbor
Your debts are paid 'cause you don't pay for labor
We plant seeds in the South. We create. Yeah, keep ranting
We know who's really doing the planting.[38]

Hamilton challenges Jefferson's motivation for creating a national bank by taking him to task for being a slaver. In his lines "Doin' whatever the hell it is you do in Monticello?" and "A civics lesson from a slaver, hey neighbor / Your debts are paid 'cause you don't pay for labor," Miranda's point of view is remixed with that of Hamilton in a way that makes the truth very murky. In highlighting Jefferson's role in slavery, Miranda rhetorically, and perhaps subconsciously, reveals the labor of the Black people who haunt the entire production. What Miranda does not take into consideration in any of his commentary surrounding this production is the residual trauma of Black actors playing the roles of White men who were directly tied to the enslavement of their (the actors') ancestors. There is no real act of subversion here because the slave masters' voices trump the presence of the actors' bodies. As an audience member of African American descent who loves hip-hop, I wanted Miranda to do more with this moment to expose the atrocities of slavery and to give Sally Hemmings's ghost the voice she deserves. But that never happened.

Staying Alive[39]

I think the most challenging point for me as an audience member of *Hamilton* was that, as a Black woman, I could not get beyond my own desire to see these amazing performers of color talking about their own freedom pursuits and quests to stay alive that were embedded in the narratives of the Founding Fathers' stories. This musical's vitality is produced through the ghosted counter-histories that the actors of color and the samples of blackness expressed in Black dance forms, from the lindy hop and the Charleston to more contemporary modern, jazz, and hip-hop moves remixed to comprise the musical's gestural landscape. American expressions of blackness and its Latinx fusions in hip-hop are connected to *Hamilton*'s narratives, and it feels exploitative. *Hamilton*'s score is built by the labor of Black and Brown people. I will not annotate each song in Act 2; I will skip around the narrative to highlight songs and performances in the musical where ghost narratives, in the varying usages of the term, are most visceral. In "Take a Break," the third number in Act 2, Hamilton's son Philip shares a rap he has been working on. He is accompanied by his mother, Eliza, who beatboxes a track for him to deliver his rudimentary raps. In this moment Miranda winks at the idea of classical music being reserved for White composers while hip-hop music, an original American music genre, is never revered in the same way.

Fast forward through establishing numbers in the musical such as "Say No to This," where we learn that Hamilton is an adulterer and has an affair with Maria Reynolds, only to be blackmailed by Maria's husband James Reynolds, to "The Room Where it Happens," where Hamilton's tensions with Burr rise as Hamilton discusses his financial plan with Jefferson and Madison, which results in the Compromise of 1790, giving support to Hamilton's plan in exchange for moving the United States capital from New York to Washington, D.C. Burr switches political parties and defeats Eliza's father, Philip Schuyler, in a race for Schuyler's seat in the Senate. This creates a terrible tension between Burr and Hamilton which is played out in the number "Schuyler Defeated."

We skim through to "Cabinet Battle #2," in which Jefferson and Hamilton rap battle it out over the United States' role in France's conflict with Britain. After the battle Madison, Jefferson, and Burr plot to take down Hamilton's squeaky-clean image in "Washington on Your Side," in which they share their envy of Washington's perennial support of Hamilton's policies. One particular lyric sung and rapped by Jefferson is quite telling:

I'm in the cabinet. I am complicit in
Watching him grabbing at power and kiss it
If Washington isn't gon' listen
To disciplined dissidents, this is the difference
This kid is out![40]

Daveed Diggs and Paris Nix are the Black actors who play the Lafayette/Jefferson role. We get to hear these amazingly talented men say "disciplined dissidents," basically mocking their own history. Miranda lends Jefferson the language of hip-hop to express his discontent and to label himself a dissident as the actors who play him must grapple with their ancestral lineage, being descendants of actual dissidents, slaves, who fought for freedom and spent their lifetimes in bondage to Jefferson before the end of the Civil War. For those audience members of color and White allies who are waiting for a musical or a play to actually address the injustice of slavery, it is very difficult to throw out the baby with the bathwater with *Hamilton* because it employs so many actors of color and is written by a Latinx writer. However, how can we uplift the amazing actors of color who performed in the original Broadway production and the national tour without making some noise about the fictions *Hamilton* perpetuates about the Founding Fathers and their relationship to what performance studies scholar Donatella Galella calls "nationalist neoliberal multicultural inclusion" that leverages the multiracial histories of Americans of color to undermine the gravity of crimes against people of color in the United States? Galella argues that much of *Hamilton*'s bipartisan work to play down race is a device that works to unite conservatives and liberals, Democrats and Republicans, in order to paint a multiracial utopic landscape:[41]

> In other words, Miranda and the musical occupy a centrist position that mobilizes performers of color and the myth of meritocracy in order to extol and envision the United States as a multiracial utopia where everyone has a fair chance to compete for access to "The Room Where It Happens," as the title of Aaron Burr's show stopping number has it. In the Obama era, people of color took center stage when they paradoxically adopted the roles of "great" white men and downplayed the salience of race and racism. They celebrated entrepreneurialism and embodied the exceptional. And then their

> exceptionalism became proof of the American Dream—how barriers could be overcome, how racial difference no longer mattered.[42]

As we visually and sonically take in *Hamilton*, our orientation to race, in an American context, is remixed through the casting. Miranda's sonic and visual cues direct the audience away from the racism and sexism that underscore inequalities embedded in the structure of the nation created by the Founding Fathers. The artists of colors' bodies remind the audience that their untold narratives are in direct conversation with the Founding Fathers' stories; however, racism and sexism are structured in the play as "ghost." In its vernacular usage in hip-hop, here ghost signifies the act of not being present, not available, not interested, and no longer reachable. There is no mention of racism in the musical, and there is limited reference to sexism. The utopic presentation of Black, Latinx, Asian, and mixed-race performers playing "White" while White performers only play the White English characters of King George and Samuel Seabury renders racism and sexism as unpatriotic fictions that have nothing to do with *Hamilton*'s "scrappy and hungry" early draft of American Dream narratives that would later be advanced by Horatio Alger in his serial "rags to riches" novels of the early twentieth century. By making all but two characters persons of color, an integrationist narrative is employed to invoke a remix of how we understand race in the show. All of the actors of color are "White." We are asked to ignore their bodies, and their histories are rendered ghost stories, incredible and highly unlikely. Hip-hop vernacular and other African American music remixed with Broadway show tunes, popular television references, and other pop culture bites, are associated with the existing words of the Founding Fathers to present a utopian ideal of America. The White characters played by White actors, Sam Seabury and King George, possess the core ideals that need to be revised to make such a utopic country. The patriotism or moral integrity are always presented as aspirational.

Further on in Act 2, we also find that women are asked to travel backwards in time. Few numbers include the voices of the female cast members. No matter how much the bodies of the women of color and their vocal delivery styles clearly indicate samples from jazz, hip-hop, and R&B music, Sally Hemmings is the only Black woman mentioned in the musical. The language of the women in the songs is decidedly standard American English, and when the women do rap they rap as "White" women who are tragically trying to be hip. Eliza's story contains no strong feminist narrative at all. The number "Burn" is a melancholy song in which Eliza appears on stage alone with a stack of letters written by the unfaithful Hamilton, in which he confesses his love for her despite all of his transgressions.

Philippa Soo is the Asian American actress who performed the part of Eliza in the Broadway version of the musical. The strongest part of this number is the conversation that Soo's White-passing Asian body is having with mainstream Broadway politics of representation. Performance studies theorist Peggy Phelan notes that reducing racial identification to phenotype forecloses the opportunity to read the multiplicity of factors that mark racial and ethnic belonging. In her discussion of African American experiences of blackness, however, Phelan notes, "the 'visibility' of Black skin is not and cannot be, an accurate barometer or identifying a community of different political, economic, sexual, and artistic interests."[43] Phelan's inference here of the multiplicity of Black identities that are composed of an intersectional configuration of class, gender, sexual identification, ability, etc., is well taken, but Black skin, similar to Asian skin, has varying degrees of visibility and threat attached to it that is not discussed. A lighter-skinned Black or Asian body has more privilege and capacity that are often untraceable for the White purview. To some White audience members many light-skinned Black and Asian actors of varying gender identification are perceived as "White" and thus ghost the audience completely.

The variances of intersectional combinations of blackness or Asianness affect fields of representation differently depending on the intra- or interracial scenario in which they are viewed or heard. Soo, representing a person of color in *Hamilton* and a White woman in the role that she plays simultaneously, is amongst an emerging group of Asian American performers in lead roles in Broadway musicals, including Diane Huey (*Little Mermaid*), Eve Noblezada (*Miss Saigon*), and Ali Ewoldt (*Phantom of the Opera*), whose bodies and racial identifications are remixed with the whiteness of the roles that they play. The roles from the plays listed here (*Little Mermaid, Phantom*) were written for White women by White men who assume that a "universal" character is always already

White. The exception is *Miss Saigon,* in which White men from France (Claude-Michel Schönberg and Jacques Boubili) write the Asian characters from their perspectives of what a Vietnamese character might be. The visibility of Asianness varies beyond the body being read as "Asian," based on who is in the audience. Different communities have different degrees of fluency to be able to hear and see select moments in which an actor may emphasize her otherness within the confines of the whiteness of the role.[44]

According to the Broadway League, the average Broadway ticket buyer has seen five Broadway shows in the past twelve months, has a median income of over two hundred thousand dollars, and is a White female whose median age is just over forty years old. The actresses in *Hamilton* are all light-skinned minorities, which makes racial translations easier for the predominantly White, female, fortysomething audiences of Broadway to see themselves in the narratives of the Schuyler sisters, despite the fact that the actresses playing them are women of color.[45] The sampling of Asian women's phenotype to physicalize and voice the experiences of White women is not a solution for Broadway's thirst for diversity. I cannot deny that playing Eliza probably did a great deal for Philippa Soo's amazing career. However, her body and the bodies of the actress I saw in Chicago (Alysha Deslorieux) and the seemingly interchangeable actresses of color who have played Eliza, Angelica, and Peggy Schuyler are always in conversation with the stories of the White women and men who did not see them or their stories as valuable contributions to the early making of America. One must ask Miranda if his strategy to sample and remix the untold cultural experiences of these actors' contemporary narratives with the historic narratives of these men and women only advances a neoliberal cultural agenda that asks us all to pretend that now is the only time that matters.

Hamilton's Ghost: Ishmael Reed's Critical Response to *Hamilton*

On August 21, 2015, cultural critic and African American author Ishmael Reed published a piece on the leftist website *CounterPunch* entitled "'Hamilton: The Musical': Black Actors Dress Up like Slave Traders." The opinion piece took Lin-Manuel Miranda to task for muting the tragedy of slavery in his musical. The musical never mentions that the Schulyer family, which Hamilton marries into, owned slaves and benefitted from slave labor. Reed also contends that Hamilton not only turned a blind eye to Thomas Jefferson's horrendous slave-owning past but also that he and George Washington participated in Native American removals across the country. After his review of Miranda's work went viral, Reed began to write a counter-narrative to *Hamilton* called *The Haunting of Lin-Manuel Miranda*, in which Miranda is visited by the people whose narratives are excluded from history in his musical. In an interview with Helena Holmes in the *Observer* on January 15, 2019, Reed discussed his musical response to *Hamilton* and was asked if he had seen it:

> I don't need to see it, because [in my play] I quote from [Chernow's] book, which is wrong. Anyway, I would find the dancing and the Hip-hop distracting. It's a global phenomenon, and people ask me, "Why take on a global phenomenon?" You know what else is a global phenomenon? *Gone With the Wind.* I think *Hamilton* is probably the biggest consumer fraud since *The Blair Witch Project.*[46]

Reed avoids the question of whether he has seen *Hamilton,* stating he would have found the hip-hop music and dancing "distracting" as he challenges the very concept of Black and Brown actors playing slave owners and conspirators becoming a global phenomenon. In an earlier interview, Reed also made a facetious claim that the actors of color portraying slave masters "must have been ignorant" and that Miranda purposely edited Hamilton's life to render him an abolitionist instead of a Founding Father who was complicit in the horrors of slavery:

> This is the case with Alexander Hamilton whose life has been scrubbed with a kind of historical Ajax until it sparkles. His reputation has been shored up as an abolitionist and someone who was opposed to slavery. Not true.[47]

Reed continued:

> When I brought up the subject of Hamilton's slaveholding in a *Times*' comment section, a white man accused me of political correctness. If Hamilton

had negotiated the sale of white people, do you think that an audience would be paying $400 per ticket to see a musical based upon his life? No, his reputation would be as tarnished as that of his assassin Aaron Burr.[48]

Reed's comment provokes a larger dialogue about what Broadway will permit and reward on its stages. The power dynamics of the Broadway producing hierarchy that reinforces narratives of exclusion, under the guise of "inclusion," are important to the metanarrative of this book. Would mainstream White audiences pay top dollar to see a play that told an American history that strategically ignored historical facts of White people being sold, enslaved, raped, and killed? Nonetheless, all of these comparisons lead back to freedom's process and its connection to White fragility and guilt. Reed highlights the haunting narratives that float in the margins of Miranda's beautifully creative, yet terribly problematic musical that is built upon Chernow's selective amnesia of American history. Miranda gestures toward these historic omissions in one-line quips, yet chooses to make hip-hop-inspired entertainment that's not a "bummer." Mirroring the economies of slavery and American popular culture, Black and Brown labor fuels *Hamilton*, yet no one wants to take responsibility for the traumatizing nature of the haunting. The bodies of the actors do the work of historical remembering by triggering reflection as to where they were and what they were doing during the historical moment of the musical and the moment in which its story is being sold to mainstream audiences across the United States, Puerto Rico, continental Europe, and, at the time of this writing, Australia.[49]

And Ya' Don't Stop[50]

Ishmael Reed did not stop critiquing Miranda in his *CounterPunch* pieces. A staged reading of his counter-narrative play, *The Haunting of Lin-Manuel Miranda*, was held in May 2019 at the Nuyorican Café, directed by Rome Neal. Reed takes his points of contention about Miranda's play and personifies them into ghost characters who all visit Miranda à la Charles Dickens's *A Christmas Carol*. The characters who haunt Miranda and interrogate his choices include slaves owned by the Schuyler family, Harriet Tubman, an indentured White servant, and

Native Americans, none of whose narratives are mentioned in *Hamilton*. Reed's play underscores the feelings of emptiness that many people of color and allied White audience members may have experienced in witnessing *Hamilton*. The identification of the ghosts of people of color in the musical and the acts of ghosting that I have identified that occur throughout are just as important as the hauntings of the White Founding Fathers whose lives are played by Black, Latinx, Asian, mixed race, and White actors. In *The Haunting of Lin-Manuel Miranda*, Reed writes Miranda as an "overwhelmed" playwright who blames his omissions about slavery, Native removal, and White servitude in his musical on the flaws in Chernow's biography of Alexander Hamilton. The reason for his negligence, Miranda's character claims, is Chernow's lack of diligence in researching his book. Ishmael Reed's Facebook synopsis of the show compares Reed's work to that of Bertolt Brecht (a White German playwright) and the New Deal-era Works Progress Administration, or WPA (also run by Whites):

> Like theater in the time of Bertolt Brecht or the WPA, Reed's new work (under the direction of multiple AUDELCO winner Rome Neal) challenges the narrative of commercial theater and mainstream historical accounts. Reed's play brings to the forefront those characters who are absent from "Hamilton, The Revolution": slaves, Native Americans, indentured servants & Harriet Tubman. Performances of "The Haunting of Lin-Manuel Miranda" take place May 23-June 16, 2019.[51]

Franklin D. Roosevelt created the WPA to put people, including artists, to work after the Depression. During this time, the word "people" was understood as referring to Whites. People of color, specifically African Americans, were working diligently in civil rights efforts to be fully recognized as American. Even though Roosevelt's WPA program designed specific job training opportunities for African American artists, access to the theater was still segregated.[52] The fact that Reed's staged reading and Miranda's play created jobs for actors of color is certain. Both playwrights create works that look directly to the audience and witness to the stories and action of the play, which winks to Brecht's alienation effect. According to the *New York Times* there was a talk-back after the first reading in which Reed appeared to backpedal a bit on his strong critique of Miranda, giving him a "pass," so to speak, so that he would not run the risk of demonizing a man of color. Cultural critics who saw *The Haunting of Lin-Manuel Miranda,* including Hua Hso of the *New Yorker* and Elisabeth Vicentelli of the *New York Times,* have suggested that Reed's play is heavy-handed and demonstrative with little nuance. In her June 2, 2019 review of *The Haunting,* Vicentelli wrote:

> Thankfully, none of it was rapped. Some of the history lessons were long-winded and meandering—and maybe slightly confusing without a basic grasp of the original musical (Reed himself has reportedly never actually seen "Hamilton"). "The Haunting of Lin-Manuel Miranda" is a minor entry in an important and sometimes overwhelming body of work.[53]

Vicentelli is a critic who knows her theater history, so she should have a clear grasp of why Reed is making the case that Miranda's musical is creative historical fiction that takes one too many leniencies. However, her discomfort with Reed's critique of the racialized and commercial aspects of Broadway's incapacity to engage slavery, Native removal, and other traumatic aspects of American history speaks to White fragility and passive aggressive attempts to dismiss the racial inequities embedded in Broadway producing structures. She refuses to directly address *why* Reed is challenging Miranda in the first place. The subtitle of her review reads, "Lin-Manuel Miranda is a character, and his hit musical is a punching bag in Ishmael Reed's didactic play about historical correctness."

Reed's points about Miranda are painful pressure points in American history. Vincentelli wants readers of the *New York Times* (assumed to be White, based on the paper's demographic) to know that they can effectively "pass" on Ishmael Reed's play for reasons that completely miss his critique. When she notes that "thankfully, none of it was rapped" we learn her politics about hip-hop and rap. She does not take hip-hop seriously as a music genre and would prefer not to talk directly about race. Since *Hamilton* began its national tour in 2018, other *Hamilton* critics have come out in droves, some taking more passive-aggressive approaches and others being more direct. Nancy Isenberg, writing for *Zócalo Public Square,* splits the difference between the two approaches:

> Thus hip-hop *Hamilton* unabashedly celebrates the American Dream; the conceit that the country has always been the land of opportunity. Hamilton represents the immigrant made good, because he was born on the Caribbean island of Nevis. Left out of the upbeat story is that Hamilton—and the Federalist Party he headed—were hostile to the idea that the United States should ever be led by newcomers.[54]

Isenberg still centers Miranda's play on a bootstraps immigration narrative, yet does concede the point that the United States was not (and, I argue, *is* not), truly comfortable acknowledging any non-White immigrant as part of American nation building.

Continuing the critiques of Miranda's positions on immigration and feminist narratives, James McMaster, writing for *HowlRound,* points out that the feminist moments in the musical fail the Bechdel test, which requires at least two female characters to talk about anything besides men:

> I am startled when I come across critics who speak in unqualified terms of *Hamilton*'s feminist merits. The female characters simply do not get enough stage time and, when they do appear onstage, their desires, fears, hopes, plans, and narratives exist only in relation to Alexander, the man at the center of Miranda's musical. I'm not even sure *Hamilton* passes the Bechdel test, the bare minimum for feminine representation in popular culture. It's arguable.[55]

McMaster also notes in his analysis of Miranda's bootstraps immigration narrative that such rhetoric is dangerous in that it projects a "work hard for success" American Dream narrative that ignores structures of inequality never addressed by Miranda:

> The assertions here, that Hamilton worked harder and was smarter, true or not, imply that other immigrants who have not experienced success in their new nation are somehow at fault. They either do not work hard enough or, simply, are not smart enough. Such logic neglects and obscures the material obstacles and violences (structural racism, predatory capitalism, long-burned bridges to citizenship) imposed on racialized immigrants within the United States in order to celebrate the (false) promise of the American dream and the nation-state.[56]

Taken together, the *Hamilton* criticism, including *The Haunting of Lin-Manuel Miranda,* asks us to question the ways in which Broadway's producing machine profits from so-called "racially progressive" strategies that utilize people of color's bodies and sample from their cultural production in the form of language, styles of self-adornment, and embodied gestures via dance and other forms, yet whitewashes their historical experiences. Despite *Hamilton*'s financial and cultural success, the musical is distributing a bootstraps narrative of the American Dream that attempts to equalize the experiences of all Americans, yet ignores the social and structural history of the racism that undergirds the Revolutionary Era. As Black and Brown youth are told that *Hamilton* is "for them," and the first Black President and First Lady of the United States celebrate it as genius, one must ask, "Why would we want to circulate a story of American history that asks historically underrepresented minorities to consume a story that renders them as ghosts?"

When Miranda toured *Hamilton* in his ancestral home of Puerto Rico to benefit hurricane relief in 2019, his goal was to share the positive attributes of the musical in a time of an American disaster. What Miranda did not speak to during his tour was his own ancestral "ghosts." Puerto Ricans have been denied full citizenship status since Puerto Rico became a territory of the United States in 1898 after the U.S. victory in the Spanish-American War. Classified as an "unincorporated territory," Puerto Rico is controlled by the U.S. government. Puerto Ricans are American citizens, yet "they do not have voting power in Congress and its citizens can't vote for the US president—but they can vote in party primaries."[57] Puerto Rican American citizenship status is almost as vulnerable as that of Black Americans living in the United States during Jim Crow. Why Miranda would want to conflate the migration and citizenship experiences of Alexander Hamilton with those of people of color is questionable.[58]

The Shady Aftermath of *Hamilton*

Professors Annette Gordon Reed at Harvard University and Lyra Monteiro at Rutgers University are astute cultural critics who have joined Ishmael Reed's historical redress of *Hamilton*. Gordon Reed, a historian who has been awarded the Pulitzer Prize, observes:

> *Hamilton* is a work of historical fiction. Creators operating in that genre have the license to make things up in order to fulfill their artistic vision. It can only go "wrong" when the license taken with facts strains credulity, and prevents the narrative from ringing true. That is not so much a failure of history as a failure of art. While imagining things that may not have happened, or did not happen exactly in the way the creator imagines it, is endemic to the process of creating historical fiction, this does not preempt historians' perfect right—even duty—to say where a given work strays from the historical record. It can do no harm to a work of historical fiction to tell people what parts of the story are, well, *fiction*.[59]

Performance studies scholar Lyra Monteiro offers a sobering critique of the *Hamilton* phenomenon that speaks directly to the state of historical denial to which many audience members consent when we fall into the Lin-Manuel Miranda virtuosity vortex of *Hamilton* and don't look closely as the "facts" that are sampled and remixed in the musical:

> America "then" did look like the people in this play, if you looked outside of the halls of government. This has never been a white nation. The idea that the actors who are performing on stage represent newcomers to this country in any way is insulting. Miranda is Puerto Rican, meaning his parents and even his grandparents were born American citizens; the African American actors in the play may have ancestors that fought in the same Revolutionary War depicted on stage—and may also be the descendants of enslaved people on whose backs the founders built their fortunes and sustained their lifestyles. More pointedly, it is problematic to have black and brown actors stand in for the great white men of the early United States in a play that does not acknowledge that the ancestors of these same actors were excluded from the freedoms for which the founders fought.[60]

Monteiro's observation of *Hamilton* challenges our complicity in perpetuating mythologies of Americanness that avoid discussion of the violence and premature death experienced by enslaved people and their descendants who are presently in pursuit of freedom as they carry the weight of their inherited trauma. Miranda's "trauma free" take on slavery in *Hamilton* took this complicit stance by focusing on a bootstraps struggle perspective that was fortified by mythical abolitionist and feminist acts of grandeur.

But when cultural critics like Reed, Gordon Reed, and Monteiro talk about the historical fiction of *Hamilton*, their critiques are quickly dismissed by the mainstream press writers who make or break American playwrights on Broadway. The critiques of these scholars are read as "angry" anomalies that attempt to detract from *Hamilton*'s global phenomenon status. The musical swept the Tony Awards of 2016 and garnered Miranda a MacArthur "Genius" Grant, work in movies and TV, and, last but not least, great wealth. *Hamilton* was also featured as a PBS special and has a national museum tour entitled *Hamilton: The Exhibition*. According to Helen Holmes writing for the *Observer* in January 2019, Miranda was in talks with Disney to cowrite the first Latina princess movie for the franchise.[61]

The overwhelming post-Broadway success of this musical has resulted in a national and international tour of *Hamilton* which distributes its idealistic and proscriptive multiracial messaging to the masses. From a hip-hop perspective, Miranda samples many messages of subversion in the musical, from controversial, yet renowned, hip-hop artists such as Biggie Smalls, DMX, and Tupac Shakur, all of whom have penned misogynist lyrics about women. To counter the haunting anti-feminist narratives from these African American male artists, Miranda borrows from influential female R&B artists such as Beyoncé, challenging the status quo with her narratives of empowerment. In an interview with Vulture in 2016, Hamilton's musical director credits Beyoncé and Destiny's Child as his muse for the Schuyler sister's musical riffs:

> A lot of reviews were saying, "The Schuyler Sisters are like the Destiny's Child of the show." I didn't feel like the music sounded enough like Destiny's Child, so I went back and listened to "Bootylicious" and "Bills, Bills, Bills." I made the arrangement a little more modern.[62]

Miranda and Lacamoire are very clear about the fact that hip-hop sells, and that they had the capacity to be subversive by giving hip-hop's language and blackness to the Founding Fathers (and sisters, in the case of the Schuyler sisters), only to find that the subversive moments may have been ignored because the predominantly White audiences of *Hamilton* have little fluency in hip-hop's vernacular. Hip-hop is voided of its political power in *Hamilton* because the musical is not intended for audiences comprised of people of color. The content of the musical is not controversial enough to speak to the residuals of slavery, immigration injustice, and Native removal that haunts the production. Miranda's intent may have been to subvert the exclusionary narratives embedded in American democracy, but ultimately, the racially conscious casting and the use of hip-hop as a lone device to denounce racism and systemic inequality are insufficient. The hip-hop in the musical often plays like Muzak versions of jazz standards. Miranda's predominantly White audiences want to believe that hip-hop is not raced at all and that America's Founding Fathers were never intentionally racist. *Hamilton*'s multiracial mash-up uses actors of color to ventriloquize the nation's denial of its racist past. In the present, we must ask, why must people of color continue to do the work for White audience members and producers who do not want to face their own fragility and responsibility for reinscribing racist tropes and power dynamics?

Conclusion: The Endgame

The end of Act 2 of *Hamilton* addresses the presidential election of 1800. President John Adams loses his fight and Thomas Jefferson and Aaron Burr are tied to win. Hamilton endorses Jefferson in a number called "The Election of 1800." The banter between Hamilton and Burr as candidates is strategically written to mirror the bitterness and angst in our current political climate. Aaron Burr brings a reality TV-style debate to the forefront in his part of the number, sung with the company as he circles the musical back to his first encounter with Alexander Hamilton:

> Break: Aaron Burr and (Ensemble)
> Talk less! (Burr!)
> Smile more! (Burr!)
> Don\'t let them know what you\'re against or what you\'re for! (Burr!)
> Shake hands with him! (Burr!)
> Charm her! (Burr!)
> It's 1800; ladies, tell your husbands, vote for Burr!

Burr continues to raise the stakes in his fight against Hamilton. Watching a Black male play Burr is important here, as his challenge to Hamilton, as manifested in the lyrical content of his songs, begins to reveal that the samples of blackness used in the musical ghost the Black subject while he plays White. When Burr challenges Hamilton to a duel, the lyrical content is in battle with the Black actor's body. In the number "Your Obedient Servant," Burr (played by Odom and Nix) references more of the actors' Black pasts than Burr's White narrative:

> Dear Alexander:
> I am slow to anger
> But I toe the line
> As I reckon with the effects
> Of your life on mine
> I look back on where I failed
> And in every place I checked
> The only common thread has been your disrespect
> Now you call me "amoral,"
> A "dangerous disgrace,"
> If you've got something to say
> Name a time and place
> Face to face
> I have the honor to be Your Obedient Servant
> A dot Burr.[63]

Burr tells Hamilton that he is tired of not being taken seriously, even as vice president, and that his identity is being criminalized by Hamilton. In the lines "you call me amoral" and a "'dangerous disgrace,'" the body of the Black actor, as Burr, shares a double meaning with the audience as the lyrical content plays against his body to reflect the ways in which Black men have been historically mythologized in the American racial imaginary. Burr challenges the Republic, paying due respect to Hamilton by calling himself "Your Obedient Servant," sampling from the written correspondence closings of the eighteenth century while, also at that time, Black men were obedient servants.

In the next number, Eliza and Alexander reconnect in "Best of Wives and Best of Women," followed by the infamous duel between Hamilton and Burr. Upon Hamilton's death after Burr issues his fatal shot, it is the Black male, playing Burr, who is left as the villain of the musical, chronicled in the heartfelt number "The World Was Wide Enough."

Then George Washington, Aaron Burr, Thomas Jefferson/Marquis de Lafayette, Mulligan, Laurens, and the Company return to tell us what was "good" about Hamilton in the closing number, which serves as a eulogy, entitled "Who Will Live to Tell Our Story." Eliza, now Hamilton's grieving widow, pulls our heartstrings to make sure that we remember Hamilton as a great man. After Eliza shares how much she will miss Hamilton and will preserve his memory, she states:

ELIZA:
I speak out against slavery
You could have done so much more if you only had—

ELIZA AND COMPANY:
Time

Eliza's character realizes in just this one line that everyone in this musical could have done more to speak out against slavery, if only there had been enough time. But time is not the answer. *Hamilton: The Musical* runs two hours and forty-five minutes. In all of that time, Miranda talks about the plight of slavery and Black people fewer than five times. Yet, the musical could not have been hip-hop or the phenomenon it is without Black people and their music and culture. Hip-hop's past and peculiar present speak the stories of the slave ancestors in the gap of the musical, haunting it with a presence.

Many people may see *Hamilton*'s success as a platform for more opportunities to empower Brown and Black youth and to open doors for more playwrights of color to create hip-hop-inspired musicals. The irony of *Hamilton* being used as a new model for Broadway success can be found in its last song, "Who Will Live to Tell Our Story." Black and Brown actors mourn the loss of Alexander Hamilton in this number as they play White characters who are literally ghosts of the production. Slaves and other historical minorities are also ghosts, defined by Merriam-Webster as "disembodied souls" who serve as "the seat of intelligence" that fuel this brilliant concept of a musical.[64] Miranda's insistence that the musical cast only American and non-U.S.-born minorities in all of these "White" roles is not the answer to change racial discontent in the United States. The answer is in living to tell our own lost ghost stories and the culturally specific *now* experiences of living while Black, Asian, Latinx, Native, and multiracial without satisfying Broadway formulas that require artists of color to build escape hatches for White audiences. In order to make it on Broadway Americans of color currently must adhere to a formula that includes race-conscious casting, celebrity stunt casting, actors of color cast in plays written by White playwrights who "don't see color," and/or plays by Black and Brown playwrights who are forced to add White characters so that they do not inspire White guilt.

"Who Will Live to Tell Our Story" is relatable for Broadway audiences because it gives a fabricated hope that we are actually all working together to make a better America. It is relatable to artists of color who strive to tell their stories because it reminds us how long we have been working to do so, only to gain access to Broadway when we tamp down our pain and suffering. We have to make the language and the culture of people of color more "accessible" for predominantly White audiences. Miranda made hip-hop accessible to the masses, yet the culture of the Black and Brown people that made hip-hop to speak truth to power was completely extracted from it.

On July 3, 2020, four months into an international COVID-19 pandemic, weeks into international anti-Black police violence protests that began after deaths of George Floyd, Ahmaud Arbery, Breonna Taylor, and on the eve of the Fourth of July, Disney+ released *Hamilton: The Movie*. News sources speculate that the musical attracted over thirty-seven million viewers, more than any other streaming platform at the time. However, Disney has yet to release the final viewing numbers. The digital release of Hamilton drew much more criticism than the play ever did by theater critics who, for the most part, raved about the genius of the musical, which I have neve disputed. However, what is not clear is how we reconcile the aftermath of *Hamilton*'s ghost story telling of history. Disney+ has over fifty-six million subscribers. White, Black, Latinx, Asian, Native American, Pacific Islander, Hispanic, Indigenous (and every racial and ethnic combination thereof) children and their parents and grandparents now rap a history of America's beginning that has ghosted the contributions of people of the global majority, specifically African American enslaved people, yet has used their bodies and artistic genius to make nearly a billion dollars. Miranda, as the creator of

Hamilton, has received only a fraction of that profit.[65] Children of color around the world who watch Hamilton are taught to believe that slavery and its aftermath were not that bad after all. As much as casting actors of various marginalized racial backgrounds works performatively to "talk back" to the White ruling powers of Broadway as we see happening in the midst of COVID-19 and Black Lives Matter protests (at this writing and hopefully in the aftermath upon this book's publication). With privileged theater artists of color who have come together to protest institutional racism and systemic inequality in the American theater with theater organizations such as "We See You White Theatre (WAT)" and the Black Theatre Coalition, one must ask, how much do people of color see that is problematic about *Hamilton* or the racial politics of Broadway? At what point does the artist of color look terribly hypocritical when they critique the politics of White theaters who exploit the stories and experiences people of color, yet benefit financially and critically from showcasing their work at theaters that continue to oppress Black and Brown artists? This was Ishmael Reed's major point in his critique of *Hamilton* when he said "I don't have to see it." Reed, like many Black Arts Movement activists before him, recognized in *Hamilton* a very familiar formula based on creating theater that has just enough controversy and to entice White audiences and critics without triggering White fragility. The frenzy around *Hamilton's* musical genius is warranted. Miranda's ability is worthy of the praise, but at what point does the very platform Hamilton used to critique Broadway turn into cultural tourism that does more damage than good for Black and Brown communities. Even Miranda admits the limitations of his work in this musical. After the Disney+ *Hamilton* film was released in July 2020, critics who were once reluctant to critique the juggernaut musical came out of the woodwork to ask questions about cultural trafficking and historical editing. Internationally recognized film critic Odie Henderson, writing for RogerEbert.com notes that the *Hamilton* film *is* one of the more controversial titles that Disney has lent its squeaky clean label:

> It's certainly raunchy in ways Uncle Walt wouldn't have approved, most notably in depicting the adulterous events that led to the Reynolds pamphlet, a Sidney Sheldon-worthy tell-all published by its protagonist, Alexander Hamilton.

Odie Henderson goes on to contextualize the release of the film in the height of a global pandemic, international protests against anti-Black violence by the police, and systemic inequality in predominantly White institutions:

> Hamilton's casting of mostly Black, Latinx and Asian performers to portray real-life people we knew were White (and, lest we forget, *slaveowners*) is questionable only if one doesn't consider that a major theme of Miranda's book is not only who gets to tell this American story, but also that the subjects themselves don't really have any control over the storyteller. With the past few weeks filled with White voiceover artists *voluntarily* stepping aside to let Black artists voice their Black characters, I'm sure this casting conceit will be litigated once again in the whataboutism court of public opinion.[66]

I support artists of color making art that can change the creative racial climate and break down barriers of access. I also understand why so many artists of color engage their capacity to create art that, conceptually, does not alienate White people and people of color who center their art choices in White legitimizing frameworks that are sanctioned by the locations of theaters frequented by critics from *The New Yorker* and *The New York Times* theater picks. Mainstream theater critics who have little fluency in the culture of African American or Latinx people often write about Black and Latinx theater as if they have "discovered" something or someone new. Such "discoveries" and acts of exploitation are at the core of American empire building, Broadway's capital building efforts, and the "American" Dream narrative. You have to conquer to be in power. You have to show that you can "blend" into the American narrative in a way that does not threaten the status quo to the point of fragility. That's what "good Broadway" theater does. I think new efforts by The Mellon Foundation in October 2020 launching an initiative with the Billie Holiday Theatre in Brooklyn called The Black Seed Project seeks to give money to Black theater leaders to fund Black theaters nationally. I am hopeful that this seed grant will be a model for paradigmatic shifts that allow theaters run by people of the global majority to decide what playwrights, plays, and artists will tell their stories.

Artists and scholars of color must question how complicit we are in reproducing the same validating systems that reward *Hamilton* as a masterpiece. It is a masterful work, to be sure. But what are the material and emotional costs? We must be careful to not regard so-called progressive casting and historical editing as the theater equivalent of "Making America Great Again." Such idealized projections of inclusivity and equity are confusing. While *Hamilton* features actors and technicians of color and uses hip-hop, a predominantly African American cultural product, its actors of color must play back an American history that is a fictional ghost story where Black people are doing anything but "rising up," to paraphrase the number "My Shot." When Vice President Mike Pence visited the Broadway show in December 2016, he was booed by many liberal audience members. The cast member who played the role of Aaron Burr that evening, Brandon Victor Dix, read a prepared statement that addressed the then-new Trump presidency. It read:

> "We, sir—we—are the diverse America who are alarmed and anxious that your new administration will not protect us, our planet, our children, our parents, or defend us and uphold our inalienable rights," he said. "We truly hope that this show has inspired you to uphold our American values and to work on behalf of all of us."[67]

As we teach *Hamilton* at universities, community colleges, and community centers, we must call attention to the silences and the omissions when we talk about "all of us" as Americans. The history and culture of Black, Latinx, Asian, Indigenous, and multiracial artists is valuable enough when it is by us, about us, for us, and near us. The Broadway versions of American history are most often more hurtful than helpful to people of color because the narratives reinforce and reward mainstream mythologies that people of color have a specific place in the racial hierarchy and that our stories should entertain, not remind us, as Duke Ellington narrated in his "Notes on the State Department Tour," discussed in the introduction, that America has "a race problem."[68] One thing *Hamilton* does ask us that is truly important is, ". . . and when my time is up, have I done enough?"

SIX

CONCLUSION / ARRESTED DEVELOPMENTS

New Arrangements of Identity in Hip-Hop Performance

> The cultural material we call black is often significant core cultural elements supplemented by many streams of incoming cultural traffic, coming from outside black cultural notions. Maybe the real genius of black cultural production has been the ability to reorganize a welter of cultural materials into innovative, arresting new arrangements.
>
> —Harry Elam, Jr.[1]

Over ten years ago, I was in graduate school trying to make sense of what I was watching around me as non-African American people began to engage with hip-hop music beyond mimicry and attempts to be "down." The 1990s was an era where White and non-African American people sampled from the African American cultural practices that dominate hip-hop's aesthetic in language, styles of self-adornment, embodied gestures, and dance to remix their own content as hip-hop, but no longer uniquely Black, culture. In my primary education at predominantly African American schools in Detroit, Michigan, I learned of famous Black artists such as Billie Holiday, Duke Ellington, Josephine Baker, Ella Fitzgerald, and so many others. I was ten years old and I was proud to be Black and American. I was proud to be a part of that rich history of performance in the United States because it was presented as something that I should be proud of and aspire towards achieving myself. As a professor of African American theater today, I rarely meet a student of any racial identity who knows anything about the history of Black music and theater. The narratives that inspired my life's trajectory have all but been erased from most mainstream, predominantly White institutions or people of color serving institutions unless they are taught by scholars who are committed to unsettling the normative whiteness of American theater history and practice. Hip-hop artists and music follow in the footsteps of many of the aforementioned jazz artists. In the age of hip-hop, will those stories ever be told as part of an American expression of blackness, or will they be subsumed under titles and headings that never mention the long history of African American music and theater as platforms for social justice and petitions for equality? Will ten-year-old Black children today be told that hip-hop music, and the theater it inspires, is "universal"—without a mention of the civil rights struggles for freedom forged by African Americans that are its foundation?

Affirming Black art as "Black" affirms Black people. We all need to feel affirmed, both as ourselves and as part of our community. Hip-hop as a Black American music form inspired me to think about the long history of Black music as a site to reimagine who we could be in the world and then have the audacity to become who we imagine. Hip-hop is part of a long legacy of Black resistance. But like blues and jazz before it, piece by piece it is being sampled away from Black people and their struggles are being used by other racial and ethnic groups to dream themselves differently, in both positive and negative ways. Whites love hip-hop music for many reasons, not all good. One reason is because hip-hop serves as a protective invisibility cloak, à la Harry Potter, which can magically "stop" them from being seen as racist or upholding racism's dependence on systemic inequality. Another genuine reason many Whites loves the music is that it is at once about and not about them. Black people sample from everyone to make hip-hop's blackness because they are taking back the thousands of parts that have been borrowed for pleasure, for pain, and for redemptive ways out of the abyss of racism. People of color who are not African American love hip-hop because it is theirs too. Even though African Americans have held the hegemony of hip-hop, other historically marginalized minorities in the United States that relate to the music learn from its creative maps as to how to survive over four hundred years of oppression and premature death,[2] and still be a generative, creative, and resilient people. To paraphrase the character Antoine Fisher in the film of the same name directed by Denzel Washington, "We're still standing. We're still strong." Black people need all of this love that the sampling of Black aesthetics in hip-hop, in the form of language, styles of self-adornment, and embodied gestures, brings back to us when these acts are done with love, empathy, and reverence; not disdain, disrespect, and greed. African American cultural production in hip-hop continues to influence Black and non-Black people around the world. Just as there are multiple blacknesses around the world, there are multiple hip-hops that are creatively connected to African American struggles for equality, which are sonically and kinesthetically embedded in hip-hop as an African American art form. No matter how many times Black people in America have to make a "way out of no way," our history says that we do this well, and that we will survive and thrive. Our present says that Black survival is dependent on claiming who we are in the present and making ourselves matter to us, for us, by us, and near us. Black futures are dependent upon us making the world as we need it to be so that we can reclaim our time and our cultural properties as valuable commodities that can help our communities come together to remember our shared humanity in a cultural moment of the twenty-first century that says, "We like your art, but we don't necessarily like you." We must remember what Black people in America have done on Broadway; off Broadway; on street corners; on dance floors; on stages big and small; in community centers, parks, churches, and libraries; in Harlem; and beyond. Hip-hop is our theater, and it is a place where we reimagine ourselves anew, for good and for bad, over and over again. Black people in America are repetition and revision. African Americans have sampled and remixed ourselves into mixtapes of forced and selective migrations that tell many stories, some not so old and some not so new, some about those who survived and thrived, others who lost their lives to the trauma of racism and its lethal weapon of anti-Black violence.

As a young Black girl in school, when I was warned that the amazing artists that I'd learned about and loved had to make "a way out of no way" because of racism and systemic inequality, I realized that I had to do something to make sure that the beautiful music that moved my heart—Negro spirituals, blues, jazz, soul, R&B, and later hip-hop—would be preserved so that other young Black children could see themselves in the possibility of it and imagine themselves as something great. Now, as a professor of African American theater and popular performance, I teach emerging artists to revere and appreciate Black culture as they consume it and study it. I teach all kids to love Black theater and music because it is part of a rich American heritage that is as much a remixed heritage as it is Black and White. Just as I was taught to love Black people, our music, and our theater, I teach my students that they can't just sample and remix the parts of hip-hop that bring them joy and pleasure; they have to be responsible and engaged with the pain that produced it, as much as the genius that sustains it. I urge these students, African American and non-African American alike, to become a part of imagining and creating an America that not only loves hip-hop theater and music as part of a creative genealogy of Black theater, music, and dance, but also rejects the idea of seeing Black people in the United States who are descendants of slavery as American when it is convenient.

Hip-hop and African American theater are moving into the "mainstream" of pop culture which, decoded, means they are consumed by White audiences and therefore must shift into the racial imaginary in the United States and the United Kingdom as "universal" stories and cultural practices. The international success of Latino actor, playwright, and composer Lin-Manuel Miranda's musical *Hamilton* brought the genre, which had been underground since the mid-1990s, to the mainstream theater world by telling the story of an American Founding Father. Alexander Hamilton's biography is ventriloquized through the bodies and voices of African American, Asian American, and Latinx American actors. Hip-hop is remixed by Miranda with other music derived from the African diaspora, such as jazz, soul, and reggae, along with historically White musical theater show tunes that had foreclosed opportunities to the very bodies and people that perform them in the Tony Award–winning musical. How do we reconcile the mashup of two genres that personify the Black–White binary and are diametrically opposed to one another in American history? Hip-hop, once regarded as the Blackest and most dangerous of all Black American music, and theater, still arguably one of the Whitest and most Eurocentric performance genres in the United States, come together in a musical that reminds us of cultural critic Greg Tate's observation in the epigraph that "much of what America sold to the world as uniquely American in character in terms of music, dance, fashion, humor, spirituality, grassroots politics, slang, literature and sports, was uniquely African-American in origin, conception and inspiration."[3]

The artistic practices and identity negotiations I have explored in *Sampling and Remixing Blackness in Hip-Hop Theater and Performance* work to reconcile my theatrical practice as an African American actor and director who must face the normative whiteness of American theater practices every day. I do not believe that I have an answer for the questions I began to have in the early 2000s about non-African American artists borrowing aspects of blackness from African Americans in their expression of hip-hop. I do have a suggestion for those who take from hip-hop without acknowledging the history of White appropriation of Black culture through acts of racial mimicry, violence, and theft. Asian and Asian American, Latinx, Native, Black artists of other nationalities and ethnicities, and Whites all can sample from blackness using the vernacular language, styles of self-adornment, and gestures that are definitely recognizable as part of "Black" American culture. Yet, we must not give "get out of cultural appropriation jail free" cards to people, regardless of racial identity, who are complicit in co-opting Black American culture, yet do not disavow the racism and residual emotional and physical trauma that Black people in the United States experience as a result of such violent acts of taking without depositing anything back into Black communities. Citing African Americans as cultural content producers who challenge racial hierarchies and systems of inequality is the baseline for Whites and other people of color who deny that short-changing any marginalized American's citizenship rights is just as bad as telling Black people in American to "get over" slavery. We must not fall into the cyclical trap of privileging the trauma or experience of one historically underrepresented group over another.

When White artists began to gain critical success in hip-hop culture in the late 1980s and early 1990s, the music and aesthetic of hip-hop became the primary source of American popular culture. All of the references to hip-hop as "African American" or "Black" music began to fall away. Hip-hop culture became less about being an African American musical and cultural form of self-expression and sociopolitical redress and more about being a site where anyone (translation: Whites) could imagine themselves differently in the world. The problem is that, unlike African Americans, Whites using hip-hop to self-reflect have the *option* to align themselves with sociopolitical quests for freedom and equality of the oppressed, or they can remain silent about racism, race, and systemic inequality even when they see it operating in all aspects of the theater and entertainment industry, and thus sustain White supremacy. When being "woke" is merely for profit and not to become allied with acts that seek to dismantle White supremacy, then we have a "love and theft problem,"[4] as Eric Lott calls it, that perpetuates the cycles of depression and denial of the anti-Black past that produces our present.

When Latinx, Native, Asian, and other historically underrepresented groups consume Black culture for entertainment and profit with little effort to actively create coalitions between groups, they not only further their own oppression, they miss opportunities to challenge the White progressive agenda that refuses to acknowledge that American race relations are not just played out on the streets in protests after young Black and Brown people are killed, but it plays out in every art institution in the nation that uses hip-hop- (or other ethnically and racially specific performance) inspired theater to help them solve their "diversity" problem; or, worse, when they add shows by African American playwrights or other people of color and cast them irresponsibly while hiring White directors who have no idea how to translate the cultural ideals embedded in the plays or musicals. These policies and practices are beyond tragic, and they just keep happening in the same fragile ways that reproduce the same hierarchies between racial and ethnic groups. Black and Brown female/non-binary/queer directors and writers of color must do twice as much to gain *one* opportunity in a venue that is legible in the White mainstream. Until we train Black critics and fund Black theater companies on a regional level and consent to make those spaces legitimizing spaces that are valued by Black and Brown artists and their friends who are not people of color, we will continue to lift up *Hamilton* as the epitome of what people of color should be aspiring towards as a measure of mainstream success.

The fact that playwrights of color have to play in White spaces, have an MFA from some White institution, or hire a White director for their plays in order to gain access to union jobs and opportunities makes the case for me. The artists in this study who utilize hip-hop to shape their artistic work vacillate between offering remixed versions of identity that use Black cultural contributions to align themselves with African American quests against systemic inequality, and ambivalence about directly challenging anti-Black racism. The problem is while everyone finds themselves within hip-hop, Black people continue to fight anti-blackness and systemic inequality within and without the music and culture of hip-hop. Black people in the United States and around the world need as many allies and as much credit and help as possible. By using hip-hop to create coalitions between other historically underrepresented communities and allied Whites, theater and performance can become powerful sites of empathy that can facilitate identification with the problems that African Americans face, not as unique to one racial group, but symptomatic of larger systems of inequality. Hip-hop has to be sampled responsibility. Remixing social conditions of oppression with those of White privilege result in the further oppression of African American people.

Like jazz, hip-hop has been a powerful outlet for African American people to express our experiences with racial discrimination and systemic inequality. When people who do not experience racial oppression use the art of hip-hop uniquely for entertainment or capital gain, the struggles against racism that Ellington identified in "Notes on the State Department Tour of 1963" as the plight of "several minority groups" becomes seemingly less urgent: "The United States has a minority problem. [. . .] Negroes are one of several minority groups but the basis of the whole problem is economic, rather than a matter of color."[5]

We cannot talk about cultural appropriation, mimicry, or cultural theft from jazz or hip-hop until we actually talk about the trauma that slavery has inflicted on race relations in the United States. To profit materially from the trauma of slavery is to profit from Black cultural production without acknowledging the contributions that African Americans continue to make to shape national identity. Sampling and remixing are empathetic tools that can help us do the work of remembering the shared trauma that people of color have experienced in the United States. These tools can also help Whites and other oppressed minorities empathize with Black oppression in ways that can empower them to action, to form coalitions that work to dismantle White privilege and anti-Black violence. The resilience of African American people to make music and theater that chronicles our journey of resistance has become an instructive blueprint that centers blackness as a site for other racial and ethnic groups to rethink how they can challenge the status quo and become aligned with social justice. More non-African American artists are producing work using Black American aesthetic practices than ever before. In the past, these acts of sampling and remixing Black cultural art during the jazz age resulted in what Kay Key observes as a reductive practice of reassigning the cultural production of African American artists to White artists who are inspired by Black cultural production. As jazz moved from Black cultural centers, neighborhoods, and clubs to become entertainment for Whites, the labels of the genre changed as well:

> In 1920s, the white Paul Whiteman was named the *King of Jazz.* In the 1930s, the white Benny Goodman was named the *King of Swing.* In the 1950s, the white Elvis was named the *King of Rock and Roll.* And in the 2000s, the white Justin Timberlake was named the *King of R&B.*[6]

These are only a few of the cultural and musical conversions from being designated as an African American cultural product to being designated as a product of the White mainstream. The result is an artistic set of coalitions, both intentional and unintentional, that exist with and without Black bodies. Many people understand the African American deposits that have shaped jazz, swing, rock and roll, R&B, and every type of American music under the sun. The current live issue in mainstream popular culture is that older generations continue to forget the legacy of hip-hop and its place in the African American musical and arts traditions, or feign selective memory based on who is listening, while generations of consumers and artists only know these music forms as connected to the White mainstream flows of popular culture, and do not necessarily relate them to African American culture at all, because African American history and cultural contributions to American theater and history are absent from most the majority of mainstream history and arts narratives delivered to American school systems, from elementary schools to universities. The result of these strategic omissions in American history and culture narratives is that American citizens across racial and class positions do not know about, let alone value, the tremendous and far-reaching impact of African American cultural practices on American popular culture. Hip-hop artists are always predicting the future as they create Black cultural products to fulfill self-designed projections of blackness that counter mainstream stereotypes, uninformed ideas, and blatant ignorance about their cultural past or present. As non-African American hip-hop theater and performance artists sample from blackness, blackness will continue to sample from other cultural expressions to remain relevant, innovative, and countercultural until such remixes are no longer necessary. Harry Elam, Jr. acknowledges the cosmopolitan influences that constitute the multicentricity of blackness explored in hip-hop theater and performance presents as a remixed hip-hop that is both Black and other. Hip-hop theater and performance by non-African American artists offers evidence of cross-cultural artistic collaborations. Hip-hop is part of the rich cultural history of Black strategies of social improvisation in the Americas that continues in the twenty-first century; it is also connected to a history of Whites trying on African American culture for pleasure and profit in acts that have been mimicked by other minorities who want to distinguish themselves from African Americans. Black people's emotions and trauma, past and present, are embedded in the music and the craft of making hip-hop. Just like sampling the beats of country music (which was derived from the blues) doesn't take it away from White musicians, their culture, or deeply personal reasons for making the music, sampling hip-hop can never dislocate it from the people and social conditions that produce it. To paraphrase hip-hop theater activist, professor, and poet Kashi Johnson in her TED Talk "Words to Live By," "Hip-hop is an art form that raises social consciousness, promotes cultural awareness, and provides us a place to protest and find our voices. Though Hip-hop begins and ends with black voices, it can inspire people across racial identities to 'find your voice, speak your truth and save your life.'"[7] Johnson also alerts us that this process of finding your voice and your truth demands that one face personal and collective trauma: "We all have emotional scars. Some may have healed over time. You may know these as lessons learned or a definitive moment in your life. But what about the other injuries? The invisible wounds that we often try to ignore even exist."[8] Racism and systemic inequality in the United States are directly connected to the trauma of slavery and its residual injuries of anti-Black racism, cultural appropriation, and mimicry. To change these narratives, we must acknowledge that hip-hop once relied on the cultural contributions of diverse racial and ethnic groups that were sampled to create its syncretic foundations.

Though subsumed under the sign of blackness, these circuits of cultural exchange helped to make hip-hop a site that attracts diverse groups back to hip-hop's blackness to identify ways of making themselves anew.

David Roediger's suggestion that the practice of trying on Black American culture for a moment and then leaving it aside for something more interesting as practiced by Whites—and here I include other marginalized groups—is more complex than appropriation or commodification:

> Whether we judge the beauty and solidarity created by the crossing of cultural colorlines in the interstices of racial capitalism to outweigh the associated slights and tragedies is on one level immaterial. The process goes on, superficially and at times deeply. If to abdicate studying it were to abdicate only understanding that mythical thing called "white culture," the consequences would be bearable. But such an abdication entails giving up on understanding the astonishing variety within U.S. culture and within African American culture, the latter having as one of its essential elements the ability to borrow creatively from others and to engender mixed and new forms.[9]

Roediger suggests that we must challenge monolithic mythologies of White and Black culture to identify places of intersection across color lines that refuse to reinforce racial hierarchies and binaries. We must embrace inspiring new ways of knowing and being that produce new forms, not reinscribe old ones. The non-African American artists sampling from samples of blackness in this book reorganize the meaning of blackness outside of its performative referential to the African American performing body. Hoch, Sax, Rosen, Lee, Jones, Jonzi D, Harris, and Miranda acknowledge that hip-hop's innovation is that it constantly troubles existing racial categories through acts of sampling and remixing that push and stretch the existing boundaries of inclusion and exclusion. Their artistic works demonstrate that identifying hip-hop's indebtedness to cultural flows from European, Asian, Latinx, and other racial and ethnic contributions is just as important as acknowledging African American samples of blackness. By exploring the transformative power of African American particularity to hip-hop music and culture, we are able to see how these acts of sampling and remixing help to forge new imaginings of racial and national identity that attempt to identify with oppression and fights against White hegemony and, in others, reify the existing racial hierarchies in complex displays of interracial/intraracial violence.

Following jazz music's influence on African American culture, hip-hop is inspiring artists around the world to forge a worldview that is committed to issues of social justice through artistic practice. These non-African American performances of blackness in hip-hop theater and performance are essential to furthering our understanding of how Black cultural practices are exchanged, translated, and reconfigured through acts of performance. Hip-hop's aesthetic practices of sampling and remixing offer alternative ways to understand the complexity of how race, ethnicity, gender, and nation are lived both locally and globally. African American artists must acknowledge the cosmopolitan identifications that Elam highlights in his assessment of cultural syncretism in African American cultural production. The fact that hip-hop renews itself by sampling from outside, yet rarely acknowledges those cross-cultural links, maintains an idea of cultural purity that is dangerous and misses opportunities to create material, cross-cultural coalitions. As Robin D. G. Kelley has posited in his discussion of polyculturalism, "black culture is not the secret root of all American popular cultures, nor has it remained pure and unaltered, nor can it be reduced to the cultural/racial binaries of African/European."[10] Another answer is found in the works of Danny Hoch, Matt Sax, Nikki S. Lee, Sarah Jones, Jonzi D, Harris, and Lin-Manuel Miranda, who suggest that non-African American identifications with African American experiences of blackness in hip-hop have the capacity to enable both powerful cross-racial, ethnic, and international coalitions and stereotypical appropriations.

By sampling and remixing blackness, many non-African Americans learn through the cultural practices of African Americans in hip-hop how to imagine alternative identities that sincerely subvert what they are socially constructed to be by the mainstream. African American cultural production is a source of inspiration for diverse groups who, through hip-hop, can begin to see Black Americans as a group of people who have historically improvised, and continue to negotiate, their social identities in the face of oppression. By identifying the impact that African American samples of blackness in hip-hop have on the artistic practices of non-African American artists, perhaps we can begin to glean strategies of artistic practice that begin to rehearse solutions for future artistic, creative, and political identities. Such strategies of improvised resistance can help us to erode the lingering systems of inequality that made the malleable categories of race, ethnicity, gender, and nation relevant to creating hierarchies of humanity in the first place.

By sampling and remixing the rituals of performance that allow experiences of centrality and liminality to intersect, hip-hop theater and performance suggest new opportunities to understand how we can free ourselves from the stagnant categories of marginalized difference and White privilege to create openings for inventive, subversive, and boundary-pushing identifications with humanity. The choices of African American and non-African American artists to perform a part of blackness through hip-hop opens conversations that can help us change how we normalize White mainstream theater practice as the benchmark by which all art is measured. Artists from many diverse American racial and ethnic identities, as well as artists around the world, have been inspired by the Black cultural expression in hip-hop. They may be inspired to imitate it, borrow it, reimagine it, consume it—but ultimately, they sample it, make it their own through their desired acts of remix, and perform it before audiences. What they are saying in these performances is that blackness is not only an expression of people of African descent that has specific national, ethnic, and cultural translations, but that the transnational reach of American blackness is significant.

No matter how much Black people in the United States strive to be legible, neither a Nobel Prize–winning Black president by way of a Kenyan father and a White mother from Kansas; nor a young, first-generation, MacArthur Award–winning Puerto Rican American making it to the White House and Broadway, respectively, can help African Americans bear the burden of blackness. African American people work each day to fight against the racist stereotypes that plague our past and present. The artists discussed in this book connect their personal and creative identity quests to hip-hop strategically because hip-hop operates as a both/and space. It allows blackness to borrow not only from itself, but from a wide variety of cultures to rejuvenate itself over time. It makes sense, then, that the artistic innovations in this book depart from the aesthetic cipher of hip-hop, which already assumes all racial and ethnic groups under its sign through acts of sampling and remixing.

Though Black, hip-hop's specific blackness departs from a regenerative African American cultural repertoire that both lives in and escapes the archive. The centrality of African American cultural and aesthetic practices within the music directly connect to and shape the identities of the non-African American artists in this book. These intertextual, cross-racial and cross-ethnic exchanges suggest that blackness is effectively and affectively remixing how race is lived and performed in day-to-day exchanges in and outside of the theater.

Hip-hop gives its audience, consumers, creators, and lovers the permission to self-identify and (dis)identify with whatever and whomever they choose. The fluidity of blackness is all-encompassing as much as it is all-consuming. *Sampling and Remixing* asks us to do similar work. Hip-hop's very specific expressions of blackness are sampled by artists around the world as a way to understand hip-hop culture and to enjoy it as a site of self-expression. Hip-hop is a place to imagine the world and one's identity differently. Because hip-hop has sampled from other cultural experiences under the sign of blackness, it is a forgiving art form that rejuvenates itself when parts are appropriated or stolen with little regard for the pain and suffering of the Black and Brown people who created it. As many of the performers in this study show us, hip-hop should be used as a tool to tell the truth, not as a site to forge historically revisionist creations for entertainment that work to reinscribe racist ideologies of anti-blackness. By locating alternative racial identifications and expressive culture that resist White supremacy and anti-Black racism within hip-hop's dominant expression of blackness, the standing testimony of African Americans making a way out of no way can serve as a blueprint for non-African American artists to accept American history as a sampled collective that renders the notion of universality one that must be resisted, reimagined, and remixed anew.

NOTES

Introduction

1. W. E. B. Du Bois, "Krigwa Players Little Negro Theater," *The Crisis* 32, no. 126 (July 3, 1926): 134–136.

2. Greg Tate, *Everything But the Burden: What White People Are Taking from Black Culture* (New York: Broadway Books, 2003) 7.

3. Macklemore and Ryan Lewis, "White Privilege II," *This Unruly Mess I've Made*, Macklemore, LLC, 2016.

4. Paul Gilroy, *Against Race: Imagining Political Culture Beyond the Color Line* (Cambridge, MA: Harvard University Press, 2002), 181.

5. Gilroy, *Against Race*, 181.

6. Eric Lott, *Love & Theft: Blackface Minstrelsy and The American Working Class* (New York: Oxford University Press, 2013), 30.

7. Lott, *Love & Theft*, 29.

8. Zhané, "Hey Mr. DJ," *Zhané*, Motown, 1994.

9. Dwight Conquergood, "Performance Studies: Interventions in Radical Research," *TDR* 46, no. 2 (2002): 146.

10. Joseph Schloss, *Making Beats: The Art of Sample Based Hip-hop* (New York: Oxford University Press, 2004), 4.

11. Mark Anthony Neal, "A Way Out of No Way: Jazz, Hip-hop and Black Social Improvisation," in *The Other Side of Nowhere: Jazz, Improvisation, and Communities in Dialogue*, ed. by Ajay Heble and Daniel Fischlin (Middletown, CT: Wesleyan University Press, 2004), 196.

12. Neal, *The Other Side of Nowhere*, 197.

13. Alexander G. Weheliye, *Phonographies: Grooves in Afrosonic Modernity* (Durham, NC: Duke University Press, 2005), 206.

14. Imani Perry, *Prophets of the Hood: Politics and Poetics in Hip-hop* (Durham, NC: Duke University Press, 2004), 10.

15. Vijay Prashad, *Everybody Was Kung Fu Fighting: Afro-Asian Connections and the Myth of Cultural Purity* (Boston: Beacon, 2002), 66.

16. Tate, *Everything But the Burden*, 137.

17. Anthony Edward Ellington, "Notes on the State Department Tour," in *Music is My Mistress* (Cambridge, MA: Da Capo Publishing, 1976), 301–330.

18. Ellington, *Music is My Mistress*, 301.

19. Stuart Hall, "Race, Articulation and Societies Structured in Dominance," in *Cultural and Literary Critiques of Concepts of "Race"*, ed. by E. Nathaniel Gates and Benjamin N. Cardozo (New York: Taylor & Francis, 1997).

20. Paul Gilroy, *The Black Atlantic: Modernity and Double Consciousness*, (Cambridge, MA: Harvard University Press, 1993), 388.

21. E. Patrick Johnson, *Appropriating Blackness: Performance and The Politics of Authenticity* (Durham, NC: Duke University Press, 2003), 3.

22. Marcyliena Morgan and Dionne Bennett, "Hip-hop & the Global Imprint of a Black Cultural Form," *Daedalus* 140, no. 2 (Spring 2011): 177.

23. Sujatha Fernandes, *Close to the Edge: In Search of the Global Hip-hop Generation* (New York: Verso Books, 2011), 4.

24. Meiling Cheng, *In Other Los Angeleses: Multicentric Performance Art* (Berkeley: University of California, 2004), 1.

25. Richard Schechner, *Between Theater and Anthropology* (Philadelphia: University of Pennsylvania Press, 1985), 52.

26. Adam Bradley and Andrew Dubois, eds., *The Anthology of Rap* (New Haven, CT: Yale University Press, 2011), 119–129.

27. John McWhorter, "Rap: Broadway's New Jazz?" *American Theater*. Accessed March 18, 2016.

28. Craig Mack, "Flava in Ya Ear," *Funk da World*, Bad Boy Records/Arista, 1994.

29. I list these rhetorical strategies of critique explored by many hip-hop artists in order to highlight how intentional African American artists in hip-hop culture are about the work that they do. Henry Louis Gates, Jr.'s classic discussion of signifyin' as a rhetorical black vernacular strategy of resignification that addresses rhetorical acts of "repetition with a signal difference" have allowed many black rappers, sonic and visual artists, and dancers to critique white hegemony, make blackness visible in seemingly invisible contexts, and to challenge the normative whiteness of modernity. See Henry Louis Gates, Jr., *The Signifying Monkey: A Theory of Afro-American Literary Criticism* (New York: Oxford University Press, 1988), 51–52.

30. Nicole Persley, "History of Hip-hop Theater," in *The Cambridge Companion to Hip-hop*, ed. by Justin Williams, (New York: Cambridge University Press, 2015).

31. Eisa Davis published an article for *The Source* magazine, "Hip-hop Theatre: The New Underground," which contextualized many works by artist of color who were making theater inspired by hip-hop. Some of the plays referenced here are Zakiyyah Alexander's *Blurring Shine* (2003); Will Power's *Flow* (2003); *In Case you Forget* (2001) by Ben Snyder; Danny Hoch's *Till the Break of Dawn* (2007); *Slanguage* (2009) by the multiracial ensemble Universes; *Angela's Mixtape* (2009) by Eisa Davis, Pulitzer Prize finalist and niece of activist Angela Davis; ensemble play *Welcome To Arroyo's* by Kristoffer Diaz (2010), also a Pulitzer Prize finalist, in 2010; the Broadway musical *Holler if You Hear Me* (2012), based on a book by Todd Kreidler and music by Tupac Shakur; and Marc Bamuthi Joseph's *red, black & GREEN: a blues* (2013).

32. The Hip-Hop Theater Festival became Hi-Arts in 2014, one of the few non-profit organizations in the world dedicated to identifying and producing art inspired by hip-hop music and culture. See www.hiarts.com for more hip-hop theater history. Many of the founders of the Hip-Hop Theater Festival are still involved in an advisory capacity at Hi-Arts. At the time of writing, Kamilah Forbes is the Artistic Director of the Apollo Theater in New York; Clyde Valentín is the Director of SMU's Meadow Arts and Urbanism foundation; and Danny Hoch is an actor, playwright, and social activist who works frequently in theater, film, and television.

33. Many credit the term "hip-hop theater" to Black British hip-hop dance theater artist Jonzi D, discussed in chapter 4, who used it to describe his unique fusion of social and concert dance styles through hip-hop dance. Holly Bass is also credited with using the term and chronicled the wide range of hip-hop-inspired performances she witnessed at the 1999 National Black Theatre Festival, and was documented in an article entitled "Blowing Up the Set: What Happens When the Pulse of Hip-Hop Shakes Up the Traditional Stage?" in the November issue of *American Theatre* magazine. Eisa Davis is also credited with being one of the first people to use and popularize the term in the theater community. Iranian performance artist and director Reza Abdoh also used the term hip-hop theater in his work.

34. *Def Poetry* featured a series of spoken word vignettes performed by nine slam poets of diverse racial, ethnic, and sexual orientations. The show premiered at the Longacre Theater and ran from November 14, 2002 to May 4, 2003. Previously George C. Wolfe and Savion Glover's *Bring in Da Noise Bring in Da Funk* (1995) featured hip-hop music as part of an African American music continuum. See Danny Simmons, *Def Poetry on Broadway* (New York: Atria Books, 2005) and Broadway World's digital remnant of the musical at https://www.broadwayworld.com/shows/Bring-in-'Da-Noise,-Bring-in-'Da-Funk-3712.html

35. See TED's speaker website space dedicated to Sarah Jones. Accessed May 20, 2019. https://www.ted.com/speakers/sarah_jones

36. *In the Heights* won Tony Awards for Best Musical, Best Musical Score, Best Choreography, and Best Orchestrations in 2010. It was nominated for the Pulitzer Prize in 2009 and won.

37. See Paul Carter Harrison, Victor Leo Walker, and Gus Edwards, eds., *Black Theatre: Ritual Performance in the African Diaspora* (Philadelphia: Temple University Press, 2002). Harrison et al. link Black American theater practices to Africa and African ritual. The scholars analyze African American Theater practices as part of a larger expression of Black theater practices in Africa and the African Diaspora. For Harrison, Black theater and performance are mutually constitutive and should incorporate both traditional conceptions of theater, as well as more improvisational styles that include spoken word, hip-hop music, and African oral traditions.

38. Exhibits of note that featured hip-hop's influence on contemporary art include the "One Planet under a Groove: Hip-hop and Contemporary Art," which was featured at the Bronx Museum in 2001. See the past exhibit archive at the Bronx Museum website: http://m.bronxmuseum.org/store/one-planet-under-a-groove-hip-hop-and-contemporary-art.

39. Harry J. Elam, Jr., "Revising the Past, Pushing into the Future," *American Theatre*, 2004, 110.

40. Danny Hoch, "Here We Go Yo: A Manifesto for a Hip-hop Arts Movement," *Hemispheric Institute.* Accessed June 8, 2018. https://hemisphericinstitute.org/en/hidvl-collections/item/2188-dhoch-manifesto.html

41. Daniel Banks, *Say Word!: Voices from Hip Hop Theater* (Ann Arbor: University of Michigan Press, 2011) 31.

42. Victor Turner, "Liminality and Communitas," in *The Ritual Process: Structure and Anti-Structure* (Chicago: Aldine Publishing, 1969), 94–113.

43. Cyndi Lauper, "Time After Time," *She's So Unusual*, Epic Records, 1984.

44. Nicole Fleetwood, *Troubling Vision: Performance, Visuality and Blackness* (Chicago: University of Chicago Press, 2011), 5.

45. Schechner, *Between Theater and Anthropology*, 52.

46. Nicole Hodges Persley, personal correspondence with Toni Blackman, April 15, 2014.

47. Henry Bial, *Acting Jewish: Negotiating Ethnicity of the American Stage & Screen* (Ann Arbor: University of Michigan Press, 2007), 87.

Chapter One

1. Frank Owen, "Paid in Full," *Spin*, October 1989, 35–36.
2. Own, "Paid in Full," 35–36.
3. A white ally is defined here as a white person using their racial privilege to work against racism. See Joan Richardson's "An Interview with Beverly Daniel Tatum," *Phi Delta Kappan* 99, no. 3, (2017): 30–36.
4. Macklemore, "White Privilege II."
5. Beverly Daniel Tatum, *Why Are All the Black Kids Sitting Together in the Cafeteria? And Other Conversations About Race* (New York: Basic Books, 2003), 365.
6. The concept of being "woke," or "wokeness," is connected to African American Vernacular English (AAVE) and discussions of the practice of challenging the status quo as an oppressed subject. According to a recent 2017 entry in Merriam-Webster's Dictionary, the term "woke" is connected to the activist work of Erykah Badu's 2008 song "Master Teacher," in which she expresses her desire to "stay woke," or acutely aware of the power of white supremacy to shadow the work of activist-minded Black people. The dictionary definition argues the phrase "stay woke" became a watch word in parts of the Black community for those who were self-aware, questioning the dominant paradigm, and striving for something better. But "stay woke" and "woke" became part of a wider discussion in 2014, immediately following the shooting of Michael Brown in Ferguson, Missouri. The word "woke" became entwined with the Black Lives Matter movement; instead of just being a word that signaled awareness of injustice or racial tension, it became a word of action. Activists were "woke" and called on others to "stay woke." The term as since been adopted by non-Black activists and allies in fights against systemic racism and inequality.
7. Lisa B. Spanierman and Laura Smith, "Roles and Responsibilities of White Allies: Implications for Research, Teaching, and Practice," *The Counseling Psychologist* 45, no. 5 (July 2017): 606–617.
8. Tatum, *Why Are All the Black Kids Sitting Together in the Cafeteria.*
9. Run-D.M.C., "It's Like That," *Run-D.M.C.*, Def Jam, 1984.
10. Cheng, *In Other Los Angeleses*, 1.
11. Ian Maxwell, *Phat Beats, Dope Rhymes: Hip-hop Down Under Comin' Upper* (Middletown, CT: Wesleyan University Press, 2003), 2.
12. Beastie Boys, "The New Style," *Licensed to Ill*, Sony/ATV Music Publishing LLC, Universal Music Publishing Group, 1986.
13. J Love, "White Like Me: 10 Codes of Ethics for White People in Hip-hop,"

Davey D's Hip-hop Corner. Accessed June 5, 2017. http://www.daveyd.com/commentarywhitelikeme.html

14. *Vogue* Magazine Video, "73 Questions with Iggy Azalea," March 24, 2015, YouTube. Accessed July 5, 2016. https://www.youtube.com/watch?v=AMh5f8xRLRE

15. Damien Arthur, "Hip-hop Consumption and Masculinity," in *GCB—Gender and Consumer Behavior Volume 8*, ed. by Lorna Stevens and Janet Borgerson (Edinburgh: Association for Consumer Research, 2006), 12.

16. See Bakari Kitwana, *Why White Kids Love Hip-hop: Wanksters, Wiggas and Wannabees and the New Reality of Race in America* (New York: Basic Books, 2006), 175. Kitwana reads the work of Hoch as social activism committed to exposing the institutional inequality embedded in old racial politics. He contends Hoch's "art as weapon of resistance approach" and lifelong engagement with hip-hop make him an anomaly amongst the white consumers and artists engaged with hip-hop who exploit hip-hop as cultural tourists.

17. Kodak Black, "Tunnel Vision," *Painting Pictures*, Atlantic Records, 2016.

18. Fred Moten, *In the Break: The Aesthetics of the Black Radical Tradition* (Minneapolis: University of Minnesota Press, 2003), 72.

19. Tom MacDonald, "WHITEBOY," Independent Label, 2018. Toni Mack has been described as a real-life version of Danny Hoch's character Flip in the film *White Boyz*, which is a 1999 independent film that was distributed by Fox Searchlight Films and written by Danny Hoch, Garth Belcon, Henri Kessler, and Marc Levin; and was also directed by Mark Levin. The comedy chronicles the experiences of a white male rapper who thinks he is black. The character was played by Hoch in his play *Jails, Hospitals & Hip-Hop*.

20. Norman Mailer, "The White Negro," *Dissent* 4 (Fall 1957): 276–293.

21. Mailer, "The White Negro," 279.

22. James Baldwin, "The Black Boy Looks at the White Boy," *Esquire Magazine* (May 1961), 104.

23. Kimberly Chabot Davis, *Beyond the White Negro: Empathy and Anti-Racist Reading* (Champaign: University of Illinois Press, 2014), 116.

24. Susan Gubar, *Racechanges: White Skin Black Face in American Culture* (New York: Oxford University Press, 2000), 248–249.

25. See the full narrative of the mission of California Grand Performances initiative at last accessed November 15, 2008. http://www.grandperformances.org/index.cfm/fuseaction/about.mission

26. Danny Hoch, *Jails, Hospitals & Hip-Hop and Some People* (New York: Villard Press, 1998), 3–4.

27. In Spike Lee's 2000 film *Bamboozled*, Lee comments on the contradic-

tion of black hip-hoppers making white designer goods famous without consideration for the ways in which their images are, in turn, commodified to sell the products. Lee cast Danny Hoch as the character "Timmi Hilnigger," a clothing designer who markets his clothes to African Americans and profits from their cultural images to sell his clothing. There is a famous urban legend in the United States that argues Tommy Hilfiger made a statement that he did not want African Americans to buy his clothing, even though they were a large part of his consumer base in the late 1990s. Hilfiger has denied this claim, yet the myth persists.

28. Jeffrey S. Podoshen, Susan A. Andrzejewski, and James M. Hunt, "Materialism, Conspicuous Consumption, and American Hip-Hop Subculture," *Journal of International Consumer Marketing* 26, no. 4 (2014): 271–283.

29. In the 2000 Spike Lee film *Bamboozled*, the director parodies the urban legend of fashion designer Tommy Hillfiger who is the subject of an urban myth that states someone interviewed Hilfiger about his late 1980s-1990s fashion line being worn by black hip-hop artists to which Hillfiger allegedly denounced that he was making clothes for the black community. After this urban tale, many African Americans swore never ot buy the Hillfigger label again. Spike Lee created a character in *Bamboozled* named "Timmy Hillnigger" to mark the ways in which many whites appropriate black culture for profit The character was is a blatant parody of Tommy Hillfiger.

30. Hoch, *Jails*, 3.

31. Hoch, *Jails*, 11–12.

32. Hoch, *Jails*, 12.

33. K. Anthony, Appiah, *The Ethics of Identity* (Princeton, NJ: Princeton University Press, 2007), 22.

34. K. Anthony, Appiah, "Race, Culture, Identity: Misunderstood Connections," The Tanner Lectures on Human Value, delivered at the University of California at San Diego, October 27 and 28, 1994.

35. Hoch, *Jails*, 12.

36. Hoch, *Jails*, 18.

37. Hoch, *Jails*, 18

38. Hoch, *Jails*, 19.

39. Interestingly, at the time of this play, Donald Trump was not the forty-fifth president of the United States, but an icon of wealth often cited by many male African American hip-hop artists, despite his known anti-Black racist rhetoric regarding "The Central Park Five." Donald Trump is on record stating that the "Central Park Five," five black men who were framed for the rape of a white woman in Central Park in 1983, were guilty, despite being officially exon-

erated by DNA evidence decades after the 1989 New York rape case. In 2019, African American film director Ava Duvernay created an Emmy nominated, limited TV miniseries for Netflix that chronicles the systematic framing of the five black youth for rape. The film series is entitled *When They See Us*, May 31, 2019.

40. David Roediger, *Colored White: Transcending the Racial Past* (Berkeley: University of California Press, 2003), 217.

41. Dorinne, Kondo, "(Re)Visions of Race: Contemporary Race Theory and the Cultural Politics of Racial Crossover in Documentary Theatre," *Theatre Journal* 52, no. 1 (March 2000): 83. Kondo's discussion of cross-racial performance and the positive and negative implications of performers of color performing the Other are insightful and inform this study.

42. John Jackson, Jr., *Real Black: Adventure in Racial Sincerity* (Chicago: University of Chicago Press, 2005), 18.

43. Johnson, *Appropriating Blackness*, 4.

44. Hoch, *Jails*, 36.

45. Hoch, *Jails*, 36.

46. Hoch, *Jails*, 40.

47. Phil Cohen, "Laboring Under Whiteness," in *Displacing Whiteness: Essays on Social and Cultural Criticism*, ed. by Ruth Frankenberg (Durham, NC: Duke University Press, 1997), 20.

48. Danny Hoch, personal correspondence with Nicole Hodges Persley, January 31, 2006.

49. Hoch, *Jails*, 96.

50. Hoch, *Jails*, 69.

51. Danny Hoch, personal communication with Nicole Hodges Persley, February 17, 2006.

52. Beastie Boys, "Fight for your Right," *Licensed to Ill*, Def Jam Columbia, 1986.

53. Lillian Ross, "The Boards: New Kid," *The New Yorker*. Accessed October 20, 2008. http://www.newyorker.com/talk/2008/10/20/081020ta_talk_ross

54. Nicole Hodges Persley, unpublished performance notes, September 12, 2008.

55. Matt Sax, *Clay*, unpublished play script, 3.

56. Matt Sax, *Clay*, unpublished play script, 6.

57. Boogie Down Productions, "You Must Learn," *Ghetto Music: The Blueprint of Hip-hop*, Jive/RCA, 1989.

58. Nicole Hodges Persley, personal correspondence with Matt Sax, February 7, 2014. Eric Rosen cofounded the About Face Theater company in Chicago,

a company dedicated to developing works that privilege lesbian, gay, bisexual, and transgender (LGBT) voices within the American theatrical canon. Sax expressed to me that Rosen was invited to see an early workshop of *Clay* at Northwestern and was so moved by Sax's performance that he offered to help him develop the play. This led Rosen to direct *Clay* and to continue his collaboration with Sax to tour the work to Kansas City, Los Angeles, and New York. Rosen later became the Artistic Director of the Kansas City Repertory Theater in 2008 and remained there until leaving in 2019.

59. Nicole Hodges Persley, personal correspondence with Matt Sax, February 7, 2014.

60. Though there are no formal training programs for hip-hop arts in the United States, community-based organizations, such as Hi-Arts in New York, are adding hip-hop arts training programs to their outreach programs. In Senegal, Hip-hop Akademy provides training for DJs and MCs.

61. Sax, *Clay*, unpublished play script, 4.

62. William Shakespeare, *The Tragedy of Hamlet, Prince of Denmark* (Online: Folger Shakespeare Library, 2015), 70. www.folgerdigitaltexts.com

63. Shakespeare, *Hamlet*, 136.

64. Sax, *Clay*, 18.

65. Sax, *Clay*, 19.

66. Sax, *Clay*, 19.

67. Sax, *Clay*, 22.

68. Sax, *Clay*, 36

69. Sax, *Clay*, 37.

70. Sax, *Clay*, 38.

71. Sax, *Clay*, 43.

72. Carl Hancock Rux, "Eminem: The New White Negro," in *Everything But the Burden: What White People are Taking From Black Culture*, ed. by Greg Tate (New York: Broadway Books, 2003), 19.

73. Harry J. Elam, Jr., "The Device of Race: An Introduction," in *African American Performance and Theater History: A Critical Reader*, ed. by Harry J. Elam, Jr. and David Krasner (New York: Oxford University Press, 2001), 4.

Chapter Two

1. Jay-Z, "Empire State of Mind," *Blueprint 3*, Roc the Mic Studios, 2009.

2. Maxine Greene, "On the American Dream: Equality, Ambiguity, and the Persistence of Rage," *Curriculum Inquiry* 13, no. 2 (1983): 179.

3. Green, "On the American Dream," 179–193.

4. Holland Cotter, "Art in Review: Nikki S. Lee," *New York Times*, 1999.

5. Charles Isherwood, "'Bridge and Tunnel': The Voices Insider the Border but Outside the Margins," review of *Bridge & Tunnel*, by Sarah Jones, *New York Times*, January 27, 2006.

6. Childish Gambino, "This is America," *This is America*, RCA Records, 2018. Donald Glover, a.k.a. "Childish Gambino" penned this Billboard 100 hit in 2018. The video, directed by Hiro Murai, sampled from Jim Crow images of black men in American iconography and parodied the nation's insensitivity to the long history of anti-Black violence, from police brutality and murders of African American men, from lynching to the Charleston Church Shooting on June 17, 2015.

7. Barbara Hodgdon, "Photography, Theater, Mnemonics; or Thirteen Ways of Looking at a Still," *Theorizing Practice: Redefining Theater History*, ed. by W. B. Worthen and Peter Holland (New York: Palgrave Macmillan, 1994), 89.

8. Philip Auslander, "The Performativity of Performance Documentation," *PAJ* 84 (2006): 1.

9. Auslander, "The Performativity of Performance Documentation," 2.

10. Rebecca Schneider, *Performing Remains: Art and War in Times of Theatrical Reenactment* (New York: Routledge, 2011), 29.

11. Schneider, *Performing Remains: Art and War in Times of Theatrical Reenactment*, 133.

12. Lil' Kim, "No Matter What They Say," *The Notorious K.I.M.*, Atlantic Records, 2000.

13. Tony Godfrey, *Conceptual Art A&I (Art and Ideas)* (New York: Phaidon, 1998).

14. Creators Project, "Nikki S. Lee," *Vice*, July 1, 2010. Accessed July 30, 2011. http://thecreatorsproject.vice.com/creators/nikki-s-lee

15. Nikki S. Lee, A&I (Art and Arirang Web Series), YouTube video, September 12, 2013. Accessed December 5, 2017. https://www.youtube.com/watch?v=YMychWgKedA&list=PL5_wvJaLQ6ddJU-6vz5yVeWB50buYodGb.

16. Nicole Hodges Persley, field notes on Nikki S. Lee Talk, USC, March 2006.

17. Lee's photographs are exhibited in the permanent collections of the Los Angeles County Museum of Art, the Metropolitan Museum of Art, the Kemper Museum in Kansas City, and other prestigious art institutions across the United States, Europe, and Asia. Lee's work is included in representations of late-twentieth- and early-twenty-first-century images of modern art that address social and political inquiries about the limitations of racial, ethnic, gender, and sexual identities in popular culture.

18. See Chisun Lee "The Assimilartist," *Colorlines* 18 (Fall 2002). Also see Cathy Covell Waegner "Ghostdog in Yellowface/Blackface," 223–240; and Deborah E. Whaley "Black Bodies/Yellow Masks: The Orientalist Aesthetic in Hip-hop and Black Visual Culture," 188–203, in Heike Raphael-Hernandez and Shannon Steen, eds., *Afro-Asian Encounters: Culture, History Politics* (New York: New York University Press, 2006).

19. Nicole Hodges Persley, field notes on Nikki S. Lee Talk, USC, March 2006.

20. Nikki S. Lee, Artist Profile, *Liverpool Biennial.* Accessed October 26, 2014. http://liverpoolbiennial.co.uk/artists/l/201/nikki-s-lee

21. The practice of tanning in various parts of Asia as a process of improvising African American racial identity to create a "hip-hop" identity is referenced in Lee's photographs, even if the artist does not mention this phenomenon. As hip-hop circulated around the world, many Asian youth in Korea and parts of Japan began to use dark makeup and tanning to "become" black in order to appear "authentically" hip-hop. Gordon Sellar, a U.S. expatriate professor and writer living in Korea, blogs about his experiences with blackface performance by young Koreans on television on March 12, 2012. See Gordon Sellar, "Blackface, Korean Media and the Context of the American Vaudeville Show," *Gordon Sellar* (blog), accessed March 12, 2018. http://www.gordsellar.com/2012/03/12/blackface-korean-media-and-american-vaudeville/

22. Billy Joel, "Just the Way You Are," *The Stranger*, Columbia Records, 1977.

23. Deborah Elizabeth Whaley discusses the marginalizing effects of blacks in yellowface and African American/Asian American coalitions in their articles. Their arguments explore the intersection of intentional coalition building through acts of identification that have both subversive and essentializing effects in hip-hop and American popular culture at large. Both are included in Raphael-Hernandez and Steen, eds., *AfroAsian Encounters.*

24. Harry Elam, Jr. and David Krasner, "The Device of Race," in *African American Performance and Theater History* (New York: Oxford University Press, 2001), 13.

25. Roland Barthes, *Camera Lucida* (New York: Hill & Wang, 1980), 31–32.

26. Carol Kino, "Now in Moving Pictures: The Attitudes of Nikki S. Lee," *The New York Times,* October 1, 2006.

27. Eunsong Kim, "Nikki S. Lee' s 'Projects' and the Ongoing Circulation of Blackface and Brownface in 'Art,'" *Contemp/orary* (blog), May 30, 2016.

28. For a cursory critical genealogy of blackface in twentieth-century Korean popular culture, see the blog *Gusts of Popular Feeling* and the post titled "3 Decades of Blackface in Korea" http://populargusts.blogspot.com/2012/03/three-decades-of-black-face-in-korea.html. Other expat blogs about American-

Korean relations include *The Unlikely Expat* at www.unlikelyexpat.blogspot.com and *Expat Hell* at www.expathell.com, a private forum dedicated to expatriate living in Korea.

29. Fleetwood, *Troubling Vision*, 127.

30. These brands have been associated with hip-hop music and culture as status symbols, along with champagnes such as Cristal and Dom Perignon. The brands have disassociated themselves from hip-hop in the United States because of their association with African Americans. An example of the type of brand association with hip-hop and blackness occurred in 2006 when Cristal champagne announced that it did not want to be associated with the culture surrounding hip-hop. Rap mogul Jay-Z made the connections between hip-hop and blackness and called for a boycott of Cristal by all African Americans in the hip-hop community at large. Lee's attention to these types of cultural details adds sincerity and credibility to her performances of hip-hop, while they stress the African American translation of blackness that she associates with hip-hop.

31. Fleetwood, *Troubling Vision*, 127.

32. "Beautiful People 2003: Nikki S. Lee," *Paper Magazine*, April 1, 2003. http://www.papermag.com/2003/04/beautiful_people_2003_nikki_s_lee.php

33. I am indebted to Richard Meyer and David Román for introducing me to Lee and inviting me to this talk and dinner.

34. Nikki S. Lee, personal conversation with Nicole Hodges Persley, Los Angeles, March 25, 2007.

35. Russell Ferguson, *Parts*, 21.

36. *Harvard Crimson*, September 28, 2001.

37. "It was all a dream" is a quote from the Notorious B.I.G.'s hip-hop classic "Juicy," which narrates the rapper's version of the American Dream, where he relates how he envisioned success into being as a young black male coming of age in the projects of New York. Sarah Jones' "Your Revolution" challenges hip-hop artists who use misogyny and materialism to advance their agendas at the expense of black women.

38. Sarah Jones's *Bridge & Tunnel* developed *at* the 45 Bleeker Street Theater, a prestigious off-Broadway venue that incubates emerging artists. The off-Broadway run of *Bridge & Tunnel* was produced by Meryl Streep. See Ernio Hernandez, "Meryl Streep Presents Sarah Jones/ new work Bridge and Tunnel," *Playbill*, 2004.

39. Marjorie Jones, "The Strange Case of Sarah Jones," National Coalition Against Censorship, *NCAC Censorship News*, issue 89, Spring 2003. Sarah Jones's spoken word poem *Your Revolution* that challenged misogyny in hip-hop was essentially banned from the airwaves in 2001 for "indecency" because

the work mentioned a black woman's body "between her thighs" and connected revolutionary practice to black women's sexual power. Jones sued the FCC and the verdict was overturned in 2003.

40. Nicole Hodges Persley, field notes for *Bridge & Tunnel* performance, Helen Hayes Theater, 2006.

41. Tony Taccone is a critically acclaimed director who was the artistic director of Berkeley Repertory Theater for fifteen years. He resigned from Berkeley Rep in 2019. He directed Sarah Jones in her off-Broadway show *Surface Transit*. He is also the director of Danny Hoch's solo show *Taking Over* (2008).

42. Gilmore, *Gulag*, 261.

43. Hodges Persley, Nicole, field notes for *Bridge & Tunnel* performance, Helen Hayes Theater, 2006.

44. Sarah Jones, personal correspondence with Nicole Hodges Persley, February 2, 2007.

45. Danny Hoch, personal correspondence with Nicole Hodges Persley, January 31, 2006.

46. Nicole Hodges Persley, personal correspondence with Sarah Jones, December 6, 2009.

47. Roberta Uno, *Total Chaos: The Arts and Aesthetics of Hip-Hop* (New York: Hachette, 2015; rep. New York: Basic Books, 2007), 30.

48. Sarah Jones, "Bio." Accessed, August 1, 2019. www.sarahjones.com

49. Nicole Hodges Persley, personal correspondence with Sarah Jones, December 6, 2008.

50. Nicole Hodges Persley, personal correspondence with Sarah Jones, December 6. 2008.

51. Key players in the Culture Project, according to its website, include Meryl Streep, Danny Glover, Mary J. Blige, Robin Williams, Marisa Tomei, Bob Balaban, Rinde Eckhert, Montel Williams, Frank McCourt, Staceyann Chin, Lynn Redgrave, and Sarah Silverman. The website describes the organization as a collective of artists "who share a passion for theater and public justice." Streep is one of the most renowned artists who lent her voice of support for Jones's *Bridge & Tunnel* as "one of the best performances I have ever seen in my life." This endorsement by Streep also gave critics and potential audience members the confidence to see a show performed by a black woman, whom many outside of the New York theater scene had never heard of and to embrace the media descriptions of her embodied multiculturalism.

52. Janine Sherman Barrois, "Tyler Perry's Madea May Lead to the Black *Little Miss Sunshine*," *Rushmore Drive*. Accessed April 12, 2009.

53. Crystal Tai, "Asian Hip-hop: An Homage to a Genre or Cultural Appro-

priation Driven by Racism or Ignorance?" *South China Morning Post.* Accessed May 28, 2018. https://www.scmp.com/lifestyle/fashion-beauty/article/2148143/asian-hip-hop-homage-genre-or-cultural-appropriation-driven

54. Ntozake Shange, "Lady in Green," in *For Colored Girl Who Considered Suicide When the Rainbow Was Enuff* (New York: Scribner, 1997), 63.

55. Various Small Fires Gallery, "Nikki S. Lee," Los Angeles. Accessed April 4, 2019. http://www.vsf.la/nikki-s-lee-parts-and-scenes/

Chapter Three

1. Thomas F. DeFrantz, "The Black Beat Made Visible: Hip-hop Dance and Body Power," in *of The Presence of the Body: Essays on Dance and Performance Theory,* ed. by Andrew Lepecki (Middletown, CT: Wesleyan University Press, 2004), 71.

2. Tricia Rose, *Black Noise: Rap Music and Black Culture in Contemporary America* (Middletown, CT: Wesleyan University Press, 1994), 83.

3. Heike Raphael-Hernandez, *Blackening Europe: The African American Presence* (New York: Routledge, 2004), 314

4. The character name "Banxsy" is should not be confused with the London-based street artist Banksy mentioned in the chapter.

5. Brenda Dixon Gottschild, *The Black Dancing Body: Geography from Coon to Cool* (New York: Macmillan, 2003).

6. Mohanalashmi, Rajakumar, *Hip-hop Dance: The American Dance Floor* (Westport, CT: Greenwood; 2012), xxx.

7. Both Barbara O'Connor and Joyce Aschenbrenner address Katherine Dunham's quests to use dance to link African Americans and other African Diasporic people with their African past. Like hip-hop music and culture, Dunham saw African American dance as a hybrid form that sampled from many African and African Diasporic dance forms. See Aschenbrenner, *Katherine Dunham: Dancing a Life* (Chicago: University of Illinois Press, 2002); and O'Connor, *Katherine Dunham: Pioneer of Black Dance* (Minneapolis: Carolhoda Books, 2000).

8. Cheng, *In Other Los Angeleses*, 12.

9. These specific "British" versions of Hip-hop often referred to as "Brit-Hop" include, but are not limited to, Trip-hop, UK Garage, Bhangra, and Grime.

10. Hernandez, *Blackening Europe.*

11. C. Lee Harrington and Denise D. Bielby, eds., *Popular Culture: Production and Consumption* (New York: Blackwell Publishing, 2001).

12. Mark Anthony Neal, "'A Man without a Country': The Boundaries of Legibility, Social Capital, and Cosmopolitan Masculinity," *Criticism* 52 no. 3, (2010), 399–411, *Project MUSE.*

13. Andy Bennett, "Hip-hop Am Main, Rapping on the Tyne: Hip-hop Culture as Local Construct in Two European Cities," in *That's the Joint: the Hip-hop Studies Reader,* ed. by Murray Forman, and Mark Anthony Neal (New York: Routledge, 2004).

14. Popping and locking are dance moves that originated in the United States with African American and Latinx dancers in California. Both are considered "funk" dance styles moves that form the foundation of hip-hop dance. "Popping" was a word given to one of several street dance styles by world famous dancer "Poppin' Pete" in the late 1970s and early 1980s. "Locking" is attributed to Los Angeles dancer Don Campbell, also known as Don Campbellock. Jorge Pabón, "Physical Graffiti: The History of Hip-hop Dance," in *Total Chaos: The Art and Aesthetics of Hip-hop,* ed. by Jeff Chang. (New York: Basic Books, 2006), 18–26. For videos of popping and locking styles, see www.thefantasticpopers.com; and Michael Holman, "Styles: Locking and Popping," *Dancers Delight.* Accessed September 15, 2008. www.msu.edu/~okumurak/styles/pop.html

15. The Rock Steady Crew, founded by b-boys Jimmy D and JoJo, is one of the most famous hip-hop dance crews in the world. Started in the United States in the Bronx, New York, in 1977, the group now has international branches and members around the world. Accessed September 9, 2018. www.rocksteadycrew.com

16. Soul 2 Soul, "'Back to Life' (However Do You Want Me)," *Club Classics Vol. One,* Virgin Records, 1989.

17. For more on African retentions in African American Dance Vernacular see Robert Farris Thompson, *Flash of the Spirit: African and Afro-American Art and Philosophy* (New York: Random House, 1983); and Jacqui Malone, *Steppin' on the Blues: The Visible Rhythms of African American Dance* (Champaign: University of Illinois Press, 1996).

18. For oral narrative accounts of the juba dance and its links to slavery and West African retentions in slave culture of the United States, see Beverly J. Robinson, *Aunt {Ant} Phyllis* (Berkeley, CA: Regent Press, 1989).

19. Suzanne Carbonneau, "Rennie Harris Puremovement: History of Hip-hop," Cue Sheet for the Lecture Series at the Jackson Hall Mondovi Center, October 10, 2003.

20. See also Robert Farris Thompson, *Flash of the Spirit* (New Haven, CT: Yale University Press, 1989); and Gottschild, *The Black Dancing Body.*

21. "Krumping" and "clowning" are terms that are used interchangeably

with slight differences in the dance styles. Pronounced *krum-pin'* (pronunciation using Hip Hop Nation Language coined by H. Samy Alim), this dance is an underground form of hip-hop dance that began in South Los Angeles in the early 2000s. Dancers compete in freestyle dance battles, improvising dance moves that sample from martial arts, hip-hop, and modern dance that culminate in a frenzied style of self-expression that often borders on Native American "trance" dance. Many dancers say krumping allows them to relieve stress in their lives. Clowning focuses on contorting the body, sampling from images in Cirque du Soleil and other "circus" type performances. Both styles focus on "feats." The dancers perform individually and collectively, yet unlike in traditional hip-hop dance, they choose to perform out of synch with one another, focusing on dancing on odd numbered beats instead of even counts. The movements are largely improvisational and have a frenetic feel that is linked to African tribal dances and Native American trance dances. Many dancers look possessed as they dance off the beat in the break of the music. David LaChapelle's 2000 documentary film *Rize* chronicles this dance tradition. Clowning may include the use of face paint and is also associated with freestyle, frenetic movements danced to hip-hop beats. The language of both dance forms includes processes of bodily communication whereby dancers engage in battles and call to one another with gestures to solicit responses. See also H. Samy Alim, "Hip-hop National Language: Localization and Globalization," in *The Oxford Handbook of African American Language*, ed. by Jennifer Bloomquist, Lisa J. Green, and Sonja L. Lanehart (New York: Oxford University Press, July 2015).

22. Grandmaster Flash and the Furious Five, "Beat Street," *Beat Street Original Movie Soundtrack*, Atlantic Records, 1984.

23. Thomas L. De Frantz, "The Black Beat Made Visible: Hip-hop Dance and Body Power," in *Of the Presence of the Body: Essays on Dance and Performance Theory*, ed. by André Lepecki (Middleton, CT: Wesleyan University Press, 2004). For more on breaking as a social dance and its conception in global popular culture, see Paul Gilroy, "Ex(or)cising Power: Black Bodies in the Black Public Sphere," in *Dance in the City*, ed. by Helen Thomas (New York: St. Martin's Press, 1997).

24. This is my term and I use it to indicate how the body is used to transmit information without the use of written or verbal texts. This is an intricate part of translating the corporeal language of hip-hop dance.

25. Joseph Schloss, *Making Beats: The Art of Sample based Hip-Hop* (Middletown, CT: Wesleyan University Press, 2004, 11).

26. In a master class on hip-hop taught by Rennie Harris, he states that hip-hop dance cannot be contained in the "counting" of beats and must be felt viscerally by the dancer. Equally, at the Hip-hop Dance Conservatory in New York,

the director, Sekka, tells his incoming classes that they are part of an ensemble and have no relationship to "individual" movement that is not always already tied to the collective. The Hip-Hop Dance Conservatory teaches dancers of all races and ethnicities hip-hop dance, while Rennie Harris's dance troupe is predominately African American.

27. See Raymond Williams, *The Long Revolution* (New York: Columbia University Press, 1984), 65–67.

28. Williams, *The Long Revolution*, 65–67.

29. A "burner" is a term used internationally to describe a piece of art put up by a graffiti artist in a public space. The term was originally used to describe full-scale graffiti pieces on the sides of subway cars.

30. Jorge Pabón, "Physical Graffiti: The History of Hip-hop Dance by Jorge 'Popmaster Fabel' Pabón of the Rocksteady Crew/ Universal Zulu Nation," in *That's The Joint: The Hip-hop Studies Reader*, second ed., ed. by Murray Forman and Mark Anthony Neal (New York: Routledge, 2012), 53–62.

31. Andrew Laidlaw, *Blackness in the Absence of Blackness: White Appropriations of Rap Music and Hip-hop Culture in Newcastle Upon Tyne—Explaining a Cultural Shift*, accessed August 10, 2019. https://hdl.handle.net/2134/8389

32. Norman Mailer, "The White Negro"; City Lights Black, 1970; Kitwana, *Why White Kids Love Hip-Hop*.

33. David Roediger, *Colored White: Transcending the Racial Past* (Berkeley: University of California Press, 2003).

34. Rose, *Black Noise*, 83; Joanna Demers, "Sampling the 1970s in Hop-Hop," *Popular Music* 22, no. 1 (Cambridge, MA: Cambridge University Press, 2003).

35. In *An Actor's Handbook*, Constantin Stanislavski argues that the "inner life" of a character is "concealed in the outer circumstances of their life, therefore in the facts of the play." See Stanislavski, *An Actor's Handbook: An Alphabetical Arrangement of Concise Statements on Aspects of Acting* (New York: Taylor and Francis, 2004), 21–22.

36. Kitwana, *Why White Kids Love Hip-hop*.

37. Joseph Roach, *Cities of the Dead* (New York: Columbia University Press, 1996), 26

38. Brent Hayes Edwards, *The Practice of Diaspora: Literature, Translation, and the Rise of Black Internationalism* (Cambridge, MA: Harvard University Press, 2003). See also Roach, *Cities of the Dead*.

39. Diana Taylor, *The Archive and the Repertoire: Performing Cultural Memory in the Americas* (Durham, NC: Duke University Press, 2003).

40. Edwards, *Practice of Diaspora*,14.

41. Pete Rock and CL Smooth, "They Reminisce Over You, (T.R.O.Y)," *Rewind Hip-hop volume* 2, Mecca the Soul Brother, Elektra Records, 1992.

42. This Philly based style of stepping is not to be confused with the African American percussive step dancing associated with African American sororities and fraternities that began in the United States in the mid-1900s. However, rhythmically, the dances share some attributes.

43. Adidas warm-up suits have become a part of African American hip-hop history due to their association with the performances of "old school" rap groups such as Run-D.M.C., who made these two-piece suits famous by wearing them in many of their concert performances. The African American rappers resignified their usage from being "track suits" used for exercise to be associated with hip-hop performance. Run-D.M.C. were one of the first hip-hop acts in American history to receive an endorsement deal from a major retailer because so many young people imitated their style.

44. Imani K. Johnson, "From Blues Women to B-girls: Performing Badass Femininity," in *Women & Performance: A Journal of Feminist Theory* 24, no. 1 (2014): 15–28.

45. Donald Huerta, "Knowing the Culture: Interview with Rennie Harris," *Dance Umbrella News*, August, 2001.

46. Deborah Jovit, "Homeboy Shakespeare," *Village Voice*. Accessed October 12, 2019. https://www.villagevoice.com/2000/09/12/homeboy-shakespeare/

47. Jovit, "Homeboy Shakespeare," 2001.

48. Jonzi D, personal discussion with Nicole Hodges Persley, Holiday Inn, London, February 2006.

49. For a complete discussion of DJ and producer ethics, see Joseph Schloss, "Sampling Ethics," in *That's The Joint: The Hip-hop Studies Reader*, ed. by Murray Forman and Mark Antony Neal (New York: Routledge, 2012), 609–628.

50. Schloss, "Sampling Ethics," 611.

51. Angela Ards, "The Harlem Renaissance and Black Transnational Culture," review of *The Practice of Diaspora: Literature Translation and the Rise of Black Internationalism* by Brent Hayes Edwards. *The Crisis*, August 2003.

52. Sabela d. Grimes and Amy O'Neal, "What Happens When You Bring Street Dance on Stage?: Interview with Nikki Klaymoon and Rennie Harris," *Dance* magazine. Accessed June 26, 2017. https://www.dancemagazine.com/hip-hop-dance-2448547007.html

Chapter Four

1. The Pan-Latinx consciousness that Miranda works to forge in the musical mirrors efforts that are occurring in education. This Pan-Latinx consciousness samples heavily from W. E. B. Du Bois. See Guadalupe San Miguel, "Embracing

Latinidad: Beyond Nationalism in the History of Education," *Journal of Latinos & Education* 10, no. 1 (2011), 3–22; and Patricia L. Price, "Cohering Culture on Calle Ocho: The Pause and Flow of Latinidad," *Globalizations* 4, no. 1 (2007), 81–99.

2. Interestingly, this was at the same time that Matt Sax, then a college student at Northwestern, developed his first play, *Clay* (discussed in chapter 1).

3. Leigh Scheps, "'In the Heights' 10 Years Later: From 'Vague Promises' to a Broadway Smash" *Entertainment Tonight*, Accessed February 1, 2019. https://www.etonline.com/in-the-heights-10-years-later-from-vague-promises-to-a-broadway-smash-exclusive-97671

4. Dick Hebdige, *Cut and Mix: Culture, Identity and Caribbean Music* (New York: Routledge, 1987), 118.

5. Missy Elliot, "Triple Threat," *Timbaland*, Goldmind/Atlantic, 2012.

6. W. E. B. Du Bois, *The Souls of Black Folk* (New York: Penguin Books, 1982), 45.

7. Memorex was a computer tape company and consumer media supplier that began in 1961 and disbanded in 1996. The company specialized in computer tape and cassette tapes, and then shifted to computers and computer products, such as CDs, DVDs, flash drives, and other accessories. See *Computer History Museum*, 2017. Accessed January 29, 2019. http://corphist.computerhistory.org/corphist/view.php?s=select&cid=9

8. Du Bois, *The Souls of Black Folk*.

9. William J. Harris, "How You Sound??": Amiri Baraka Writes Free Jazz," *Jazz Studies On Line* (January 28, 2011): 313.

10. Danny Hoch, "Here We Go, Yo: A Manifesto for A New Hip-hop Arts Movement Tells It Like It Is," *American Theatre Magazine*, December 2004, 21.

11. W. E. B. Du Bois, "Krigwa Players Little Negro Theatre," *The Crisis* 32, no. 3 (July 1926): 134–136. "The plays of a real Negro theatre must be: 1. 'About us.' That is, they must have plays which reveal Negro life as it is. 2. 'By us.' That is, Negro authors who understand from birth and continued association just what it means to be a Negro today must write them. 3. 'For us.' That is, the theatre must cater primarily to Negro audiences and be supported and sustained by their entertainment and approval. 4. 'Near us.' The theatre must be in a Negro neighborhood near the mass of ordinary Negro peoples."

12. Danny Hoch, "Here We Go, Yo," 21.

13. Danny Hoch, "Here We Go, Yo."

14. Lin-Manuel Miranda and Quiara Alegría Hudes, *In the Heights; The Complete Book and Lyrics of the Broadway Musical* (Lanham, MD: Applause Books, 2013), 1. Use of capitals indicates the performer is singing or rapping, as used in the original text of *In the Heights*, 1–2.

15. Brian Eugenio Herrera, "Compiling *West Side* Story's Parahistories, 1949–2009," *Theatre Journal* 64, no. 2 (2012), 234. Herrera maps the interconnecting histories of Stephen Sondheim's 1957 musical *West Side Story* and the 2009 Broadway revival that included lyrics translated from English to Spanish by Lin-Manuel Miranda. Miranda's charge was to keep the integrity of the original English version, but to translate the narrative into Spanish, keeping the rhyme schemes and meaning. Herrera's discussion of Puerto Rican identity in *West Side Story* translation works through and against Latinx stereotypes as much as it questions the gendering of Latinoness by Arthur Laurents (author of the original version's book) to fit some type of Broadway formula that mirrors the double consciousness reflected in the expression of Latinx identity in language from both outsider (White) and insider (Latinx) perspectives.

16. J Balvin and Willy William, "Mi Gente ft. Beyoncé," *Vibras*, Universal Latin, 2017.

17. Juan Flores, *From Bomba to Hip-hop: Puerto Rican Culture and Latino Identity* (New York: Columbia University Press, 2000), 116.

18. Lin-Manuel Miranda, "Lin-Manuel Miranda Gives Keynote Speech Address at NAHJ Scholarship Banquet 2009," YouTube video. Accessed February 6, 2009. https://www.youtube.com/watch?v=1lYLi906z60

19. Miranda, "Lin-Manuel Miranda Gives Keynote."

20. Miranda and Hudes, *In the Heights*, 54–58.

21. Miranda and Hudes, *In the Heights*, 116–127.

22. Pierre Bourdieu, *Distinction: A Social Critique of the Judgement of Taste*, translated by Richard Nice (Cambridge, MA: Harvard University Press, 1987), 170–171.

23. Quiara Alegría Hudes is a prolific playwright of Latinx and Jewish descent who won the Pulitzer Prize for her play *Water by the Spoonful* in 2012. While I do not discuss Hudes's work on *In the Heights* in detail in this chapter, her book for the musical is an integral part to the intervention that Miranda makes to unsettle superficial representation of Latinx life written by white playwrights on the American theatre stage.

24. REM, "The End of the World," *Document*, IRS, 1987.

25. The publicity of the musical is most often focused on Sax and his relationship to hip-hop culture. Sax wrote the music and Rosen collaborated on the lyrics and the book. Rosen also directed the musical.

26. Matt Sax and Eric Rosen, *Venice*, unpublished play script, courtesy of the authors, May 2013, 3.

27. Sax and Rosen, *Venice*, 5

28. Sax and Rosen, *Venice*, 33.

29. Sax and Rosen, *Venice*.

30. In "'All That You Can't Leave Behind': Black Female Soul Singing and the Politics of Surrogation in the Age of Catastrophe," *Meridians: Feminism, Race, Transnationalism* 8, no. 1 (2007): 180–204. Daphne Brooks focuses on performance by hip-hop/R&B mash-up singers Beyoncé Knowles and Mary J. Blige, comparing their songs as anthems to the survivors of 2005's Hurricane Katrina. Brooks revels in the ways that the women improvise strategies of resistance that make black women's voices audible and bodies visible within sonic and visual artscapes that silence and erase black feminist discourses performed by academic and pop culture black feminist intellectuals.

31. Shoshana Greenberg, "A World Divided: Tracing the Origins of Matt Sax and Eric Rosen's *Venice*," *Huffington Post*. Accessed May 28, 2013. http://www.huffingtonpost.com/shoshana-greenberg/a-world-divided-tracing-the-origins_b_3344278.html

32. Elizabeth Vincentelli, "The 5 Worst Theater Shows of 2013," *The New York Post*, December 23, 2013. http://nypost.com/2013/12/23/the-5-worst-theater-shows-of-2013/

33. Ben Brantley, "Of Shakespeare and Super Heroes: *Venice* by Matt Sax and Eric Rosen," *New York Times*. Accessed June 13, 2013.

34. Richard Zoglin, *Venice*, by way of Kansas City: The Year's Best Musical," *Time*, May 14, 2010.

35. Stuart Hall, "Cultural Identity and Diaspora," in *Colonial Discourse and Post-Colonial Theory: A Reader*, ed. by Patrick Williams and Laura Chrisman (London: Harvester Wheatsheaf, 1994), 392–401.

36. Raul A Reyes, "Chicago: 'In the Heights' Non-Latino Lead Stirs Controversy," *NBC News*. Accessed August 25, 2016. https://www.nbcnews.com/news/latino/chicago-heights-non-latino-lead-stirs-controversy-n637266

37. Banks, *Say Word!*, 6.

Chapter Five

1. Lin-Manuel Miranda, White House Performance of Alexander Hamilton, PBS.

2. Lin-Manuel Miranda, White House Performance of Alexander Hamilton, PBS.

3. *Urban Dictionary*, s.v. "Ghost," by miggelzworth, last updated October 10, 2010. https://www.urbandictionary.com/define.php?term=Ghost

4. *Urban Dictionary*, "Ghost."

5. *Oxford Dictionary Online*, s.v., "ghost," accessed August 3, 2018. https://www.bing.com/search?q=ghosting&FORM=ATUR01&PC=ATUR&PTAG=P-TAG00RAND.

6. Suzan-Lori Parks, "Elements of Style," in *The America Play* (New York: Theatre Communications Group, 1992), 12.

7. Kylie Umehira, "All Hammed Up: All Hammed Up: How *Hamilton: An American Musical* Addresses Post-Racial Beliefs," *WR: Journal of the CAS Writing Program*, no. 9 (2016–2017). Accessed June 21, 2017. https://www.bu.edu/writingprogram/journal/past-issues/issue-9/

8. Kylie Umehira, "All Hammed Up."

9. "The First Time Ever I saw Your Face" was made famous by soul singer Roberta Flack in the 1970s and is from her 1969 album *First Take*. The song originated as a folk song penned in 1957 by British singer/songwriter Ewan McColl for Peggy Seeger. Flack won a Grammy Award for "Record of the Year" in 1972 for the song. I use this reference here to reinforce the ways in which Flack's black body and cultural narrative is grafted onto a song written by a white British songwriter for a white female folk singer. Flack's presence on the song offers a completely different narrative, as Flack's history as a black woman from the American South haunts the song's meaning and context. See "Roberta Flack Biography" at *The Great Rock Bible*. Accessed April 15, 2018. http://thegreatrockbible.com/portfolio-item/roberta-flack-biography/

10. Miranda and McCarter, *Hamilton*, 16

11. Miranda and McCarter, *Hamilton*, 16.

12. Miranda and McCarter, *Hamilton*, 26–27.

13. Hamilton and McCarter, *Hamilton*, 24.

14. *The Musical Lyrics*, "Hamilton, 2015." Accessed April 1, 2018. http://www.themusicallyrics.com/h/351-hamilton-the-musical-lyrics/3704-my-shot-lyrics-hamilton.html

15. Jacqueline Howard, "The Disparities of How Black and White Men Die in Gun Violence, State by State," *CNN.com*, April 24, 2018. Accessed May 23, 2018. https://www.cnn.com/2018/04/23/health/gun-deaths-in-men-by-state-study/index.html

16. Miranda and McCarter, "*Hamilton*: The Revolution, chapter II, discusses "Aaron Burr, Sir." Miranda and McCarter utilize footnotes to the commentary on the song to highlight that Burr may have received preferential treatment because his father was the college president. The one major thing that Miranda leaves out here is that that "little college" was Princeton. Princeton continues to reproduce systemic inequality and favor White admits to this day. According to 2019 statistics posted on Princeton's website, African American student per-

centages for the freshman class of 2019 were at eight percent, and the percentage of Latinx students that comprised the freshman class was ten percent. See "African Americans and Princeton University: A Brief History," *Princeton University Library Web*. Accessed May 1, 2018 https://libguides.princeton.edu/c.php?g=84056&p=544526; And "Princeton University Undergraduate Admission Statistics for the class of 2022," last updated July 2018. Accessed February 10, 2018. https://admission.princeton.edu/how-apply/admission-statistics

17. Miranda and McCarter, *Hamilton*, 25.

18. Miranda and McCarter, *Hamilton*, 16.

19. Arnold Rognow, *A Fatal Friendship: Alexander Hamilton and Aaron Burr* (New York: Macmillan, 1999), 59–60.

20. E. Patrick Johnson, "Snap! Culture: A Different Kind of 'Reading,'" *Text and Performance Quarterly* 15, no. 2 (1995): 122–142.

21. Mark Binelli, "'Hamilton' Creator Lin-Manuel Miranda: The Rolling Stone Interview," *Rolling Stone*, June 21, 2016. Accessed August 5, 2017. https://www.rollingstone.com/culture/culture-news/hamilton-creator-lin-manuel-miranda-the-rolling-stone-interview-42607/

22. John McWhorter, "The Exhausting and Useless Accusations of Racism in 'Hamilton,'" *Daily Beast*, April 16, 2016. https://www.thedailybeast.com/the-exhausting-and-useless-accusations-of-racism-hamilton

23. McWhorter, "Accusations of Racism in 'Hamilton.'"

24. Jerneja Planinšek Žlof, "Lin-Manuel Miranda's Musical *Hamilton* and Early Feminism: Rapping Gender Equality," in *Ethnic and Cultural Identify in Music and Song Lyrics*, ed. by Victor Kenney and Michelle Gadpaille (Newcastle upon Tyne: Cambridge Scholars Publishing, 2017).

25. *Genius*, "Right Hand Man," lyric notes to the Original Broadway Musical Hamilton (2015). In the Genius notations, Lin-Manuel offers the following on this number: "The reference to *In the Heights* and '96,000' was totally subconscious. One of the interns on the show, was like, 'Did you mean to put in 32,000 three times?' I'm like, 'What?' And she pointed it out to me and it's a total coincidence. Actually, there use to be more of them—more echoes of it. It just whittled down to three instances where we said, 'thirty-two thousand,' which adds up to 96,000," July 28, 2019. https://genius.com/7860623

26. Miranda and McCarter, *Hamilton*, 80.

27. Tony Castro, "How Hispanics Helped Win the American Revolution," *La Opinión*, July 14, 2014.

28. Peter Fitzpatrick, "Latino Patriots of the American Revolution, Donde Estan?" *Al Dia*, April 14, 2017. https://aldianews.com/articles/opinion/op-ed-latino-patriots-american-revolution-donde-estan/47408

29. Castro, "How Hispanics Helped Win the American Revolution."

30. Aretha Franklin, *A Different World*, Arista Records, 1989.

31. Edward Delman, "How Lin-Manuel Miranda Shapes History," *The Atlantic*, September 25, 2015. Accessed May 25, 2016. https://www.theatlantic.com/entertainment/archive/2015/09/lin-manuel-miranda-hamilton/408019/

32. According to the White House's website, Executive Order 13769 contends that immigrants who come to this country should not only support the constitution, they also should "not admit those who engage in acts of bigotry or hatred (including 'honor' killings, other forms of violence against women, or the persecution of those who practice religions different from their own) or those who would oppress Americans of any race, gender, or sexual orientation." However, such a law is ironic, specifically because these qualities are sought in people entering a country that cannot extend these expectations of protection to new immigrants to the U.S. or its existing citizens. Accessed June 5, 2019. https://www.whitehouse.gov/presidential-actions/executive-order-protecting-nation-foreign-terrorist-entry-united-states/

33. Ralph Ellison, "The Shadow and The Act," *The Reporter*, December 6, 1919.

34. Ellison, "The Shadow and The Act," 18.

35. Ellison, "The Shadow and The Act," 18.

36. The relationship between Thomas Jefferson and Sally Hemmings has been romanticized in many works of historical fiction, including but not limited to Barbara Chase-Riboud's *Sally Hemmings* (1979), *Thomas Jefferson and Sally Hemmings: An American Controversy* by Annette Gordon-Reed (1998); and several films, including *Belle* (2014), dir. by Amma Asante, and *The Courage to Love* (2000), dir. by Kari Skogland.

37. Miranda and McCarter, *Hamilton*, 161.

38. Miranda and McCarter, *Hamilton*, 161.

39. Bee Gees, "Staying Alive," Capital Records, 1977.

40. Miranda and McCarter, *Hamilton*, 199.

41. Donatella Galella, "Being In 'The Room Where It Happens': Hamilton, Obama and Nationalist Neoliberal Multicultural Inclusion," *Theatre Survey* 59, no. 3 (September 2018): 363–385.

42. Galella, "Being In 'The Room Where It Happens,'" 364.

43. Peggy Phelan, *Unmarked: The Politics of Performance*, (New York: Routledge, 2007), 10.

44. We must ask if the use of colorblind casting of Asian Americans in parts that were written for white actresses (save *Miss Saigon*) is an example of what Faedra Chatard Carpenter calls "aural whiteness." When Asian American

actresses (and all actresses of color, for that matter) take on roles that ask them to erase themselves racially and ethnically and to dissolve into a fictional or non-fictional representation of a white character under the guise of equal opportunity, something is lost in translation for the performers of color, as their experiences in portraying white characters are always deemed as "progress" towards a post-racial or colorblind state. The normative whiteness of the so-called universal character (in plays, television shows, films, and other performance platforms created by white writers) is an unproductive approach to arriving at a more equitable field of representation and remains "unmarked," as Peggy Phelan has theorized. See Faedra C. Carpenter, *Coloring Whiteness: Acts of Critique in Black Performance*, (Ann Arbor: University of Michigan Press, 2014), 94–224. *Project MUSE*, 2014.

45. The 2017–2018 Broadway League "the business, demographics, and economic impact of Broadway theatre throughout North America." The Broadway League's "Demographics of the Broadway Audience" report for 2017–2018 reports that over seventy-five percent of the Broadway audience is overwhelmingly White and female. These statistics also show that a large percentage of Broadway audience members had experiences with theater during their childhood. The disparity between White and non-White theatergoers is racial, socioeconomic, and generational. The current audience configuration is also representative of what is produced on Broadway stages. The percentage of shows on Broadway that are by and about people of color factor for very little of the productions (plays or musicals) or the representations of actors of color. For access to the full report, see "The Demographics of the Broadway Audience." Accessed May 16, 2019. https://www.broadwayleague.com/research/research-reports/

46. Helena Holmes, "Ishmael Reed on Why He Thinks *Hamilton* is a Total Fraud," *The Observer*, January 15, 2019. Accessed May 6, 2019. https://observer.com/2019/01/playwright-ishmael-reed-on-why-he-thinks-hamilton-is-a-total-fraud/

47. Ishmael Reed, "'Hamilton: The Musical;' Black Actors Dress Up Like Slave Traders . . . And It's Not Halloween," *Counterpunch*, August 21, 2015.

48. Reed, "'Hamilton: The Musical.'"

49. The cities of Brisbane, Melbourne, and Sydney were in a bidding war to bring *Hamilton: The Musical* to Australia. Sydney won the rights and will premier Hamilton in February 2021 at the Lyric Theater in Sydney, Australia. Ironically, the sites of Hamilton's tour dates are directly connected to the slave owning history of the Founding Fathers of the United States. At the time of this writing, Hamilton is not scheduled to tour any countries in Africa or South America. For more on the Hamilton tour in Australia, see Nathanael Cooper, "Sydney Secures Australian

Premier of Hamilton," *Sydney Morning Herald*, May 22, 2019. Accessed May 23, 2019. https://www.smh.com.au/entertainment/musicals/sydney-secures-australian-premiere-of-hamilton-20190522-p51pvf.html

50. Warren G, "And Ya' Don't' Stop," *Regulate: G Funk Era*, Violator Records, 1994.

51. Nuyorican Poets Café Facebook Page, "The Haunting of Lin-Manuel Miranda," Facebook Page, May 23, 2019 through June 16, 2019. https://www.facebook.com/events/nuyorican-poets-cafe/the-haunting-of-lin-manuel-miranda/326437058023520/

52. Franklin Roosevelt took office in 1933. The "New Deal" promises were for all Americans, yet African Americans were still segregated in public and private life from White Americans. While women, African Americans and other historically underrepresented groups gained access to employment based on New Deal programs, it was Eleanor Roosevelt that helped to advocate for inclusive representation for artists of color. According to the *History Channel*, many women, Blacks, and other minorities found employment with the WPA. *History Channel* reports that "in 1935, the WPA employed approximately 350,000 African Americans, about 15 percent of its total workforce. The Federal Music and Theatre projects also supported black musicians and actors." *History Channel* Editors of the WPA history note that the WPA made "significant contributions to the preservation of African American culture and history with the Federal Writers' Project. The program collected interviews, articles and notes on African American life in the South, including oral histories from former slaves." Accessed June 9, 2019. https://www.history.com/topics/great-depression/works-progress-administration

53. Elisabeth Vincentelli, "The Haunting has a Big Problem with 'Hamilton,'" *New York Times*, June 2, 2019. Accessed May 29, 2019 https://www.nytimes.com/2019/06/02/theater/the-haunting-of-lin-manuel-miranda-review.html

54. Nancy Isenberg, "Let's Not Pretend That 'Hamilton' Is History," *Zócalo Public Square*, March 16, 2018. Accessed April 2, 2018. https://www.zocalopublicsquare.org/2016/03/17/lets-not-pretend-that-hamilton-is-history/ideas/nexus/

55. James McMaster, "Why Hamilton Is Not the Revolution You Think It Is," *Howl Round*, February 23, 2016.

56. McMaster, "Why Hamilton Is Not the Revolution."

57. Rachel Lewis, "Is Puerto Rico Part of the U.S?" *Time*, September 26, 2017.

58. Lewis, "Is Puerto Rico Part of the U.S?"

59. Annette Gordon Reed, "The Intense Debates Surrounding Hamilton Don't Diminish the musical—They Enhance it," *Vox*, September 13, 2016. Accessed May 18, 2016.

60. Lyra Monteiro, "Race Conscious Casting and the Erasure of the Black Past in Lin-Manuel Miranda's *Hamilton*," *The Public Historian* 38 (February 2016): 93.

61. Helen Holmes, "Lin-Manuel Miranda's Next Big Move? Giving Disney Its first Big-Screen Latina Princess," *The Observer*, January 22, 2019. Accessed February 25, 2019. https://observer.com/2019/01/lin-manuel-mirandas-next-move-giving-disney-its-first-ever-latina-princess/

62. Nate Jones, "Nerding Out with Hamilton's Musical Director, Alex Lacamoire," *New York Magazine*, "Vulture," January 13, 2016. Accessed March 15, 2016. https://www.vulture.com/2016/01/hamilton-alex-lacamoire-interview.html

63. Miranda and McCarter, *Hamilton*, 266–267.

64. *Merriam Webster English Dictionary*, s.v., "Ghost (noun): the seat of life or intelligence soul, give up the ghost 2: a disembodied soul especially: the soul of a dead person believed to be an inhabitant of the unseen world or to appear to the living in bodily likeness," accessed February 1, 2018. https://www.merriam-webster.com/dictionary/ghost

65. According to *Broadway World, Hamilton* has grossed over five hundred million dollars since its premier on Broadway in 2015. Payout reports for Lin-Manuel Miranda are reported at six million dollars per year, an estimated one percent of the overall gross of the musical's profits. See "Broadway Grosses—Hamilton." Accessed June 20, 2019. Lin-Manuel Miranda's net worth including profits from Hamilton is estimated at eighty million dollars as of October 8, 2020. thttps://www.broadwayworld.com/grossesshow.cfm?show=HAMILTON&year=2019&allall=on

66. Odie Henderson, "Hamilton," *Roger Ebert*, July 3, 2020. Accessed October 13, 2020. https://www.rogerebert.com/reviews/hamilton-movie-review-2020

67. Christopher Mele and Patrick Healy, "'Hamilton' Has Some Unscripted Words for Pence. Trump Wasn't Happy," *New York Times*, November 19, 2016.

68. Harvey Cohen, "Chapter 12 U.S State Department Tour," in *Ellington's America* (Chicago: University of Chicago Press, 2010), 441–442.

Chapter Six

1. Harry J. Elam, Jr. and Kennell Jackson, *Black Cultural Traffic: Crossroads in Global Performance and Popular Culture* (Ann Arbor: University of Michigan Press, 2005), 17.

2. Ruth Wilson Gilmore, *Golden Gulag: Prisons, Surplus, Crisis and Opposition in Globalizing California* (Berkeley: University of California Press, 2007).

3. Tate, *Everything but The Burden*, 7.

4. Lott, *Love and Theft*.

5. Ellington, *Music is My Mistress*, 308.

6. Kel Kray, "Dear Fellow White People: Loving Hip-hop Doesn't Make You Anti-Racist," *Everyday Feminism*. Accessed August 21, 2105. www.everydayfeminism.com

7. Kashi Johnson, "'Words to Live By' TED Talk Le High River," YouTube, April 23, 2013. Accessed June 28, 2015. https://www.youtube.com/watch?v=ffMhrY1sOZI

8. Johnson, "'Words to Live By.'"

9. David Roediger, *Colored White*: *Transcending the Racial Past* (Berkeley: University of California Press, 2003), 228.

10. Robin D. G. Kelley, "People in Me," *Color Lines* 1, no. 3 (Winter 1999): 5–7.

INDEX

Note: Page references in italics indicate photographs.